WITHDRAWN

Language and Control in Children's Literature

Children's literature has received little serious linguistic analysis despite its widely acknowledged influence on the development and socialisation of young people. In this important and timely study, Knowles and Malmkjær examine the work of some of our most popular nineteenth- and twentieth-century children's writers in order to expose the persuasive power of language.

At the heart of their analysis lie two surveys of children's favourite reading: the first carried out in 1888, the other a hundred years later by the authors themselves. By analysing the vocabulary and grammar patterns in the most popular children's texts of each period, the authors examine the ways in which children's writers use language to support or challenge particular views of the social world. For example, by examining the work of nineteenth-century English writers of juvenile fiction, the authors expose the colonial and class assumptions on which the books were predicated.

An invaluable book for anyone concerned with children and what they read, whether parent, teacher or students of language and literature.

Murray Knowles lectures in Applied English Linguistics at the Centre for English Language Studies, University of Birmingham. **Kirsten Malmkjær** is Assistant Director of Research at the University of Cambridge Research Centre for English and Applied Linguistics. Her previous publications include *The Linguistics Encyclopedia* (Routledge, 1991).

Language and Control in Children's Literature

Murray Knowles and
Kirsten Malmkjær

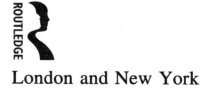

London and New York

First published 1996
by Routledge
11 New Fetter Lane, London EC4P 4EE

Simultaneously published in the USA and Canada
by Routledge
29 West 35th Street, New York, NY 10001
© 1996 Murray Knowles and Kirsten Malmkjær

Typeset in Times by J&L Composition Ltd, Filey, North Yorkshire
Printed and bound in Great Britain by Mackays of Chatham PLC,
Chatham, Kent

British Library Cataloguing in Publication Data
A catalogue record for this book is available from the British Library

Library of Congress Cataloguing in Publication Data
A catalogue record for this book has been requested

ISBN 0–415–08624–8 (hbk)
    0–415–08625–6 (pbk)

To
Stella
Katie Mary, Claire and Patrick
MK

To
David
Nils, Amy and Tomas
KM

Contents

Preface

This book arises from our joint interest in literature written, if not exclusively for children, then at least with child readers in mind. Almost everyone has been exposed to such literature in childhood, almost all parents revisit it with their own children, and very many teachers use it in their everyday work with children. Child educators, along with publishers of books for children, repeatedly stress the importance for success in the education system, and in life in general, of the acquisition of good reading habits early in life, and adult concern about the influence, good and bad, which literature may exert on child readers has a long history. It was such concern, in part, which prompted Edward Salmon, in the nineteenth century, to conduct a survey of children's reading habits (see Salmon, 1888). Salmon judges such literature chiefly for its moral content, however, and it is commonly agreed that the first scholarly work on English literature for children is Harvey Darton's *Children's Books in England*, published in 1932. As Carpenter and Prichard (1984: 142) point out, however, the value of this work was not recognised until long after Harvey Darton's death in 1936, and it is only relatively recently that children's literature has come to the fore in academic disciplines such as literary criticism, stylistics and translation studies.

There is, then, a curious discrepancy between the ubiquity and perceived importance of children's literature, and scholarly research in the field. We set out intending to add to the latter a study with a specific focus on language, because it seemed to us indisputable that the effects, whatever they might be, which literature might work on children, must be mediated largely through the language which constitutes the texts in question.

In fiction, the reality-creating potential of language comes to the fore particularly clearly, and writers have a heightened degree of creative licence. It seemed to us worth while to try to highlight the ways in which adult writers use this degree of linguistic licence when writing for children, and the degree to which such writers are themselves constrained by the modes of expression current at their time. Both relationships, that between adult writers and child readers and that between current modes of expression and writers, can, as we hope to have made clear in the body of this book, be considered relationships of control. We hope, further, that our discussion of texts produced by writers of different persuasions, and those writing at different times, might draw attention to these relationships particularly clearly, in offering the opportunity for comparison.

Acknowledgements

A great many people have, in various ways, helped to shape this book. We are indebted to colleagues, friends and students too numerous to mention for what they have taught us during friendly discussions, whether in seminars or in less structured contexts.

A personal thank-you, however, must go to Malcolm Coulthard for his continuing support in all sorts of ways; to Michael Hoey for being both friend and teacher; to Chris Kennedy for his encouragement; and to Gillian Brown, Viggo Hjørnager Pedersen and John B. Thompson for reading and commenting on earlier versions of chapter 2. To Enid Rose-Betts, Jane Gardiner and Susanna Lu, a special thank-you for their tolerance, particularly of word-processing blunders.

We are grateful for the interest and practical help we have received from the COBUILD team, in particular from Gwynneth Fox and Ramesh Krishnamurthy.

We thank staff at Routledge for their help and patience, in particular Claire L'Enfant, who commissioned this book, and Julia Hall who saw it through with the aid of Alison Foyle.

We are very grateful indeed to all the children who answered Murray Knowles' questions about what they like to read, and to the teachers who encouraged them to do so. We are especially grateful to Patrick, Claire and Katie Mary Knowles, and to Tomas, Amy and Nils Downes for guiding us back to their books, and to Stella Knowles and David Downes for their love and support.

We thank the following publishers and individuals for permission to use work for which they hold the copyright: Blackwell Publishers for permission to print Table 1.2 from *Ideology and Modern Culture* by John Thompson 1990. Curtis Brown on behalf of Nina Bawden for permission to print excerpts from *Carrie's War*, Copyright © 1973 Nina Bawden. Campbell Books for permission to reprint *Dear Zoo* by

Rod Campbell, first published in 1982 by Abelard-Schuman Ltd, re-issued in 1987 by Campbell Books, published in paperback by Picture Puffins in 1984. Jonathan Cape Ltd and Penguin Books Ltd for permission to print excerpts from *Danny the Champion of the World*, *Matilda* and *The BFG* by Roald Dahl 1975, 1988, 1982. HarperCollins Publishers Limited for permission to print excerpts from *The Lion, the Witch and the Wardrobe* by C.S. Lewis 1950. Orion Children's Publishing and J.M. Dent for permission to print excerpts from *The Borrowers* by Mary Norton 1952. Oxford University Press for permission to print excerpts from *Oscar Wilde: Complete Shorter Fiction*, edited with an introduction by Isobel Murray, World Classics Edition 1980, Copyright © 1979 Isobel Murray. K.M. Paynton for permission to print excerpts from *Seventeenth Summer*, Copyright © 1970 K.M. Paynton. Penguin Books Ltd for permission to print excerpts from *James and the Giant Peach* by Roald Dahl 1961. Alison Prince for permission to print excerpts from *Nick's October*, Copyright © 1986 Alison Prince. Victor Gollancz Ltd and Simon & Schuster Books for Young Readers, an imprint of Simon & Schuster Children's Publishing Division, for permission to print excerpts from *Forever* by Judy Blume, Copyright © 1975 Judy Blume. Victor Gollancz Ltd and Pancheon Books, a division of Random House, Inc., for permission to print excerpts from *The Chocolate War* by Robert Cormier, Copyright © 1974 Robert Cormier. Walker Books Limited for permission to print excerpts from *Jane and the Dragon* by Martin Baynton, Copyright © 1988 Martin Baynton; and from *The Dragon's Purpose* by Martin Baynton, Copyright © 1990 Martin Baynton; both published in the UK by Walker Books Limited.

1 Children's literature in England

INTRODUCTION

It is often felt that it is right and proper to begin the discussion of a particular subject area by providing a definition, and commentators on literature written for children have provided a host of definitions over the years. John Rowe Townsend is one of the best known of those commentators and assigns responsibility to the publisher in deciding what is a children's book:

> In the short run it appears that, for better or worse, the publisher decides. If he puts a book on the children's list, it will be reviewed as a children's book and will be read by children (or young people), if it is read at all. If he puts it on the adult list, it will not – or at least not immediately.
>
> (1980: 197)

Aidan Chambers also addresses himself to the question and makes the point that obviously some books are intended for children while others which are not attract child readers. Chambers goes on, however, to point out that it is not so much definitions that are needed but the development of a critical method 'which will take account of the child as reader' (1980: 250–1). In this study we are concerned with linguistic description rather than literary criticism but we take note of Chambers' point because we believe that an understanding of linguistic patternings in texts will help in taking account not only of the child reader but the (usually) adult author who produces the text.

The consideration of literature written for children from a linguistic perspective is a comparatively new field of study. The critical study of language, however, has acquired considerable impetus in the last twenty years and a focus on such a large and important area of social life as children's fiction in this country seems long overdue. The history of children's literature, in terms of publishing, is relatively short, with the bringing out of *A Little Pretty Pocket Book* by John Newberry (1713–67) in 1744 as the generally agreed starting point. Modern children's literature has its roots in the mid nineteenth century as authors turned to writing for entertainment and publishers realised there was a considerable market waiting to be tapped. But the evolution of children's literature should not simply be considered in crude economic terms, important though capitalism is as a controlling principle. We feel that Zohar Shavit makes an important point when she says (1992: 2): 'Children's literature evolved from the convergence of and interaction among several cultural fields or systems.' It seems to us that to make any sense of this 'convergence and interaction' account must be taken of the linguistic structures of the texts and their importance in realising author/reader relationships. In children's literature this is highly significant as it is a 'more than unusually balanced power relationship' (Hunt, 1988: 164). It is, therefore, a relationship which raises questions about domination or authorial control. After all, children's books are controlled by adults in that they can determine what children read and, in the main, produce what children read. As Julia Briggs states:

> Children's books are written for a special readership but not, normally by members of that readership; both the writing and quite often the buying of them, is carried out by adult non-members on behalf of child members.
>
> (1989: 4)

In this chapter we wish to consider the evolution of children's literature and to comment on its traditions or 'strands' which have resulted in the late twentieth century in such a diverse and creative range of publications for young readers. We shall also consider the nature of the author/reader relationship referred to above. For us children's literature is any narrative written and published for children and we include the 'teen' novels aimed at the 'young adult' or late adolescent reader, very much a tradition of the last three decades of the twentieth century. In our considerations we shall refer to two surveys of children's reading habits. The first, carried out in 1884, was published by Edward Salmon (1865–1955) in 1888 and the second was compiled as part of an ongoing research project initiated by Murray Knowles in 1989–90 to establish a part-computerised corpus of children's literature. Neither survey is regarded as being absolute in its findings but they should be seen as providing useful points of location as we proceed with our discussions.

THE NINETEENTH CENTURY: TRADITIONAL JUVENILE FICTION

It is in the nineteenth century that we witness a proliferation of literature written for children and the beginning of the modern age. In the early years of the century authors began to write for entertainment and we see the advent of what became a mass output of popular juvenile fiction. This fiction was first characterised by the adventure story, which, while it did not exclude female readers, was located in a particularly male world or what the authors of this type of fiction perceived as a male reality. Thus, the 1800s gave us the types of stories contained in magazines like *The Boys' Own Paper* and in books by writers such as R.M. Ballantyne (1825–94), W.H.G. Kingston (1814–80), Captain Marryat (1792–1848), T. Mayne Reid (1818–83), G.A. Henty (1832–1902) and a host of lesser-known authors such as Gordon Stables (1840–1910). With the school story we have the two interlocking wings of what we shall refer to hereafter as traditional juvenile fiction. Before we discuss that tradition in more detail it is useful to take note of the background from which it eventually emerged.

The beginnings

Narratives of adventure were appearing in England from round about the fourteenth century and while they were not written specifically for children they became popular with a young readership. They belong to the Romance tradition, usually rooted in French or other European sources, and were invariably in verse. Later, prose narratives appeared in the form of chapbooks, the first cheap printed books for a popular market. Few chapbooks before the late eighteenth century were written or printed with children in mind but towards the century's end reading material was being produced in some quantity for children. This 'consisted of a cheerful medley of old tales from the chapbooks, and lively new ones which stated how good children were rewarded and naughty ones were punished with frightful fates calculated to satisfy the most bloodthirsty infant mind' (Avery, 1975: 15).

By the end of the eighteenth century a new element had entered the world of children's books. Three books written at this time have been described by Avery as 'the foundation stones of the nursery library of the next hundred years' (1965: 13). These were Thomas Day's (1748–89) *The History of Sandford and Merton*, Mrs Trimmer's (1741–

1810) *Fabulous Histories* and John Aikin's (1747–1822) and Mrs Barbauld's (1743–1825) *Evenings at Home*. Each was published many times in the next hundred years, most likely an indication of their popularity with adults as suitable reading for the young. It is worth commenting briefly on these narratives as they reflect strongly the prevailing belief, best summed up by Mrs Trimmer herself, that children's literature should be comprised of works 'by which curiosity was gratified at the same time that religion, loyalty, and good morals were inculcated' (Salway, 1976: 20).

In *Sandford and Merton* (1783–9) Day's intention was to present Rousseau's *Emile* to English children. He wrote a series of stories, some of which were based on classical myths while others were tales with a moral such as 'The Good-Natured Little Boy' and 'The Ill-Natured Little Boy'. The stories were connected by a linking narrative centred upon three main characters: Harry Sandford, the sturdy, honest son of a poor farmer, Tommy Merton, the spoilt, snobbish son of a rich merchant and Mr Barlow their clergyman teacher. It was this narrative that gave the book its reputation as a major work for children.

Mrs Trimmer's *Fabulous Histories* (1786) later published as *The History of the Robins* was described by her in the introduction as providing for her young readers 'a series of Fables, intended to convey moral instruction applicable to themselves' (see Darton, 1932/1982: 158). The aim of the stories was, by encouraging kindness to animals, to promote moral behaviour as perceived by Mrs Trimmer. This meant that the emphasis was on the dutiful. Writing a century later, Edward Salmon saw her style as being characterised by 'the pomposity of its tone' and considered that in the book there 'is nothing unusually meritorious' (1888: 163).

Evenings at Home (1792–6) was a collection in six volumes (eventually published in one volume) of a miscellany of facts, stories and moral and religious teaching.

There was now a moral, indeed didactic, flavour as children's books were seen as a necessary part of children's education and while the moral tale as exemplified above reached its zenith in the early decades of the nineteenth century its influence never completely died out. This is important, as we shall see in Chapter 3, when we consider the linguistic features of traditional juvenile fiction.

The adventure story

In the first years of the nineteenth century there were a few writers producing less overtly didactic texts for young readers. There was not, though, an identifiable collection of books written for children which presented more 'entertaining' narratives than the types of works we have just considered. By the early 1840s, however, there was a major addition to the types of books available to older children, especially for boys. It is in this decade that there commenced the writing and publishing of what became known as the *adventure* story, the genre which lays the foundations of modern children's fiction.

The adventure story has its tradition firmly rooted in Defoe's *Robinson Crusoe* published in 1719. What are known as the 'Robinsonnades' became, for a time, 'the dominant form in fiction for children and young people' (Carpenter and Prichard, 1984: 458). One of the best known of these writers – indeed we can regard him as the 'founding father' of the adventure story – was Captain Marryat, whose *Peter Simple* was published in 1834 and *Mr. Midshipman Easy* in 1836. The latter work is regarded as one of the most popular of nineteenth-century children's stories and was indeed widely read by boys. It was not, however, written for children. As Avery comments:

> It is innocent enough, but Marryat's racy humour is given full rein and we get a picaresque novel (of a refined sort), a purged *Roderick Random*, with breezy jokes about debagging midshipmen masquerading as the devil, and using female disguise to get access to young ladies' apartments.
>
> (1965: 140)

We note also the references to Mrs Easy's pregnancy:

> It was at the finale of the eleventh year of their marriage that Mrs. Easy at first complained that she could not enjoy her breakfast. Mrs. Easy had her own suspicions, everybody else considered it past doubt, all except Mr. Easy; he little 'thought good easy man, that his greatness was ripening'; he had decided that to have an heir was no easy task, and it never came into his calculations, that there could be a change in his wife's figure.
>
> (Marryat, 1836: 6)

The lack of explicit moralising is further exemplified by the nurse's defence of her illegitimate baby with the words, 'If you please Ma'am it was a very little one' (*ibid.* 10). The discourse hardly seems compatible with the work of Mrs Trimmer or the lack of humour and the moral intent that Thomas Day delivered to his young readers in *Sandford and Merton*. Marryat, however, had two styles of writing and, as Avery points out (1965: 140): 'one can make a direct comparison of his official style for boys with the sort of book that was spontaneous Marryat'. Certainly, there are very distinct differences in the styles of narrative between *Mr. Midshipman Easy* and *Masterman Ready*, which was published in 1841 as the first of his books written specifically for young readers.

In *Masterman Ready* we have the typical 'Robinsonnade' structure fashioned on *Robinson Crusoe* and its best-known imitator *Swiss Family Robinson*. Indeed, Marryat's children had asked their father for a story which was a continuation of this latter work (Carpenter and Prichard, 1984: 344). The Seagrave family are voyaging to Australia and are shipwrecked on an island with an old seaman, Masterman Ready. Ready provides long didactic passages in which there is much reference to thanking God for His mercies and the comfort to be found in the Bible. Mr Seagrave also contributes substantially to the moral and pious flavour of the book. Thus, although we now have a narrative in which dangers threaten and in which 'adventures' clearly occur, the opportunity for moralising on a range of activities and behaviour is not lost. The elements of moral instruction *à la* Trimmer and Barbault have by no means disappeared. Indeed, Tommy, the six-year-old of the family, is responsible, through his thoughtless behaviour, for Ready's death. Ready, however, dies murmuring, 'Poor little Tommy, don't let him know that he was the cause of my death' (Marryat, 1841/1889: 325).

Overall, though the moral earnestness of the 1780s is still present – Mr Seagrave's didacticism is particularly manifested 'by haranguing his children about reasoning power in animals, the history of the British colonies, and economics' (Avery, 1965: 141) – Marryat does present a story with interesting details about strange places and, while a writer 'of moral purpose', wished also to 'excite and amuse' as well as 'instruct' (see Leeson, 1985: 76). Marryat's example was soon followed by a number of writers who from the start aimed at the adolescent boy. By 1888 Marryat was listed (see Salmon, 1888: 14) as one of the three most popular boys' writers along with W.H.G. Kingston and R.M. Ballantyne. There was not in England a similar pioneering movement in creating a lasting body of fiction for girls. It is also worth noting that while 'harangue' Marryat did, he ought also to be remembered, as we shall see in chapter 3, for his rather untypical views on colonisation and empire.

R.M. Ballantyne, like Marryat an ex-naval officer, drew upon his real-life experiences as a trapper and fur trader in North America in some of his story-telling. He is probably best remembered for *The Coral Island* (1858), which was to become one of the most popular children's books ever written and a strong influence on the young

Robert Louis Stevenson. Again we note the debt owed to Defoe, the story being centred upon the adventures of three friends who are shipwrecked on a desert island and who survive because of their initiative. According to Avery, Ballantyne's contribution as a writer for boys was that he was able to combine 'instruction and moral and religious precepts with an exciting plot' (1965: 229).

W.H.G. Kingston was one of the most prolific writers for a juvenile readership and, according to Salmon (1888: 14), the most popular. Kingston's best-known works are *Peter the Whaler* (1851) and *The Three Midshipmen* (1873). *Peter the Whaler* is a story very much in the Marryat tradition. The narrative concerns the adventures of the son of a Church of Ireland clergyman who goes to sea and survives fire, piracy and being marooned on Arctic ice. Avery states, 'like Ballantyne, his heroes were pious, and this piety pervades all his adventure stories' (1965: 145). Actually, in our view, Peter is not really pious until the end of the story (see chapter 3). According to Salmon (1888: 15) *The Three Midshipmen* was the most popular adventure story book written for boys, and this nearly forty years after being published.

Kingston, Marryat and Ballantyne are the most prominent of the early adventure story-writers. According to Carpenter and Prichard, they were responsible for taking a stage further the 'Robinsonnade' format in that they

> introduced another motif into the adventure story, that of the young Englishman (often a mere boy) who goes out into the wilds, mingles with natives and hunters, and comes back toughened, having learnt their ways.
>
> (1984: 6)

This motif should be borne in mind as a salient feature of the adventure story at this early stage in its development as it absorbed other features by the end of the century, as we shall see. However, it is now time to consider briefly traditional juvenile fiction's other wing; the *school* story.

The school story

The narrative regarded as establishing, if not immortalising, this tradition in children's fiction is Thomas Hughes's (1822–96) *Tom Brown's Schooldays*. The book was published in 1857 and was immediately successful. Although school stories had been published earlier in Britain it was *Tom Brown's Schooldays* set in the Rugby of

Thomas Arnold ('the Doctor' in the narrative) that is regarded as the classic work of the tradition and as marking its true beginning. Arnold, as well as being the father of Matthew Arnold, is regarded as responsible for the evolution of much of the British public-school system which, in general, had not been held in high regard.

As we have seen, much of the earlier work for children was decidedly didactic in tone and this narrative does not lack a moral, decidedly 'muscular' Christian flavour. This is particularly interesting in that while Thomas Hughes appeared to hero-worship Dr Arnold, Arnold himself was not inclined towards the heartiness of the team spirit so much admired by Hughes. Hughes was very much influenced by his close friend Charles Kingsley who 'earned for his views the sobriquet of "muscular Christianity"' (Musgrave, 1985: 50). Hughes himself in the preface to the sixth edition of his book stated: 'My sole object in writing was to preach to boys: if ever I write again it will be to preach to some other age' (1857/1880: xiii). The value systems esteemed by Hughes are presented to the young reader in a series of episodes or set pieces without a closely knit plot. Thus, we see Tom from his earliest days at home to his return to Rugby as an old boy on hearing of the death of Arnold. At various stages the author holds forth on 'games, fights, country pastimes, lessons, sickness and health, and Christianity' (Musgrave, 1985: 57) to present the world view he felt his readers ought to have, a view centred upon family, patriotism and God. John Rowe Townsend (1965: 58) sees *Tom Brown's Schooldays* as a documentary and a moral documentary at that.

If Thomas Hughes produced a 'moral documentary' at least there were episodes in his book which provided entertainment as well as preaching. The second great school classic, though nowadays much less known, *Eric, or Little by Little*, was excessive in its concentration on morals. The book by F.W. Farrar (1831–1903) was published the year after *Tom Brown's Schooldays* in 1858. Farrar produced *Eric*, as Hughes did *Tom Brown*, to preach but delivers a continuous moral exhortation whereas, as Isabel Quigley informs us:

> Hughes got in first with his cheerful, attractive preaching, which reconciled his readers to the didactic approach. Had *Eric* been the first school story it might, as founder of a genre, have been still-born.
>
> (1984: 68)

The story concerns how Eric Williams, a boy of noble character, fights a losing battle with temptation. 'Little by Little' refers to the progress of his moral decline as a schoolboy at Roslyn School. First, he is involved in cribbing – he was actually passing the crib to another boy – and from then on it is a downward path. Eric wishes to be popular and eventually he is swearing, smoking and drinking. He reforms but soon yields again to temptation, drinking and attacking a master. Eventually, wrongly suspected of theft, he runs away to sea. His health is broken under intolerable conditions and he returns home to die. It is a book that today's young reader would find difficult to read without laughing. Nevertheless, it was popular throughout the nineteenth century and the author sums up his purpose in writing it in the preface to the 1889 edition:

> The story of *Eric* was written with but one single object – the vivid inculcation of inward purity and moral purpose, by the history of a boy who, in spite of the inherent nobleness of his disposition falls into all folly and wickedness, until he has learnt to seek help from above.
>
> (cited by Musgrave, 1985: 67)

Farrar also wrote *St. Winifred's, or, the World of School* which was published in 1862. This also has a theme of moral decline though the hero eventually redeems himself.

Manliness and empire

By the 1880s the tradition of English authors producing a male-orientated juvenile fiction was well established. As the century entered its final decades the 'clichés of the genre' were established and the author best remembered for doing so must be G.A. Henty (see Carpenter and Prichard, 1984: 7). Henty takes the adventure story a stage further than Ballantyne, Kingston and Marryat. For Henty the Empire and the concept of 'Englishness' or 'Britishness' were essential ingredients in his writing for boys. Henty was 'a propagandist – for Empire and British interests – and a highly successful one too, in his way' (Arnold, 1980: 79). Henty's favourite setting was one of the many colonial wars of the nineteenth century which permitted him to present his ideal of resourceful and patriotic young manhood. This ideal was also manifested in his historical novels, which often focused on a crucial point in English history. Indeed war, be it in the nineteenth, eighteenth or seventeenth century, was an essential backcloth for Henty's narratives. His heroes, invariably upper middle class, were 'brave' and 'dashing' though his portrayal of characters from the lower social orders or other racial backgrounds was often less than sympathetic.

Henty's writing epitomised the culmination of the public-school ideal and the public schoolboy's place in the Empire. The books were written to a formula so much so that

> if you have read only two or three of the eighty-odd books he wrote for boys you know most of the rest, even if you like one first encountered better than those you met later when you could recognise the formula.
>
> (Darton, 1932/1982: 302)

To a large extent the boys' adventure stories from the 1840s on can all be seen, to some extent, in formulaic terms. Henty adds, however, to the distinguishing features of the tradition his staunch patriotism and belief in the system of empire. According to Avery, when comparing Henty with the earlier writers, Henty's heroes were cast in a similar mould but 'he made them more British, more conscious of the might of the Empire which they served and which to a certain extent replaced the Kingdom of Heaven in their emotions' (1965: 145).

As the adventure story flourished in terms of appealing to a mass readership so too did the school story. In 1881–2 Talbot Baines Reed (1852–93) wrote *The Fifth Form at St. Dominic's* for *The Boys' Own Paper*, which was published as a book in 1887. Reed's subsequent work was based largely on public-school settings and he is responsible for popularising this type of children's fiction originally created by Hughes in the same way that Henty and his imitators popularised the adventure story. The public school is now a well-established and respected institution. Its function is to produce the type of young men necessary to govern and defend the Empire, the heroes of Henty's books. Good examples must be set and 'honour' and 'decency' are key concepts; they form the basis of the code of behaviour which binds all the boys together as members of a hierarchical society with a particular system of dominance. Should a boy offend against the code then his peers will make their disapproval known. The writers who modelled themselves upon Reed perpetuated the stock ingredients of a stolen examination paper, the sneak and the bully, the triumphant win in cricket or rugger and the characteristics of loyalty to one's friends and the school. The later school story has, for Isabel Quigley, 'everything to attract the hack and the humdrum (as well as the occasional Kipling, who presumably took a hack humdrum subject to see what he could do with it)' (1984: 99). What Kipling did with it was to produce *Stalky and Co.*, whose three main characters H.G. Wells referred to as 'mucky little sadists' (see Quigley 1984: 109). *Stalky and Co.* was published in 1899 and was thus too late to be a possible inclusion in Salmon's survey. Rudyard Kipling (1865–1936) presented in a series of linked stories 'some tracts or parables on the education of the young' (see Musgrave, 1985: 171). Many of the incidents and characters are based on Kipling's own experiences and relationships at school. Much criticised, and it does contain scenes of violent behaviour and attitude which lends support to Wells's criticism, *Stalky and Co.* is very different from the world of *Eric*. It is made quite clear on several occasions in the book what Stalky and his friends think of Farrar's world and the statement 'we ain't going to have any beastly Erickin'' (1899/1987: 118) indicates that whatever Kipling's views on the 'education of the young' they were not going to be couched in the same moral tone; Kipling's is a different didacticism. Certainly, as John Rowe Townsend points out, *Eric* and *Stalky* operate on different planes, with Kipling's boys being depicted much more realistically and convincingly. Like Wells, Townsend is concerned about the values of the book. Attitudes towards the working class, for example, as represented by a gamekeeper who is demoted for shooting a fox and attitudes towards violent behaviour as noted above (1965: 65). Like *Tom Brown's Schooldays*, *Stalky and Co.* is about power relations and the hierarchy of the school. At the top is the revered headmaster. By and large all other levels are fair game for Stalky and his friends, who are quite ruthless in their campaigns against those who incur their disapproval.

    Stalky appeared at the height of empire. In one story the boys are disgusted by a visiting MP whose speech has him referred to as the 'jelly-bellied flag slapper'. This would appear to be pejorative yet the criticism is not of the notion of the Empire and service to it but rather of the fact that the visitor has with his raucous speech on honour and glory 'profaned the most secret places of their [the boys'] souls with outcries and gesticulations' (Kipling, 1899/1987: 175). It is not the notion of empire that the boys are objecting to; rather, it is the speaker's vulgarity. He is not, it is made clear, of the right pedigree; he has offended the code, the 'dream of glory that boys do not discuss even with their most intimate equal' (*ibid.* 175). At the end Stalky leaves school to take his rightful place as servant of the Empire in India. The book was extremely popular and not just with boys. Townsend regards it as 'an unpleasant though vigorous piece of work' (1965: 65) and Isabel Quigley sees it as 'The school story as imperial manual' (1984: 109–25).

Traditional juvenile fiction, as manifested by Henty, Reed and their imitators, did not produce anything that could be regarded as a classic. As Carpenter comments:

> During the 1880s such writers as G.A. Henty turned out sheaves of stories about brave British lads abroad; but this optimistic school of fiction was to produce no classic, no narrative of any more than trivial interest.
>
> (1985: 15)

He goes on to comment that 'Probably the nearest one can come to an "Empire" classic for children is Kipling's *Stalky and Co.*' However, he gives support to Quigley when he says that *Stalky*, 'an apparently amoral book . . . is in fact subtly organised to demonstrate that boyish anti-authoritarian pranks are a good training for *manly* service in the cause of one's nation'.

Dual readership

In our discussion on traditional juvenile fiction we have considered the significant landmarks of the two wings. There are works which we have not mentioned: F. Anstey (1856–1934), for example, who made a unique contribution with his *Vice Versa*, published in 1882. This story was based upon school and highly critical of both schoolmasters and private schools. Anstey, though writing in a most realistic manner, introduces the elements of fantasy and magic. His book has more in common with that strand of children's literature which we can designate fantasy fiction and which we consider in more detail a little later. Anstey, in one sense, straddles both camps but we feel that his use of fantasy locates him more properly within the other tradition. Furthermore, it would appear that though he became popular with children Anstey had adults in mind (Musgrave, 1985: 86) when he wrote his book. Certainly, his use of satire would indicate this and the book is very different from the tradition as exemplified by Talbot Baines Reed, being an excellent comic fantasy.

No discussion of traditional juvenile fiction can omit mention of Robert Louis Stevenson (1850–94) and *Treasure Island*. Although there are considerable differences between Stevenson's work and the work of the writers discussed above there is still the ideal of the young hero that did not vary, did not 'change in the hands of . . . writers in the genre, from Ballantyne to Stevenson' (Avery, 1965: 144). *Treasure Island*, published as a book in 1883, also provides an example, like Anstey's *Vice Versa*, of dual readership. It was written for boys but was to prove a great favourite of adult readers. Stevenson acknowledges the influence of both Ballantyne and Kingston but produced an entertaining novel which is not explicitly didactic, in offering either scientific or other educational facts as part of the story. Nor does it preach Christianity in the manner of Kingston, for example. The book contrasts with other examples of the tradition in having what would appear to be a degree of moral ambiguity. Note the character of Long John Silver 'the villain with something heroic about him' (Townsend, 1965: 52). Carpenter and Prichard (1984: 542) comment on the role of Long John Silver as the book's true hero and how he 'possesses a degree of courage and ingenuity not shown by the "good" characters'. Harvey Darton (1932/1982: 295) calls it 'the very apotheosis of the penny dreadful [cheap and sensational mass-produced magazines] which the virtuous and healthy magazines had been founded to dethrone'. Robert Leeson comments, however, on what he calls the book's 'supreme quality of moral logic' and contrasts the character of Jim Hawkins when invited to make a run for it from Silver with how Ballantyne's, Kingston's or Henty's heroes might have behaved. For Leeson *Treasure Island* is 'a comment on the greed of its "respectable adult hero"' and 'Jim Hawkins is as much a comment on Victorian rapacity as Carroll's Alice is a comment on Victorian hypocrisy'. The book, he says, is 'the exception that underlines the rule of the genre, and is best remembered where the rest are forgotten' (1985: 98).

As a final comment on dual readership we should not forget the influence of Sir Walter Scott (1771–1832) on the tradition of the adventure story. He only wrote one book specifically for children but his historical adventure novels were as popular with children as they were with adults. Edward Salmon (1888: 14) cites Scott as the third most popular author with boy readers.

Juvenile magazines

As the nineteenth century progressed the adventure and school stories were to reach a much wider audience through the popularity of weekly magazines. These are a comparatively late feature in writing produced for young readers. In the case of male readers the magazines were very much a reaction to earlier low-priced publications which became known as the 'penny dreadfuls'. These were not initially aimed at boys but provided an escapism in terms of cheap and sensational fiction for a mass readership. Penny dreadfuls were sold not only by newsagents but by all kinds of shopkeepers who were attracted by the high rate of discount allowed by the publishers (see Turner, 1976: 20–72). In terms of subject matter they were directly descended from the sensational type of chapbook and from Gothic novels. Many of the stories romanticised the exploits of notorious criminals or boasted titles such as *Varney the Vampire* (its alternative title was *The Feast of Blood*). The penny dreadfuls saw the creation of *Sweeney Todd the Demon Barber of Fleet Street* (*ibid.* 38–50) and the legends of characters such as Dick Turpin, Spring Heeled Jack and Jack Sheppard.

Many of the stories were lurid in terms of both narration and illustration. and they were soon courting a juvenile market. They provoked much criticism from concerned commentators as the century progressed. Salmon, for example, referred to the 'degrading and debilitating dreadful' (1888: 188). Salmon was writing in praise of boys' magazines of a more 'high minded' type, many of which had been founded to counteract the influence of the penny dreadfuls. *The Boy's Own Paper* (*BOP*), published for eighty-eight years from 1879, was created by the Religious Tract Society and provides the best-known example.

Magazines such as the *BOP* were to elevate the notion of 'manliness' and to make it available to a mass readership. Authors published in the *BOP* included Talbot Baines Reed, who published *The Fifth Form at St. Dominic's* as a serial for the magazine. The adventure writers were well represented with W.H.G. Kingston appearing in the first issue with the first instalment of a serial called *From Powder Monkey to Admiral*, which, according to Avery, 'startlingly suggested that poor boys might after all rise in the world' (1975: 192). Stories by Ballantyne and Henty were to appear in its pages and successive editors concentrated on providing 'healthy' boys' stories and advice. For Salmon the *BOP* was 'the only first-class journal of its kind which has forced its way into the slums as well as into the best homes' (1888: 186). Other magazines appeared in the 1890s with the Harmsworth series of boys' adventure weeklies which perpetuated the Kingston–Henty tradition.

Stories for girls

It will be apparent in our description of nineteenth-century juvenile fiction that the two wings were clearly intended for a male readership. Certainly, as we noted above, British writers for girls did not establish a tradition for a female readership in the same way that Ballantyne, Hughes, Henty and others managed to do. Girls' stories that were to become 'classics' were pioneered in the United States, the two best known being *Little Women* by Louisa M. Alcott (1832–88), published in 1868, and *What Katy Did* by Susan Coolidge (1845–1905), published in 1872. There were British writers, however, although their names are unlikely to be universally familiar with young readers today. Stories for girls were rooted in domesticity and the didacticism exemplified by Mrs Trimmer, for example, was persistent throughout the century.

While boys' books had their particular codes to impart to the reader, at least they were imparted in narratives which did contain exciting events and descriptions of strange places. For girls the work of such writers as Charlotte Yonge (1823–1901), Juliana Ewing (1841–85) and Mary Louisa Molesworth (1839–1921) continued to reflect the moral and religious purpose of the earlier writers. Of the three Ewing had probably the greatest literary talent; Margarita Laski (1950) in *Mrs. Ewing, Mrs. Molesworth and Mrs. Hodgson Burnett* refers to her as 'the most nearly great of my three ladies' (cited by Townsend, 1965: 69). E. Nesbitt was a great admirer and Ewing's writing was considerably more sophisticated than many of her evangelical co-authors. Gillian Avery (1975: 82) makes the point that many of her stories were far too difficult for other than an educated adult readership.

The nineteenth century was very much defined by gender and this is reflected in children's fiction. In novels created by writers such as Charlotte Yonge 'the father was elevated and remote. . . . The mother had a special role and status midway between father and children' (Leeson, 1985: 79) and, as Leeson goes on to point out, this meant 'a division not merely of social responsibility but of human qualities' (*ibid*. 80) where males are equated with courage and wisdom and females with love and purity. The pioneering work of Louisa M. Alcott's *Little Women* was also family-based but narrated in a much more informal and down-to-earth style and in a way that meant female characters were presented 'as having a strong sense of individual identity' (Wall, 1991: 89). It is interesting to note, however, that Charlotte Yonge's *The Daisy Chain* was a likely influence on Alcott.

Of some interest are examples of what were popular with girl readers in the late nineteenth century. According to Salmon (1888: 21–3) Sir Walter Scott and Charles Kingsley (1819–75) were the second and third most favourite authors after Dickens. Kingsley's historical adventure story *Westward Ho!* (1855) was cited as the most popular book and W.H.G. Kingston ranked above Alcott in the list of favourite authors, though *Little Women* was the seventh favourite book. Ballantyne and Marryat were also cited and *The Boys' Own Paper* was listed as the second most favourite magazine after *The Girls' Own Paper*. In addition Anstey and Farrar were listed. The popularity of several boys' writers and the BOP is, according to Salmon (1888: 28), because 'they [girls] can get in boys' books what they seldom get in their own – stirring plot and lively movement'. Be this as it may, it does appear that the tradition had taken hold with a growing number of female readers and we shall consider later how English writers in this tradition viewed the role of the female in the world that they represented to their young audience.

THE NINETEENTH CENTURY: FANTASY AND IMAGINATION

One of the most significant features of children's fiction today is that the presentation of adventures does not require a 'real-world' setting. Recognisable adventures can occur in narratives that are also good examples of another tradition, namely that of the fantasy story. It is this tradition that marks that 'other strand' in the development of modern children's literature.

> To this strand belong most of the great names of the late Victorian and Edwardian nursery: Kingsley, Carroll, MacDonald, Grahame, Potter, Nesbitt, Barrie with Milne as a late comer.
>
> (Carpenter, 1985: 16)

The 1860s is the focal decade for most commentators in that they regard it as the genesis of the 'Golden Age' of children's literature, for others the 'First Golden Age'. The publication of Charles Kingsley's *The Water Babies* in 1863 represents what Carpenter and Prichard (1984: 181) call 'an eloquent defence of works of the imagination' as opposed to those who argued for children to be given facts. It is also a good example of the tradition being presented as the moral tale reshaped, for Kingsley, as Leeson points out (1985: 85), 'feels the poor need to be redeemed and cleansed ready to enter paradise alongside the already clean and respectable'. In many respects *The Water Babies* is a moral tale presented as a fairytale, a tradition closely related to that of fantasy, and indeed it is not always a simple task to differentiate between them. For us Carpenter and Prichard (1984: 181) provide a useful description where fantasy is seen as a term used (in the context of children's literature) to describe works of fiction, written by a specific author (i.e. not traditional) and usually novel length, which involve the supernatural or some other unreal element.

The traditional fairytale, on the other hand, is seen as a sub-genre of the folktale, itself a sub-genre of folklore, 'traditional verbal materials and social rituals that have been handed down solely, or at least primarily, by word of mouth and by example rather than in written form' (Abrams 1957/1971: 63). There is also the literary fairytale which is perceived as based on, or at least as sharing certain features of the traditional fairytale and to which we shall return. For the moment we shall define fairytales as 'narratives predicated upon magic'. The fairytale assumes magic in the same way that the realistic novel asumes its absence, fantasy fiction may incorporate a magical element, but when it does, that element, far from being assumed, is fantastic relative to the realistic aspects of the work. In *Alice's Adventures in Wonderland* (1865), for example, as Leeson points out, 'Fantasy allows Alice to challenge family authority by providing animals, playing cards, chesspieces, to take the place of adults' (1985: 102–3).

Many, if not most, of the books published in this tradition are books which commanded a dual readership. For Barbara Wall the classic children's writers of the time did not share a narrative manner:

> They were innovative, skilful and original writers who sought individual solutions to the problems of how to address children in fiction, and found, at least when they were most successful, individual, indeed sometimes highly idiosyncratic, voices.
>
> (1991: 40)

More importantly, she claims that although they were very conscious of the fact that 'they were writing for children, they needed also to satisfy adult standards of what was considered appropriate for children'.

The great period of children's books with a dual, and durable, audience began with the publication of *Alice's Adventures in Wonderland*. Though *Alice* was written for children perhaps no book has ever had an audience so evenly divided between children and adults. Lewis Carroll (1832–98) is anarchic where Kingsley is didactic notwithstanding that both books have resemblances that 'are by no means superficial' (Townsend, 1965: 42). Both authors have reversed worlds and indulge in absurd logic and word play. *Alice* is, of course, the classic fantasy story and a classic of children's literature. For many commentators *Alice* was a turning point in children's literature because

> The directness of such work was a revolution in its sphere. It was the coming to the surface, powerfully and permanently, the first unapolegetic, undocumented appearance in print, for readers who sorely needed it, of liberty of thought in children's books. Henceforth fear had gone, and with it shy disquiet. There was to be in hours of pleasure no more dread about the moral value, the ponderable, measured quality and extent, of the pleasure itself. It was to be enjoyed and even promoted with neither forethought nor remorse.
>
> (Darton, 1932/1982: 260)

For Darton the two 'Alices' (*Through the Looking Glass* was published in 1871) moved completely from the moralising tone of earlier works for children. It is worth noting, however, as Carpenter reminds us (1985: 68), that *Alice* was by no means an immediate success. Indeed, initially it appeared to be not much liked by children but by 1898 in a poll conducted by *The Pall Mall Gazette* into the reading habits of ten-year-olds *Alice's Adventures in Wonderland* came easily first (Avery, 1965: 137).

The so-called 'First Golden Age' of children's literature was to begin with Carroll and was to last until the early 1900s. Amongst those writers who are commonly agreed to be representative of it we can list George MacDonald (1824–1905) and in particular his *At the Back of the North Wind* (1871), which was didactic but did not preach overtly, Richard Jeffries (1848–87) and *Bevis, the Story of a Boy* (1882), Edith Nesbit (1858–1924) and her comic fantasy *Five Children and It* (1902), Kenneth Grahame (1859–1932) and *The Wind in the Willows* (1908), Francis Hodgson Burnett (1849–1924) and *The Secret Garden*, published in 1911. A.A. Milne's (1882–1956) *Pooh* books, published in 1926 and 1928, and Beatrix Potter (1866–1943) would also be included though the audience here is much younger.

It will be noted our concept of fantasy includes anthropomorphism as an element. Thus, adventures may be had by animals with identifiable human feelings as well as by human children where there is some supernatural or other unreal element. It is perhaps worth noting with Crouch (1962: 43) that we differentiate between the type of story where animals appear as types of human characters and the realistic animal narrative which typifies another genre, a good example of which would be Henry Williamson (1895–1977), author of *Tarka the Otter* (1927) popular with, though not written for, children.

THE FAIRYTALE

We commented earlier on the close relationship between the fairytale and the stories found in the tradition of fantasy writing. The fairytale, of course, has never been a tradition of works exclusively, or even primarily, for children. This is not remarkable in itself except that, as Zipes (1991: xi) points out, it is so often taken for granted that fairytales are 'largely the domain of children'. This perception may derive in part from certain features typical of fairytale narrative (see chapter 5) and in part from the marketing and dissemination of fairytales. Today collections of fairytales are popular gifts for very young children (Hallett and Karasak, 1991: 6–7), and the tales are widely told in infant and nursery schools. As Steedman (1982: 142) points out, attractively produced and priced editions of individual tales like *Cinderella*, *Snow White* and *Little Red Riding Hood*, specifically designed to appeal to children, are available in newspaper shops and supermarkets as well as bookshops. In addition Disney cartoon adaptations on video have contributed to the genre's popularity.

In fact, most traditional fairytales came to British children in translations in which some adaptation had taken place (see also Ellis, 1983, for an account of the types of adaptation the Grimm brothers made to the tales they collected). Throughout the nineteenth century earlier disapproval of the fairytale (Mrs Trimmer was a fierce opponent) faded as more and more tales from a variety of nations became available to young readers. The brothers Grimm (Jacob, 1785–1863; Wilhelm, 1786–1859) were first published in English in 1823 and Hans Christian Andersen (1805–75) appeared throughout the 1840s. Both Andersen and the brothers Grimm were cited as popular reading matter in the 1880s (see Salmon, 1888: 14, 21). By the end of the century the genre was firmly established with the collections and translations of Joseph Jacobs (1854–1916) and Andrew Lang (1844–1912) amongst others.

Of course it is the tales as children read and hear them that are important in this study, but the traditional tales exist in different versions, and there are a number of difficulties for a project such as ours in using translated texts. For example, it is not always possible to establish (i) who the translator/adaptor is, (ii) whether the translator has worked from a version of the text in its language of origin or whether he or she has used an existing translation into English or into another language as the basis for the new text, (iii) the likely motivation for selecting one rather than another version of the story as Source Text for the translation. We therefore limit discussion in chapter 5 to literary fairytales written in English by identifiable authors whose social setting and background is known. 'The genre cuts across all ages' (Zipes, 1991: xi), but we shall limit discussion to examples which are not primarily directed at adults.

The nineteenth century saw the fairytale arise as a new European literary genre partly as a result of the efforts of collectors of traditional folktales, and partly out of a desire among writers to use their craft in the service of child socialisation (Zipes, 1983: 3). As fairytales regained their respectability (for an account of the loss of respectability during the seventeenth and eighteenth centuries of the original folk- and fairytales see Zipes, 1987: Introduction). Many Victorian writers came to consider the genre as the ideal vehicle for influencing the minds and morals of the reading and read-to middle classes, and it was, according to Zipes (1987: xi), 'through the fairytale that a social discourse about conditions in England took form'.

The Industrial Revolution in England created what seemed to many writers a wholly materialistic society founded on greed and self-interest and benefiting the few at the expense of the many with a new mass of urban poor having come into existence. Nature appeared to have fallen into neglect, and human freedom seemed unduly curtailed by the institutionalisation which accompanied the rise of the new middle classes. In this climate a series of controversies arose about the spiritual and material foundations of English life, nature, child-rearing practices, the possibility of human freedom and about possible sources of social cohesion. These questions formed the basis of the so-called 'Conditions of England Debate' to which both the novel and the literary fairytale began to relate (Zipes, 1987: xv–xvi).

Zipes (1987: xxiii) perceives two basic trends among fairytale writers during the period 1860 until 1900. The majority of writers embraced conventionalism, while a minority engaged in overt, non-conformist utopianism. According to Zipes (xxiii–xxiv), conventionalist writers of the period

> conceived plots conventionally to reconcile themselves and their readers to the status quo of Victorian society. Their imaginative worlds could be called exercises in complicity . . . for there is rarely a hint of social criticism and subversion in their works. . . .

After a brief period of disturbance, . . . extraordinary creatures generally enable the protagonists to integrate themselves into a prescribed social order.

Zipes considers Edith Nesbit (1858–1924) conformist, while George MacDonald and Oscar Wilde (1854–1900) figure among writers he considers non-conformist utopians. These

> reveal a profound belief in the power of the imagination as a potent force that can be used to question the value of existing social relations. There is also a moral impulse in this second direction. However, it does not lead to reconciliation with the status quo – rather, rebellion against convention and conformity. Fairy-tale protagonists are sent on quests which change them as the world around them also changes. The fairies and the other magical creatures inspire and compel the protagonists to alter their lives and pursue utopian dreams.

(1987: xxiv)

Amongst the most popular of the literary fairytales were Nesbit's 'The Book of Beasts' (1900), MacDonald's *The Princess and Curdie* (1883 – as a book), Wilde's 'The Happy Prince' (1888a). Examples of all these writers' fairytales are still available in children's bookshops today, which suggests that their work continues to inspire imaginations beyond the scholarly.

THE TWENTIETH CENTURY: THE FIRST HALF

The tradition of the adventure and school stories persisted into the twentieth century. Narratives of the Henty mould were being produced by any number of imitators. The tradition, however, 'had become in fact a piece of manufactured goods' (Darton, 1932/1982: 303). Writers such as F.S. Brereton (1872–1957) and Percy F. Westerman (1876–1960) were amongst the more popular and were succeeded in turn by W.E. Johns (1893–1968), the creator of Biggles. Boys' adventure magazines also made much use of the type of adventure story and adult popular authors like John Buchan (1875–1940) and Sapper (1888–1937) were also read by adolescent boys.

The 1920s and 1930s produced little that was original in terms of the adventure story. The narratives were stereotypical with both plots and characters fossilised in the 1880s and 1890s. The Biggles books contain recognisable Henty characters and situations and in Johns and the writers cited above 'there is a range of moral attitudes which have hardly been made obsolete by the march of history since they were always clearly repellent' (Inglis, 1981: 53).

The school story too produced little that was creative in the first half of the century. The early years saw established the tradition of the girls' school story most closely associated with Angela Brazil (1869–1947) and so well described by Cadogan and Craig (1976). For most people today the school story means, as Isabel Quigley (1982: 254) points out, the 'pop' school story and the mythical world of Billy Bunter, and Frank Eyre (1971) writes of the tradition having been brought to a 'perfection of unreality'. The tradition of the public schoolboy narrative had run its course by the end of World War II and by the 1960s and 1970s writers were, and still are, producing novels set with day-school backgrounds with characters and situations that are credible.

The inter-war years were not entirely barren. A different type of adventure emerged. Rather than the 'manly', public-school-educated, clean-limbed young hero fighting against the stereotyped odds in far-flung corners of the world, there was produced what might be called the 'local' adventure. Carpenter and Prichard refer to 'small scale and entirely plausible adventures that could hold just as much excitement as more melodramatic adventures' (1984: 7). Arthur Ransome's (1884–1967) *Swallows and Amazons* was published in 1930 and represents the new fiction at its best while Enid Blyton (1897–1968) with her *Famous Five* shows it at its most ordinary and unoriginal. Ransome's characters are overwhelmingly middle class and possessed of what Avery calls a 'calm efficiency and capacity for coping without adults' (1975: 121). Indeed their middle classness has provoked strong criticism of Ransome. Dixon (1977: 58) comments:

> *Swallows and Amazons*, a 'classic' . . . is another typical example . . . in which the children are exclusively middle class and in which, if members of the lower classes appear at all, it's decidedly on the fringe.

The narrative is structured, he says, like most children's literature so that it 'has the overall effect, whether conscious or not, either on the part of the writer or on that of the reader, of indoctrinating children with a capitalist ideology' (*ibid.* 70). Be that as it may, Ransome's contribution should not be overlooked. Apart from the fact that he was not appealing to a gender-specific audience there was his 'conscientious realism' (Leeson 1985: 117). There was now something identifiable as a 'real life' although Trease's view that the Ransome books depict 'a fantasy world, disguised under a wealth of realistic practical detail' (1964: 139) seems to us to be a more complete description. Ransome, however, offered a new formula in the writing of adventure stories which might be summed up as 'localisation'. Thus adventures could be experienced during children's holidays in surroundings that were neither exotic nor fantastic. For Fred Inglis, Ransome 'straddles the years between the wars, and is the dominating writer for children during that period' (1981: 129).

The middle-class family world was very much the scenario for children's adventures in the 1930s and 1940s. That is, with the exception of *The Family From One End Street* by Eve Garnett, published in 1937. This purported to depict working-class life as it really was. It won the Carnegie Medal (the major award for children's literature) and was much hailed as a 'classic of reality'. That this should be so, according to Leeson (1985: 112), 'is an indication of the level of unreality that pervaded the family story'. In similar vein Frank Eyre had commented earlier:

> We praised too highly *The Family From One End Street* because it was all we could find of that sort to praise. . . . Unhappily the shadow of One End Street hangs over much contemporary realistic writing for children.
>
> (1971: 24)

By and large the first half of the twentieth century was not notable for the production of children's stories of any quality. The period marks the drawing to an end of the Ballantyne–Henty inspired tradition and in the years following World War II we see the emergence of narratives where traditional juvenile fiction gives way to 'novels of character' with writers like Alan Garner, for example, 'showing how mythology and magic could be used to create a children's adventure' (Carpenter and Prichard, 1984: 8).

The fantasy story continued to appear in Britain though the period between the wars is not, as we noted, universally regarded as a particularly creative one. A time when, as John Rowe Townsend puts it 'the general standard of children's books had been low for several years, and when interest in the subject was at an equally low ebb' (1965: 105). In 1937, however, *The Hobbit* by J.R.R. Tolkien (1892–1973) was published although it did not gain fame as a classic until the mid 1960s when the subsequent trilogy *The Lord of the Rings* (1954/1955) had acquired a cult following.

In many respects Tolkien's approach was closer to the genre of science fiction in which he took a great interest (see Carpenter and

Prichard, 1984: 255). In *The Hobbit* he recreated the world with minute detail. There were maps, there was natural history, there was geology, there were languages and in this world adventures took place. Inglis comments:

> *The Hobbit* is the . . . best link between a present day child and the world which made these stories up in order to describe the early colonizing of England. Its pace and fullness, its good temper, the scale of its protagonists, its manageable horrors and disasters, its simple triumphs and morals, all fit it to the child's eye view.
>
> (1981: 199)

The Lord of the Rings as a sequel to *The Hobbit* began life as a children's book but Tolkien had not intended the finished version to be such. It has, however, been read by many children and it is in so many ways a book for a young readership. The narrative in many respects would fit easily into the genre of traditional juvenile fiction we discussed earlier and this is important as it underlines how different traditions in children's literature are not mutually exclusive. Tolkien provides a quest to be undertaken by the hero (a male) and his companions. They sustain many adventures as they undertake the long and dangerous journey. Good and evil are presented without subtlety and moral choices are easily perceived but not always easily made (Kirkpatrick, 1978: 1233). Tolkien's medieval background is obvious in the narrative structure but it is interesting and important to note with Carpenter and Prichard (1984: 325) that '*The Lord of the Rings*, like *The Hobbit*, also shows traces of more contemporary influences including Stevenson's *Kidnapped* and Buchan's *The Thirty Nine Steps*' and that Tolkien very much enjoyed the works of Rider Haggard (1856–1925) whose adventure story *King Solomon's Mines* was published in 1885. In addition he was strongly influenced by the fairy books of Andrew Lang and the works of George McDonald (*ibid.* 255, 325).

A further point of interest is made by Michael Wood (1976: 168) in terms of the theology of the book. 'Tolkien believes in Providence both in and out of his fiction. He never mentions chance without a pious parenthesis – "if such it be".' A theological, often didactic, element is also very evident in the work of Tolkien's friend C.S. Lewis (1898–1963). Indeed, the purpose of the first of the Narnia books *The Lion, the Witch and the Wardrobe* (1950) and its successors was to 're-imagine Christianity in terms of a children's fairy story' (Carpenter and Pritchard, 1984: 310).

Whatever the allegorical nature of the Narnia books there is again the clearly recognisable adventure motif in a fantasy setting. Lewis was also dealing with subjects that in the 1950s were regarded as taboo for children. 'These books ran directly across a number of attitudes and taboos in children's fiction. . . . They contain violence, pain and death' (Kirkpatrick, 1978: 769). Overall, for the young reader, however, there are clear divisions between right and wrong, the concepts of 'nobleness' and of evil and stirring deeds courageously executed without, necessarily, for that reader a conscious perception of religious imagery.

In sum, we can note the fact that from the 1860s literature written for children diverged so that, as Humphrey Carpenter informs us,

> Kipling was almost the only writer who straddled the two streams of children's literature which divided in about 1860 and never really came together again until the 1950s. On the one hand was the breezy, optimistic adventure story, set firmly in the real world (though greatly exaggerating certain characteristics of that world). Stories of school life pioneered by Thomas Hughes and then mass produced by hack writers from the 1880s, belonged in this category, . . . 'Realistic' fiction of this kind attracted few writers of any quality. . . . The other strand of writing for children . . . was introspective, and is generally described as 'fantasy'. . . . While it was not overtly realistic and purported to have nothing to say about the 'real' world, in this fantastic strain of writing may be found some profound observations about human character and contemporary society and (strikingly often) about religion.
>
> (1985: 15–16)

Kipling also, it should be noted was a purveyor of fairytales of the type exemplified in *Puck of Pook's Hill* (1906) and *Rewards and Fairies* (1910).

THE TWENTIETH CENTURY: THE SECOND HALF

In one sense contemporary children's literature has acquired what Humphrey Carpenter calls a 'dual purpose' (1985: 1). That is that books not only provide an exciting narrative but also contain 'some moral truth or lesson', without necessarily reverting to the didacticism of an earlier period. The 1950s and 1960s are generally regarded as seeing a vast improvement in the form and content of literature written for children – a 'Second Golden Age' or, as Inglis puts it in writing of Philippa Pearce (1920–), 'I take *Tom's Midnight Garden* (1958) to inaugurate the present "golden age" of children's literature' (1981: 259). Naomi Lewis (1978: vii) writes of the second 'flowering'. One clear reason for the emergence of a new 'class' of children's writing in the 1950s and 1960s was that publishers were beginning to build up their lists in this area and it was attracting writers of recognised literary merit. Indeed, as Blishen comments: 'Writing for children grows stronger and bolder, as writing for adults grows more . . . inward, marked by self doubting intricacy' (1975: 11). We now see established adult writers entering the field. As early as 1946 Elizabeth Goudge (1900–84) won the Carnegie Medal for *The Little White Horse* and Rumer Godden (1907–) followed suit in 1947 with *The Doll's House*. Later Joan Aiken (1924–), Nina Bawden (1925–) and Penelope Lively (1933–) were to swell the ranks of children's writers. The general lack of creativity that marked the inter-war years appeared to be over.

One of the characteristics of much of post-war children's writing is how mythology and magic became dominant influences in the writing of stories of adventure. Alan Garner (1934–) was one of the most widely discussed writers of the 1960s and 1970s. His earliest work *The Weirdstone of Brisingamen* (1960) and its sequel *The Moon of Gomrath* (1963) were very much in the Tolkien mould or, as Inglis puts it, 'ready examples of the Tolkien formation' (1981: 238). Magic and myth informs so much of Garner's work as in *Elidor* (1967), for example, *The Owl Service* (1967) and *Red Shift* (1973). Neither of the latter two, both of which work on three layers of narrative, can be regarded as an 'easy read'. In *The Owl Service* the layers involve the present time, a time past and a mythical time. In *Red Shift* the layers are three independent stories operating at different periods of time. For Inglis, Garner has 'a strong bookish atavism' and this means that, according to him, '*The Owl Service* remains fixed in the forcefield of myth, and the characters distinct in the stereotypes of upper and working class and the eternal triangle' (1981: 245).

The very great variety of contemporary children's writers makes it impossible to mention them all even if such were our intention. However, the undoubted originality and evident popularity (the two are not always compatible) of some authors warrants a brief focus of attention. Penelope Lively began writing for children in the 1970s and her *The Ghost of Thomas Kempe* (1973) proved to be very popular. It also won for her the Carnegie Medal in 1974. The book is still popular and was cited in Knowles's 1989–90 survey. Lively's main contribution to children's fiction, according to Carpenter and Prichard, is that her writing 'shows the author attempting to get away from the conventions of the children's adventure novel' (1984: 322).

For Inglis Penelope Lively is one of a group of writers who he takes as 'breaking the ranks of the Tolkien formation' (1981: 226) in her pursuance of an historical theme.

Nina Bawden was also cited by Knowles's respondents and by a much smaller survey of 100 second-year women undergraduates asked (in 1992–3) to recall their favourite reading matter between the ages of eleven and fourteen. Bawden's first book for children, *Devil by the Sea* was published in 1957 and was a conventional adventure story. Her later work, however, concentrates more on emotions and motives for actions and 'adventures' rooted in the experiences of childhood. The two best known of Bawden's books, *Carrie's War* (1973) and *The Peppermint Pig* (1975), portray most skilfully a child's view of the world and combine realism with the ability to construct an entertaining narrative with the right balance of plot, characters and suspense.

Another popular post-war writer is Robert Westall (1929–). Westall's best-known work, *The Machine Gunners* (1975), has been recognised classroom reading for a number of years and this may well have influenced our respondents. Westall, it has been said, produced a book which 'has an intensity and energy on the page which is the mark of a true writer' (Paton-Walsh, 1978b: 1315) and Robert Leeson (1985: 137) praises him for being one of a group of writers who 'gave for the first time on any scale authentic pictures of working class children'. *The Machine Gunners* is set in Newcastle upon Tyne during World War II and concerns the theft by a group of children of a machine gun from a crashed German fighter 'plane. Paton-Walsh's and Leeson's sentiments have been echoed by many critics who praise Westall's ability to write modern adventure stories that are realistic in terms of the characters and their relationships. Others of Westall's books deal with sexuality and he has been criticised severely by David Rees (1984) for what Rees calls his elevation of 'macho-man', his stereotyping of females and social class divisions and for perpetuating racist attitudes. Rees is himself a well-known children's author, having won the Carnegie Medal for *The Exeter Blitz* in 1978.

The change in direction of writing for children in the last thirty years is exemplified by a range of authors which it is beyond the scope of this study to other than briefly mention. There is the work of Leon Garfield (1921–), for example, or Jan Mark (1943–), Peter Dickinson (1927–) and Margaret Mahy (1936–), who are all worthy of note. William Mayne (1928–) is an author regarded by John Rowe Townsend as one of 'a new generation of writers' and his contribution as a talented, creative and original writer must be acknowledged. We feel, however, that it is no accident that none of his works were cited by our respondents in 1989–90 and this might lend weight to Pamela Cleaver's comment that: 'His work is much admired by critics and librarians, but whether it is much enjoyed by children is often questioned. He is, perhaps, a minority taste' (Kirkpatrick, 1978: 848).

One author who is most definitely not a minority taste is Roald Dahl (1916–90), who was the most popular author cited by our respondents. Dahl had been producing children's stories since 1961 when *James and the Giant Peach* was published. Notice here again the fusing of the strands with adventure, fantasy and magic. *Charlie and the Chocolate Factory* (1964) is a world best seller though it has attracted criticism for its portrayal of the Ompa-Loompas and its depiction of Charlie's aged grandparents. This work illustrates what Inglis (1981: 236) feels is the essential contribution of Dahl in that he has 'a vigorous feel for the raucous, crude vengefulness of children'. Dahl's stories often do focus on the grotesque and the cruel and many adults have objected to them on these grounds. However, they are unfailingly popular and our respondents listed virtually all his works, the most popular being *Danny, the Champion of the World* (1975), *The Twits* (1980), *George's Marvellous Medicine* (1981), *The BFG* (1982), *The Witches* (1983) and *Matilda* (1988) as well as the two cited above. Because of his very great popularity and the fact that he is very much, in our view, an amalgam of all the traditions Dahl will be the focus of our attention in terms of linguistic description more than once in succeeding chapters and we reserve further comment for now.

The great expansion in children's literature has produced a host of authors, themes and settings. The 'teen novel', for example, is very much a post-war phenomenon. In the 1970s the adolescent reader began to be catered for in a manner hitherto unknown in publishing for young readers. Previously children would have been expected to graduate to 'serious' adult literature via Sir Walter Scott or Dickens. There was a 'gap' in the market, it was perceived, for readers too old for children's stories and not yet ready for adult literature. A gap, in other words, ready for exploitation. Post-Salinger American writers were in the forefront in this new wave of 'realistic' writing and they include Judy Blume (1938–), with the first explicit description of a heterosexual encounter, Betsy Byars (1928–), Robert Cormier (1925–), S.E. Hinton (1950–) and Paul Zindel (1936–). In Britain Robert Leeson (1928–) is one of the best known of writers for adolescents as well as being the author of a series based on the television school series *Grange Hill*.

GENRE AND CHILDREN'S LITERATURE

We have referred on more than one occasion during our description of literature written for children to 'traditions' or 'strands' which go to make up that body of fiction. In one sense this would appear to be saying that all literature written for children is a genre in its own right. That, initially, might be useful as a very general starting point but less than rigorous for the purposes of language description. It is obvious from what we have already discussed that the concept of a strand of traditional juvenile fiction or of fantasy fiction does allow us to classify, to say that there are identifiable features shared by texts. It is also obvious that over a 100-year span the textual strategies adopted by writers for young readers and their narrative frameworks are going to differ considerably in their form and purpose. Texts can only be evaluated within the social framework that produces them or what Gunther Kress calls the 'social occasions':

> Genres have specific forms and meanings, deriving from and encoding the functions, the functions' purposes and meanings of social occasions. Genres therefore provide a precise index and catalogue of the relevant social occasions of a community at a given time.
>
> (1985: 19)

Genre, then, can be used to refer to text categorisations made on the basis of external criteria relating to authorial purpose and a range of social, cultural and historical influences. What we have to bear in mind as a general observation is that genres or 'types of texts' are not without their complexities. Not least of these is the fact that many genres are not determined by clearly differentiated elements but rather by an interaction between several. There are important implications here for writer/reader relationships, what we can call the relations of expectations:

> Because of the constraints of these relations of expectations 'the writer always reveals or writes from a certain *position* . . . in relation to [the] ideological climate' (Maceherey, 1978: 195). He will, knowingly or not, represent part of an ideology and he will be read, consciously or not, through ideological spectacles.
>
> (Musgrave, 1985: 3)

The categorisation of 'types' of discourse has been a focus of literary and rhetorical scholarship since Aristotle presented his three central means of differentiating the various 'kinds' of poetry. These are: (i) the medium for imitating reality; (ii) the representation of men or what Aristotle calls the 'object of imitation'; (iii) the 'manner of imitation' or the manner of narration. Together these three reflect Aristotle's central assumption that art is a *mimesis*, an imitation or representation of nature. In sum, as the centuries progressed, the central issue was whether genres are fixed in their rules and limited in their number.

In the first three decades of the twentieth century the work of the Russian formalists and the structuralists were innovative in their approach to genre (see chapter 5 for our discussion of Vladimir Propp (1895–1970) and his theory of the story structure of fairy-tales). One reason for this is the debt owed to certain developments in modern linguistics. The linguistic concepts formulated by Saussure were heavily influential in both formalism and structuralism. Roman Jakobson, who personifies the link between the fields of criticism and linguistics, states: 'Poetics deals with the problems of verbal structure. . . . Since linguistics is the global science of verbal structure, poetics may be regarded as an integral part of linguistics' (1960: 350). For Jakobson poetics is not simply the application of linguistic theory to the analysis of poetry but includes any aesthetic or creative linguistic use of the spoken or written medium.

Jonathan Culler upholds the significance of the concept of genre in his *Structuralist Poetics* and is concerned with, amongst other matters, the relations of expectations that we referred to above. For the writer this means that s/he will, in creating a poem or a novel, 'engage with a literary tradition or at the very least with a certain idea of the poem or the novel. The activity is made possible by the existence of the genre, which the author can write against, . . . but which is none the less the context within which the activity takes place' (1975: 116).

For the reader the concept offers a 'norm of expectation to guide the reader in his encounter with the text' (*ibid.* 136). Thus, there will be 'a certain idea' in the decoding of the text for the receiver of the message just as much as for the producer. All works must be read in relation to the literary system in which they occur. As Culler puts it, 'Comedy exists by virtue of the fact that to read something as a comedy involves different expectations from reading something as a tragedy' (*ibid.*).

Genre, then, can be considered traditionally as 'types' of literature

– ballads, sonnets, tragedies, fairytales, etc. Any description of a 'type' of text, however, in a study such as ours must take account of the intertextual element of literature written for children or the ways in which any one text is linked to other texts. This could mean, for example, that in reading a Victorian adventure story we recognise features which we would perceive as belonging to other traditions or genres. The elements of friendship and the journey or quest, for example, are not only elements of the adventure story but also of many fantasy narratives and fairytales. Thus, across traditions there may well be a common stock of literary and linguistic procedures and conventions. 'Texts always refer to, incorporate or displace other texts, in a continuous process of intertextuality. The act of reading situates one text among others in terms of genre, context or purpose' (Hodge, 1990: 110). No text can operate independently of other texts and generic labels such as adventure, fantasy, school, etc. need not be mutually exclusive but are useful if for no other reason than, as Hawkes tells us:

> A genre-word, 'novel', 'poem', 'tragedy', placed on the cover of a book 'programmes' our reading of it, reduces its complexity, or rather gives it a knowable shape, enabling us literally to read it, by giving it a context and a framework which allows order and complexity to appear.
>
> (1983: 103)

Thus, if we use the term genre rather than tradition in succeeding pages we are talking about the 'knowable shapes' of texts, the recognisable conventions wherein characters, situations and behaviour are represented to readers. In doing so it may be that a differentiation between 'genre' and 'text type' might be a useful one to keep in mind:

> I use the term 'genre' to refer to categorisations assigned on the basis of external criteria. I use the term 'text type', on the other hand, to refer to grouping of texts that are similar with respect to their linguistic form, irrespective of genre categories.
>
> (Biber, 1991: 70)

In the texts we focus on as representative of the genres or traditions we have discussed previously we would suggest that there are certain *institutions* which the author uses to locate the reader and which can serve as channels for that author's representation of a world view. These institutions, we suggest, are not mutually exclusive and while some will be shared by some texts there are those which may not occur in others. Thus, some institutions which are prominent in children's fiction are *family, friendship, gender, home, race* and *religion*. We may, as indeed we do, find all of these in traditional juvenile fiction but not in the fairy story. The fantasy story will share institutions in common, though separately, with both the adventure story and the fairy story as well as others which may be common to all three. *Friendship*, with its attendant concepts of loyalty and trust (not to mention betrayal and faithlessness), could well be a shared institution but the *journey* or *quest* might not. We have already commented on the role of the *family* in nineteenth-century fiction where it was very much a social agency teaching and supporting a particular code. Through the family the author can convey to his/her reader the meaning attached to the concepts of fatherhood, motherhood, maleness, femaleness and so on. The latter two concepts showing how the institutions interweave as *gender* assumes significance. Equally, time may alter the view that some authors have of these institutions or, rather, how they represent them to their readers. In chapter 4, we shall see a very different portrayal of *family* in Roald Dahl's *Matilda* as compared, for example, to its representation in *Tom Brown's Schooldays* or any one of the Victorian texts. Institutions should be seen as the woven threads of the text and by naming them we facilitate a linguistic description which should enable us to approach an understanding of the messages conveyed by authors to their child readers and we have already commented on how differently child and adult readers were regarded in the nineteenth century by an author such as Marryat. The notion of institutions, we maintain, is more useful than genre particularly when we discuss contemporary children's texts in chapter 4 as conventional generic labels are not always precise in the message that they convey to the reader. *Carrie's War*, for example, is a narrative of 'adventure' but very far removed from the world of Captain Marryat.

THE AUTHOR, THE READER AND THE TEXT

We have referred to relations of expectations that exist between author and reader and the implications these have for the encoding and decoding of texts. There is involved here an interaction between author and reader and 'out of this interaction of authors and readers the meaning of what is written emerges' (Musgrave, 1985: 4). While our work is based on linguistic description (see chapter 2 for a detailed discussion of this) the development of a theory of narratology over the last thirty years has provided a new set of terms for the criticism of fiction. The implications of this development for the textual analysis of children's literature are considerable but particularly in the consideration of author–reader relations. Rimmon-Kenan (1983: 2), for example, sees narratology as 'a communication process in which the message is transmitted by addresser to addressee'. This is almost identical to Seymour Chatman's view that 'A narrative is a communication; hence, it presupposes two parties, a sender and a receiver' (1978: 28). An earlier definition of narrative also lays emphasis on two participants where narrative is 'all those literary works which are distinguished by two characteristics: the presence of a story and a story teller' (Scholes and Kellogg, 1966: 4).

With specific reference to literature written for children the development of a theory of narratology has not only provided a new set of terms for criticism but has 'made possible the precise and methodical examination of an aspect of fiction until recently almost totally ignored – the relationship between narrator and narratee' (Wall, 1991: 3). In her examination of the narrator's voice or 'the description and discussion of the manner of communication between addresser and addressee' in children's fiction Wall adapts Seymour Chatman's model as first proposed in *Story and Discourse* (1978). Wall's work is chiefly concerned 'not with the "message" but with the nature of the addresser and of the addressee and with the manner in which the message is transmitted' (1991: 3). The 'message' and the representation of it in text is of concern to us but even though we focus on linguistic analysis, a set of terms for the participants in a narrative process is important and we shall also use Chapman's terms (1978: 151) as illustrated below:

Narrative text

real author → | implied author → narrator → narratee → implied reader | → real reader

In presenting Chapman's terminology we shall adapt so that we understand the following when we refer to the participants contained therein. The real author is the creator, the producer of the text; the real reader is the child who holds the text and reads the words. By implied author we mean an image of the author which may be constructed by the reader as s/he reads the text and by implied reader we mean the reader the author has in mind as s/he constructs the narrative.

The concept of the implied reader and the critical method that follows from it . . . help us establish the author's relationship with the [child] reader implied in the story, to see how he creates that relationship, and to discover the meaning(s) he seeks to negotiate.

(Chambers, 1980: 253)

It is the four participants described above that are most useful to us though we recognise that a narrator may well be present in a text as distinct from the author and addressing someone in that text as distinct from the reader. Wall (1991: 5) cites Salinger's *Catcher in the Rye* as an example where a narrator is a character in the story (Holden Caulfield) and a narratee (Holden's psychiatrist) is also a character. The choice of a first-person narrator was a favourite device of a number of Victorian children's writers and, as Leech and Short (1981: 265) point out, such a choice 'tends to bias the reader in favour of the narrator/character'. We shall mainly refer to author and reader but it should be borne in mind that the term author includes implied author as well as real author and reader includes implied reader as well as real reader.

THE DATA

We noted above Barbara Wall's (1991) concern with the addresser, addressee and the way in which the 'message' is communicated between them. For us the text as a whole is the message. We are concerned with both the text as a chronological ordering of events (what the Russian formalists called the *fabula*, which approximates to Chatman's term *story*) and the way in which the story is moulded (the *sjuzet* or *discourse*) and characters and settings represented to the reader (see Chatman, 1978: 19–20) as the author gets on with the business of narrating the story. In our subsequent discussions and descriptions we are concerned less with narrative theory than with the grammatical and lexical selections made by an author to portray characters, their relationships and the settings in which these occur. A detailed explanation of our descriptive apparatus and the thinking behind it is given in the next chapter. We would just say at this stage that M.A.K. Halliday's work on transitivity and the representation of participants and the things participants 'do' to each other in situations is of major importance in describing authors' 'views of the world' (see Halliday, 1985: 101–57). We focus on vocabulary choices and why characters or participants are described in certain ways and not others and why, in the representation of actions and thoughts, certain verb forms are chosen rather than others. It is by means of the choices available to us that 'we characterize our view of reality' (Toolan, 1988: 112).

When we talked earlier about 'facilitating a linguistic description' we meant that naming institutions provides us with a list of key lexical items. Some of our selected texts form part of a computerised corpus of children's literature which is currently being compiled. While not all our analysis is reliant upon computational techniques we maintain that the use of concordance lines showing the occurrences of selected items in their lexical environment, that is, with a set number of words to either side of the key word (a word such as *friend*, for example), is invaluable in drawing conclusions about lexical relations in text. We discuss this in more detail in chapter 2. To this end we make use of *Microconcord* (M. Scott and Johns, 1993), a computer software program designed to search through large amounts of text to find all the occurrences of a word or words and from which concordance lines can be obtained and thus information about the collocational properties of an item or 'the company a word keeps' (see Carter, 1987: 36). In addition, in chapter 3 where it seemed appropriate, comparison is made with much larger databases so we can see how words are actually used in context and how that usage may have changed. For the English of the 1970s and early 1980s we refer to the Birmingham Collection of English texts (BCOET), which constituted the COBUILD (Collins Birmingham University International Language Database) corpus. This corpus of naturally occurring data provided lexicographers with a database of about 20 million words from a wide range of spoken and written sources. We take examples from the *COBUILD English Language Dictionary*, which is a tradition-breaking publication in the field of lexicography.

We also make reference to the current corpus, the Bank of English (HarperCollins/Birmingham University), for examples of usage of the late 1980s and the 1990s. This corpus was standing at around 167 million words at the time of this study and allows the further investigation of lexical items in their normal linguistic environments, as they are actually used. In particular we were interested in the British books section of this corpus, around 23 million words, which includes 128 books of post-1985 popular (mainly crime) fiction.

For nineteenth-century usage we turned to the *Oxford English Dictionary* (compact edition). This allowed us, when considering traditional juvenile fiction, to consider words in appropriate nineteenth-century contexts.

In selecting our texts for consideration we have been guided by the fact that we wanted to be as representative as possible of the traditions that we have been discussing in this chapter. In our discussions on the nature and development of literature written for children we have, on more than one occasion, made reference to Salmon's 1888 survey and Knowles's 1989–90 survey. These have been most informative and were also influential, though not our sole guiding principle, when it came to choosing the texts to be analysed. It seems appropriate at this stage that, having made reference to these surveys, we comment in a little more detail upon their findings.

Edward Salmon published *Juvenile Literature as it is* in 1888 and he states his aim for doing so with some precision: 'To give all charged with the mental and moral welfare of the rising generation an idea of the books written for girls and boys, has been my object' (1888: 9). The book's opening chapter contains a survey of children's reading habits carried out by a Charles Welsh in 1884. Welsh had 'despatched to numerous schools for girls and boys a circular containing several questions such as "who is your favourite author?", "who is your favourite writer of fiction?" and "which of his books did you like best?"' (*ibid.* 13). There were at least twelve of these questions. Approximately two thousand replies were received from boys and girls aged eleven to nineteen representing a range of schools and social backgrounds. These were then categorised according to gender. Seven hundred and ninety replies were received from boys. When works that are obviously written for adults are filtered out (Dickens was first choice and Sir Walter Scott third) remaining titles represent what we have classified as traditional juvenile fiction with its two interlocking wings of the adventure story and the school story. W.H.G. Kingston was favourite boys' author (179) and second overall. Captain Marryat was second favourite boys' author and fifth overall (102) while R.M. Ballantyne was third favourite (with 67) and sixth overall. G.A. Henty polled one vote as did Thomas Hughes, the author of *Tom Brown's Schooldays*.

The favourite books section of the poll had *Robinson Crusoe* (43) first and *Swiss Family Robinson* second. This is important but we do not concentrate on either text in our subsequent analyses as the first was not written primarily for children and its universal popularity with a young readership was arrived at mainly through abridged editions (see Carpenter and Prichard, 1984: 457–8) and abridgement is not part of our focus. The importance of Defoe's work is what it inspired, which we have discussed earlier in this chapter. *Swiss Family Robinson* was not originally written in English and was 'subsequently much enlarged by translators and editors' (*ibid.* 510). Again, we acknowledge its considerable influence on the tradition.

The first English children's book in the poll was *The Boys' Own Annual* (17) which was fifth overall. This annual was a year's collection of *The Boys' Own Paper* and contained many school and adventure stories including those of Henty. The *BOP* was overwhelmingly the favourite magazine of Welsh's boy respondents (404) and Henty wrote extensively for it (see Avery, 1965: 236). He was also a regular contributor to and editor of *The Union Jack*, the respondents' fourth favourite magazine, the second and third choices being publications for adults. *Tom Brown's Schooldays* was the second favourite book (15) if we discount Anstey's *Vice Versa*. Farrar's *St. Winifred's* (11) was third favourite, followed by Kingston's *The Three Midshipmen* (8). Salmon offers no explanation for the lack of correlation between favourite authors and writers of fiction and favourite books. The figures given for the former are based on the answers to the first two of the three questions cited above, however, with Salmon commenting that the distinction between them is 'rather subtle' (1888: 14) without entering into detail.

The replies from girls numbered just over 1,000 and, like the boys, Dickens was cited as favourite author (355). Sir Walter Scott (248) and Charles Kingsley (103) were numbered second and third favourites overall and, as we discussed earlier, this is interesting as *Westward Ho!* (34) was listed as favourite book with Scott's *Ivanhoe* (18) as eighth choice (it was fifth favourite with the boys). While both books were written for adults they were widely read by children and are historical adventure stories demonstrating further just how popular this type of fiction was with young readers. Of children's writers Charlotte Yonge (100), Hans Christian Andersen (33), A.L.O.E. (32) (A Lady of England; the pseudonym of Charlotte Maria Tucker (1821–93)) were first, second and third with Welsh's respondents and fourth, eleventh and twelfth overall. Favourite books listed were *Little Women* (21), seventh overall; and Yonge's *The Daisy Chain* (13) and *The Heir of Radcliffe* (12), tenth and eleventh overall though the latter was, arguably, written for adults. Kingston, Ballantyne and Marryat all figured prominently as did *The Boys' Own Paper*. The brothers Grimm (20) and Lewis Carroll (5) were also cited by the female respondents.

Knowles (1989–90) conducted a survey as a preliminary for the construction of the part-computerised corpus of modern children's fiction referred to earlier in this chapter. He had already constructed a Victorian corpus based on Salmon's survey and standing at around

760,000 words. The institutions to which the questionnaires were despatched were junior and secondary schools, sixth-form colleges and colleges of further education. The secondary schools included comprehensive, grammar, independent day and public schools. Seven hundred and fifty questionnaires were despatched initially. Others have been sent out since as this survey is being conducted over a number of years in an to attempt to take account of new authors as the century draws to a close and also of authors made popular by dramatised versions of their works presented on television. The years 1989–90, therefore, should be seen as the first stage in an ongoing project and the modern fiction corpus referred to in this study is the original corpus based on that survey and stands at around 750,000 words.

Seven hundred and twenty six completed questionnaires were returned. The age range was ten to eighteen. Knowles used Welsh as a model but restricted himself to five questions: (i) 'Who is your favourite author?'; (ii)'What books of his/hers have you read recently? (up to 3 titles)', (iii) 'What other authors do you like? (up to 3 authors)', (iv a) 'What *magazines, journals, comics* do you read?', (iv b) 'Why do you like them?', (v) 'Do you read any non-fiction? If so list up to three books you have read recently?' Of these questions we are concerned mainly, when we refer to this data, with (i) and (ii), with reference being made to (iii) and (iv) where appropriate.

The responses to Knowles's questionnaires demonstrated overwelmingly the popularity of Roald Dahl with all age groups. In the 10–12 group there were 246 responses to the survey. Twenty-six of these selected adult narratives (18 were female respondents) and 10 were spoiled. Of the remainder 80 selected Dahl as favourite author and Enid Blyton was second with 34 nominations. In third place there were different selections according to gender, with the girls choosing Carolyn Keene (the Nancy Drew mystery stories) as third preference with Judy Blume fourth and Nina Bawden and Francine Pascale (Sweet Valley High series) fifth equal. For the boys Franklin W. Dixon's Hardy Boys mystery series was third, C.S. Lewis was fourth and Michael Hardcastle was fifth equal with Robert Westall.

In the 13–15 age range there were 244 returns with 63 adult selections. These latter varied from Austen, Bronte and Dickens to popular thrillers and romantic melodramas. There were 9 spoiled papers. Dahl was first choice with 45 nominations. For the girls Judy Blume was second choice, with Bawden and Keene equal third, C.S. Lewis fourth and Tolkien and Lois Duncan equal fifth.

The boys selected C.S. Lewis, Franklin W. Dixon with Joan Lindgard and Blyton and Tolkien equal fifth. These were followed by Robert Westall, Leon Garfield and Nina Bawden. Joan Lingard was also popular with girl readers as was Michelle Magorian and Robert Cormier.

The 16–18 age group, not surprisingly, had the biggest selection of adult narratives. There were 236 returns of which 89 can be classified as children's literature. Dahl scored 28 overall. For the male respondents Tolkien, Cormier, C.S. Lewis and S.E. Hinton were next favourite in that order whilst females nominated S.E. Hinton, Judy Blume and Robert Cormier with Enid Blyton and Jan Mark being fifth equal.

It is recognised that this preliminary survey is smaller than Salmon's. Nevertheless it presents a very strong indication of the reading habits of the total age range. Data currently being processed as a result of subsequent surveys would indicate a considerable degree of consistency with the above findings.

CONCLUSIONS

It was our intention in this chapter to outline the development of literature written for children over the last 150 years, to discuss this development briefly within some form of generic framework, to stress the importance of author–reader relationships and to give some indication of the sources which helped influence our choice of texts.

The 1840s witnessed the birth of modern children's fiction with the establishing of traditional juvenile fiction and stories that were not solely didactic treatises. It is important also to remember that while written with a male readership in mind they were also read by many girls. Authors such as R.M. Ballantyne were still recognised reading matter in post-war Britain and many forty- and fifty-year-old men and women have recalled *The Coral Island* as a favourite narrative of their youth.

English girls' writers of the second half of the nineteenth century did not produce anything that has lasted in quite the same way. Rooted in domesticity and the institution of the family, the works of Yonge, Ewing and Molesworth never achieved the status of children's 'classic' awarded to narratives such as Ballantyne's. This status was reserved for Louisa M. Alcott and perhaps this is because, as Wall (1991: 90) tells us about *Little Women*, while the book may be 'preachy', unlike its British counterparts 'the preaching is made acceptable by the quality of the voice in which it is uttered. . . . This story of four sisters is told, quite simply, by one of themselves . . . who uses the same easy colloquial language that the girls themselves use in their conversation.' *Little Women* is not one of our selected texts as we feel it represents a different tradition and one worthy of study in its own right. Of British writers, British girls in the nineteenth century, while showing an inclination for traditional juvenile fiction, also indicated the popularity of writers of fantasy and of fairytales and this is reflected in our discussions in chapters 5 and 6.

If we appear to have given less attention to the developments of the last forty years this is solely for reasons of space. The great proliferation of texts available for children in contemporary Britain make it impossible to do other than summarise the new quality of children's literature and the drawing together of the traditions in producing this quality. We have endeavoured to remedy any such shortcomings by giving considerable and detailed attention to our analyses and discussions of our selected twentieth-century texts in chapters 4 and 6.

Finally, we hope we have succeeded in locating our own readers in terms of our subject matter and that they have a view of the development – and a very rapid development it has been – of a fascinating aspect of our culture. It is now our responsibility to consider notions of control and of ideology and to discuss these in relation to the application of a linguistic analysis to our selected texts.

2 Literature as a carrier of ideology: children's literature and control

THE IDEA OF IDEOLOGY

The term ideology was coined by Destutt de Tracy (1754–1836) to refer to 'the radically empirical analysis of the human mind' (Aiken, 1956: 16). The emphasis on the mind remains in the twentieth-century tendency to link ideology with belief systems, political persuasions and the like, even though, in the twentieth century, analyses tend to be primarily socially orientated, and to take a distinctly linguistic turn.

In this book, too, we use the notion of ideology in linguistic analysis. However, we agree with Thompson (1984; 1990) that it is desirable to reserve for the term ideology a sense of its own, distinct from the senses attached to terms like belief system and political persuasion. In order to clarify the distinction between these senses and the sense in which the term is used here, it will be useful to provide a brief sketch of the evolution of ideological analysis.

Towards the end of the eighteenth century, western philosophers began to question the notion of an independent objective reality which could be examined and understood, if only the right method of examination and thinking were employed. In the philosophy of Immanuel Kant (1724–1804), the human mind – reason – was given a crucial role in our perception of the world. The world existed as a thing in itself, irrespectively of how humans might perceive it, but it was no longer considered available for inspection by humans in its pure form. The human mind had its own structure which crucially influenced the way in which humans understood and interpreted the world.

Kant, however, believed that human reason was a constant: all humans were rational, so the world as perceived by humans, although it might not be the world as it actually was, was at least the same world for them all, and was perceived in more or less the same manner by every human being. It was with the addition of Georg Wilhelm Friedrich Hegel's (1770–1831) conception of human nature and human reason as subject to historical development and therefore open to influence from the changing conditions of individual and social life, that it became possible to conceive that different individuals might understand the universe in radically different ways. So while 'ideology' might still be used in de Tracy's sense, it became possible to entertain the notion of a plurality of ideologies. In addition, the Hegelian emphasis on the influence on reason of social factors implied that the study of ideology should include the study of those socio-historical conditions which might influence 'rational' human behaviour.

During the Napoleonic era, the term acquired the negative connotations which may follow it even today, as it was used to refer to 'virtually any belief of a republican or revolutionary sort, that is to say, any belief hostile to Napoleon himself' (Aiken, 1956: 17). These pejorative associations were reinforced in the usage of Marx (1818–83) and Engels (1820–95), in whose *The German Ideology* (1845–6/1939) the term was used to refer to any mode of thinking inimical to their own revolutionary philosophy of history. The notion of a plurality of ideologies, then, is also present in the writings of Marx and Engels, where ideologies are, in addition, conceived as echoes of the 'material' or actual, efficient causes of social change.

Our own century has seen a growing preoccupation, in an increasing number of fields of enquiry, with questions of personal identity, rationality, socialisation and the nature of society itself; and the notion of ideology has been invoked in the service of numerous scholarly pursuits. The term ideology remains in frequent use as a plural noun, a near-synonym of 'belief system'. Political parties, pressure groups of various persuasions, social classes and even individuals are said to act according to their separate, often mutually opposed, ideologies, which inform and influence their behaviour and modes of expression, and which reflect the conditions under which people live. Since any sane person behaves in accordance with a more or less coherent set of beliefs, everyone has an ideology, in this sense of the term, and scholars who embrace this 'neutral' conception of ideology (Thompson, 1984: 4; 1990: 53–67) tend to be careful to outline their own 'ideological' standpoint before setting out to examine and criticise that of others, if that is their purpose.

It is clear that the idea that any person can observe and criticise the behaviour of others impartially is untenable. It is equally obvious that different social groups, religious, ethnic, political and so on, behave according to different sets of beliefs. However, it is useful to keep the notion of a belief system separate from the notion of ideology and reserve for the latter term a sense which will allow for critical investigation of phenomena that are intersubjectively available to observation. In this 'critical' conception of ideology, '*to study ideology is to study the ways in which meaning serves to establish and sustain relations of domination*' (Thompson, 1990: 56). While the sense in which Thompson uses the term meaning remains unclear at this point (though see below), the definition provides a clear link with relations of domination.

Relations of domination are systematically asymmetrical relations of power. A systematically asymmetrical power relationship, a relationship of domination, obtains where individuals or groups are endowed with power which, for whatever reason, is inaccessible to certain other individuals or groups. There are many such relationships of domination in every society and in the world as a whole:

> In studying ideology we *may* be concerned with the ways in which meaning sustains relations of class domination, but we may also be concerned with other kinds of domination, such as the structured social relations between men and women, between one ethnic group and another, or between hegemonic nation–states and those nation–states located on the margins of a global system.
>
> (Thompson 1990: 58)

To these relationships we can add the structured social relationships between adults and children as these obtain in homes, schools, secular and religious clubs and societies and in society in general. In the overwhelming majority of cases, adults establish, structure and maintain these relationships. In spite of the powerful emotional hold which children have over their parents and over many other adults, it is generally the case that adults, in virtue of their greater experience, strength, access to the media and to the essentials and luxuries of life (via money and position), and as designers of educational systems, are more powerful than children socially, economically and physically.

Adults see it as their task to socialise children, that is, to make them behave in ways that are generally acceptable to adults – in ways that will fit the children to take their proper place in society, as adults perceive it. Obviously, adults have many means towards this end available to them. They might, for example, consciously exercise their superior physical strength, or employ a regime of reward and punishment. However, they also inevitably influence children more subtly, often subconsciously, and, many would argue, most effectively, through language. As Halliday (1978) points out, language is a powerful socialising agent, because it is through language that the child learns about the social world, about social customs, institutions and hierarchies. The language of social texts – including those texts which we read to our children or give them to read for themselves – is therefore a particularly effective agent in promoting the acceptance by the child of these customs, institutions and hierarchies.

The notion of ideology as meaning in the service of power, then, highlights the role language plays in establishing and sustaining socio-historically situated relations of domination. It is important to stress that the mobilisation of meaning in the service of power not only sustains relations of domination, but can also establish these relations. If you 'get your meaning to stick' (Thompson, 1984: 132), you gain power, and a relationship of domination can be established. Consider the following interaction which takes place between Arrietty and the boy in *The Borrowers* (1952; page references to the Puffin edition, 1993) by Mary Norton (1903–92):

Arrietty burst out laughing; she laughed so much that she had to hide her face in the primrose. 'Oh dear', she gasped with tears in her eyes, 'you are funny!' She stared up at his puzzled face. 'Human beans are for Borrowers – like bread for butter!'

The boy was silent a while. A sigh of wind rustled the cherry-tree and shivered among the blossom.

'Well, I don't believe it,' he said at last, watching the falling petals. 'I don't believe that's what we're for at all and I don't believe we're dying out!'

'Oh, goodness!' exclaimed Arrietty impatiently, staring up at his chin. 'Just use your common sense: you're the only real human bean I ever saw (although I do just know of three more . . .). But I know lots and lots of Borrowers: . . .

He leaned closer. 'Then where are they now? Tell me that.'. . .

'Oh,' said Arrietty, 'they're somewhere.' But where? she wondered. And she shivered slightly in the boy's cold shadow which lay about her, slant-wise, on the grass.

He drew back again, his fair head blocking out a great piece of sky. 'Well,' he said deliberately after a moment, and his eyes were cold, 'I've only seen two Borrowers but I've seen hundreds and hundreds and hundreds and hundreds and hundreds – '

'Oh no – ' whispered Arrietty.

'Of human beans.' And he sat back.

Arrietty stood very still. She did not look at him. After a while she said: 'I don't believe you.'

'All right,' he said, 'then I'll tell you – '

'I still won't believe you,' murmured Arrietty.

'Listen!' he said. And he told her about railway stations and football matches and racecourses. . . . He told her about India and China and North America and the British Commonwealth. He told her about the July sales.

'Not hundreds,' he said, 'but thousands and millions and billions and trillions of great, big, enormous people. Now do you believe me?' . . .

'I don't know,' she whispered.

'As for you,' he went on, leaning closer again, 'I don't believe that there are any more Borrowers anywhere in the world. I believe you're the last three. . . . And you'll be the very last because you're the youngest. One day,' he told her, smiling triumphantly, 'you'll be the only Borrower left in the world!'

He sat still, waiting, but she did not look up. 'Now you're crying,' he remarked after a moment.

(pp. 71–4)

This passage comes from the tenth of the twenty chapters of *The Borrowers*. It is a central chapter, not only structurally, but also in the sense that it is here that the relationship between Borrowers and humans is defined and redefined between the boy and Arrietty. In the passage quoted, it is clear that the boy succeeds in 'getting his meaning to stick'; Arrietty finally believes his 'story', not her own; having set out with tears of triumph in her eyes at the boy's lack of 'understanding' of his subservience to Borrowers – 'Human beans are *for* Borrowers', by the end she is crying over humans' domination of Borrowers.

The scene for the linguistic power struggle which takes place in chapter 10 is set in chapter 9, where the boy and Arrietty meet and he threatens to beat her with a stick and to break her in half, that is, to exercise his superior physical strength, if she does not stay still and tell him where she lives. At this point, however, Arrietty remains bravely defiant, and her position is further strengthened when it turns out that she is four years older than the boy and a better reader. The chapter ends with Arrietty introducing her 'story', or 'meaning', that humans are dying out, which is a good thing, and that only a few are needed 'to keep us' (p. 67). By the end of chapter 10, however, it is the boy's story that predominates.

It is possible to identify typical *strategies of symbolic construction* through which the general *modes of operation* of ideology may be realised (Thompson, 1990: 60–7). However, it should be borne in mind that since no linguistic item or structure is 'ideological' in and for itself, it cannot be assumed that the presence of one form or another in a given text is an indicator that ideology is in operation at that point. It is necessary also to provide some reasoned argument to support any suggestion that such a form, in its surrounding co-text, serves the ideological purpose in its given socio-historical context. Obviously, it can be helpful in this respect to compare the representation of social institutions in texts of similar genres produced in different eras, or, for that matter, in the same era, since writers often oppose relationships of domination. Such opposition may be stated more or less explicitly, and may be expressed through parody or satire. But to recognise the opposition, it is necessary to understand what it is opposed to, and to be familiar with the ideological function of those modes of expressions which are being satirised (Thompson, 1990: 68).

Another important point is that the ideological purpose is not accompanied by a guarantee of success. Neither adults nor children are passive recipients of ideology; people are active interpreters of the social world around them and of its symbolic forms. They evaluate, judge and distance themselves from these symbolic forms. Our project is merely to make more explicit the linguistic means writers employ in their efforts to support, undermine or simply comment on particular relationships of domination, including those which obtain between children and their adult mentors.

IDEOLOGY AND NARRATIVE

Thompson (1990: 59–67) lists five general modes of operation of ideology together with a number of associated strategies of symbolic construction. All of these modes and strategies may be carried by narrative, the telling of what happens to characters over a relatively well-defined stretch of time, a form taken by or found within a great deal of literature for children (although other forms are, of course, not excluded from the genre).

Among the general modes of operation of ideology, and the strategies associated with them, are the following (from Thompson 1990: table 1.2).

Mode	*Associated strategies*
Legitimation	Narrativisation
	Rationalisation
	Universalisation
Dissimulation	Displacement
	Euphemisation
	Trope
Unification	Standardisation
	Symbolisation of unity
Fragmentation	Differentiation
	Expurgation of the other
Reification	Naturalisation
	Eternalisation
	Nominalisation
	Passivisation

The strategies Thompson lists are realised through stretches of discourse of varying length. Some involve at least a clause and usually substantially more than that. These 'macro-linguistic' strategies include Rationalisation, Universalisation, Narrativisation, Standardisation, Symbolisation of unity, Naturalisation, Eternalisation and Passivisation. Others are typically realised by stretches of discourse smaller than the clause, that is, single words or phrases. These 'micro-linguistic' strategies include Displacement, Euphemisation, Trope and Nominalisation. Differentiation and Expurgation of the other can be realised both macro- and micro-linguistically, and micro-linguistically realised strategies may be carried within those realised at the macro-linguistic level. Below, (pp. 65–8) we shall relate Thomson's scheme to Hollindale's (1988; Hunt, 1992: 19–40) three 'levels' of ideology in children's books, and outline certain features of the linguistic system through which the ideological purpose may be served, or through which writers may express opposition to relations of domination. Here, however, we shall illustrate each of Thompson's strategies, beginning at the top of his list of typical modes of operation of ideology.

As we can see, *narrativisation* itself is a strategy which may serve *legitimation*, the representation of relations of domination as legitimate. As Thompson points out, narratives provide particularly fertile ground for the portrayal of social relations and the unfolding of consequences of actions 'in ways that may establish and sustain relations of power' (1990: 62). Moreover, fiction in general is an excellent vehicle for all of Thompson's other strategies. For example, both dialogue between characters and narrator discourse are well suited to carry *rationalisation*, the presentation of relations of domination as justifiable on rational grounds. This typically involves the production of a chain of reasoning which explains why certain social relations and/or institutions should be supported. For example, in *The Railway Children* (1906; Sainsbury edition 1992) by Edith Nesbit (1858–1924), the weakness of women and the need for men to be protective of them is carefully explained to Peter by Doctor Forrest, as follows:

> 'Well,' said the doctor, 'you know men have to do the work of the world and not be afraid of anything – so they have to be hardy and brave. But women have to take care of their babies and cuddle them and nurse them and be very patient and gentle.'
>
> 'Yes,' said Peter, wondering what was coming next.
>
> 'Well then, you see. Boys and girls are only little men and women. And *we* are much harder and hardier than they are . . . and much stronger, and things that hurt *them* don't hurt *us*. You know you mustn't hit a girl – '
>
> 'I should think not, indeed,' muttered Peter, indignantly.
>
> 'Not even if she's your own sister. That's because girls are so much softer and weaker than we are; they have to be, you know,' he added, 'because if they weren't, it wouldn't be nice for the babies. And that's why all the animals are so good to the mother animals. They never fight them, you know.'
>
> 'I know,' said Peter, interested, 'two buck rabbits will fight all day if you let them, but they won't hurt a doe.'
>
> 'No; and quite wild beasts – lions and elephants – they're immensely gentle with the female beasts. And we've got to be, too.'
>
> 'I see,' said Peter.
>
> > (*ibid.*: 228–9)

The third strategy Thompson lists under legitimation is *universalisation*. This strategy is realised in claims that universal benefit will accrue if the relations and institutions in question receive support. The quotation from *The Railway Children* implies universal benefit to the species of upholding the differentiation between men and women, but more explicit statements also abound. For example, In 'Uncle David's Nonsensical Story about Giants and Fairies' (1839; Mark, 1993: 56) by Catharine Sinclair (1800–64) we read that 'luckily for the whole world, the fairy Teach-all got possession of immense property, which she proceeded without delay to make the best use of in her power'. Fairy Teach-all encourages physical and mental exertion aimed at enabling children 'to know the world in which they live and to fulfil the purposes for which they have been brought into it' (Mark, 1993: 51).

Dissimulation is the mode of operation of ideology in which relations of domination are hidden, denied or obscured. This can be done through *displacement*, referring to a phenomenon by a positively or negatively loaded term normally used to refer to some other phenomenon. In *The Borrowers*, just before the passage cited on pages 44–5 above, there is an interesting debate between Arrietty and the boy about the correct term for the activity from which the Borrowers take their species name:

> The boy sat thoughtfully on his haunches, chewing a blade of grass. 'Borrowing,' he said after a while. 'Is that what you call it?'
>
> 'What else would you call it?' asked Arrietty.
>
> 'I'd call it stealing.'
>
> Arrietty laughed. She really laughed. 'But we *are* Borrowers,' she explained, 'like you're a – a Human Bean or whatever it's called. We're part of the house. You might as well say that the fire-grate steals the coal from the coal-scuttle.'
>
> 'Then what is stealing?'
>
> Arrietty looked grave. 'Supposing my Uncle Hendreary borrowed an emerald watch from Her dressing table and my father took it and hung it up on our wall. That's stealing. . . . But Borrowers don't steal.'
>
> 'Except from human beans,' said the boy.

It is the boy's last remark in this quotation which leads Arrietty to explain that humans are *for* Borrowers, the remark which sparks off the competition to have one's story believed which Arrietty loses (see above).

The strategy of displacement is also employed extensively in stories in which the intention is to show that it is better to be poor than rich, and to discourage overindulgence of children, a type fairly common in the nineteenth century. For example, in 'The Green Velvet Dress' (1858; Mark, 1993: 93–101) by Charlotte Maria Tucker (1821–93), the main character, Jenny, is taught by her visit to the rich but sad Lady Grange to transfer the positive terms she had previously reserved for conditions of wealth to conditions of poverty and to transfer the negative terms she had previously reserved for conditions of poverty to conditions of wealth. She sets out to deliver to Lady Grange 'a dress which, to her [Jenny], appeared the very perfection of beauty and splendour' (p. 94), thinking, on the way (pp. 94–5):

> 'It must be a pleasure . . . even to touch that lovely soft green velvet; and what must it be to wear it? I could never fancy any one's ever feeling unhappy in such a dress!' . . . 'How nice and warm and comfortable it feels. I don't believe that the lady who will wear it ever knows what it is to be hungry or cold. She's never tired, for she has a fine coach to ride in – oh! how grand it must be to ride in a coach! And then to dress like a queen, and feast on good things every day! How very, very happy she must be!'

Here, the sensations of unhappiness, hunger, cold and tiredness, which Jenny dissociates from the Lady Grange of her imagination, are those which she associates with her own life (see the quotation from the beginning of the story below). With the life of Lady Grange, Jenny associates grandness, health and happiness.

However, the real Lady Grange gives quite a different impression (pp. 95–6):

> Her manner was gracious and gentle; but Jenny could not help noticing how mournful was its tone; and when she ventured to raise her eyes to the face of the lady, she saw on it an expression of melancholy and care, which raised a feeling of pity as well as of surprise. . . . Jenny happened to glance at Lady Grange. There was an anxious frown on the gentle face, a flush on the lately pale cheek, which gave an impression of keen suffering not unmixed with anger.

Faced with the actual Lady Grange, Jenny now associates with her mourning, melancholy, care, anxiety, suffering, pallor and fever-like flushes, and anger.

Still, Jenny is taken to the kitchen, where she meets the servants with whom she continues to associate grandness and pride (p. 96):

> 'How proud one would be, too, to have so many servants, some of them looking themselves so very grand!' thought Jenny.

She is, however, soon disillusioned, as the servants begin to gossip about the family. The 'many servants' become redefined as 'a set of people' who, far from being 'grand', exhibit the unpleasant characteristics of domestic spies, and Jenny begins to associate contentment with her own lifestyle (p. 97):

'I'm glad we've our own little cot to ourselves,' was the thought which crossed Jenny's mind; 'and that we have not a set of people about us to watch every look, listen to every word, and make our troubles known to all the world!'

By the time Jenny leaves, the reordering of terms, and of Jenny's ideas and emotions, is complete (p. 100):

Jenny having finished her cold meat, now rose and left the house – left it with ideas how changed from those with which she entered it! The feeling of envy was changed for the feeling of pity; and the young girl, as with light step she made her way towards the home where she was sure of kind smiles and a pleasant welcome, thought how much happier was her own lot than that of the lady of fortune. Even the robe of rich green velvet had lost its attractions for Jenny – was it more beautiful than the fresh turf over which she sped with so light a heart?

Pity for herself has been transferred to Lady Grange, and the impression of happiness has been transferred from Lady Grange to Jenny herself. The beauty of the dress has been transferred to the turf, one of those delights of life to which, we are reminded, the poor share access with the rich. So 'Mother is right – the best blessings are as free to the poor as to the rich' (p. 100). *Ergo*, the rich are not dominant in any way that truly matters.

This story also employs *tropes* in its effort at dissimulation. As in many narratives involving poor characters, there are strong hints of feebleness of health and the possibility of death hastened by under-nourishment and the lack of adequate clothing and fuel. The tale begins (p. 93):

'Wrap your cloak tight round you, my lass, for the wind's bitter cold this morning: and here – see – you wouldn't be worse of my bit of a shawl under it.'

'Oh! but, mother, remember your rheumatics.'

'I'm a'most right again, Jenny, and I be n't out in the cold,' said the poor woman, stirring the few glowing embers which scarcely gave even the appearance of a fire.

'And come back soon again, Jenny dear,' cried a pale, bare-footed little boy, running from the corner; 'I hope the grand lady won't keep you long.'. . . And the little thin arms were thrown round her neck . . .

'Oh, Tommy! I wish I were a grand lady! – I wish I had plenty of money! Shouldn't you have meat enough, and all kinds of food, to make you strong and hearty again!'

This Tommy does not receive (though his sister brings him home some early violets). In any case, by the end of the story, where it is also somewhat perversely suggested that having sufficient food would not improve Tommy's prospects – money cannot buy health – death is presented, in poem form, by the metaphor of a happy home above:

> N'er will I sigh for wealth,
> Such wealth as coffers can hold:
> Contentment, union, and health,
> Are not to be bought for gold!
> The costly treasures I prize
> Are treasures of family love –
> A happy home here, and the hope so dear
> Of a happier home above!

The strategy of *euphemisation*, using a term which deliberately highlights the positive aspects of a phenomenon, abounds in literature for children. An example of euphemisation in the service of power occurs early on in *The Secret Garden* (1911; Sainsbury edition, 1992: 33) by Frances Hodgson Burnett (1848–1924), when Mary recalls that her servants in India had been taught to refer to their masters as 'protectors of the poor'. Because the particular abuse of power instantiated by the 'un-natural' subsection of the master class in question here is heavily criticised in this novel (see below), this particular instance of euphemisation is understood as satirical. However, the notion of the landed gentry as protectors of the poor rustic is upheld in the novel as a whole, and instantiated, for example, in scenes like the following (1992: 320):

> Mr Craven looked over the collection of sturdy little bodies and round, red-cheeked faces . . . and he awoke to the fact that they were a healthy, likeable lot. He . . . took a golden sovereign from his pocket and gave it to 'our 'Lizabeth Ellen', who was the oldest. 'If you divide that into eight parts there will be half a crown for each of you,' he said.
> Then amid grins and chuckles and bobbing of curtsies, he drove away, leaving ecstasy and nudging elbows and little jumps of joy behind.

This particular master is, indeed, a protector of the poor, with the power to keep an old servant, the gardener, Ben Weatherstaff, on 'by favour – because she [Colin's dead mother] liked me' (p. 253) – or, by implication, to dismiss servants if they fail to please.

Unification is the mode of operation of ideology through which diverse social groups are brought together through various efforts at *standardisation*, for example of language, or by creating *symbolisations of unity*, such as national flags and anthems (Thompson, 1990: 64–5). Literature itself can, of course, serve as a symbol of national unity, or it can be written or collected in order to create an impression of a common standard. For example, Ellis (1983) claims that a prime motivation for the Grimms' effort to present their stories as collected from the common people was to create a sense of unity and identity of spirit among the German people.

On the other hand, *fragmentation* – a 'divide and rule' policy – may serve ideology. Fragmentation can be promoted by *differentiation*: emphasising the differences between groups. This is clearly seen in the quotation above from *The Railway Children*, part of which is repeated here for convenience. Some of the differentiating pronouns are italicised in the original:

> 'Well then, you see. Boys and girls are only little men and women. And *we* are much harder and hardier than they are . . . and much stronger, and things that hurt *them* don't hurt *us*.'

Interestingly, in this passage, there is also unification of adults and children: 'Boys and girls are only little men and women.' This, while reinforcing the differentiation between the sexes, also serves, on the one hand, to obscure to a certain degree the fact of adult control over children. On the other hand, however, it justifies the socialisation effort: if boys and girls are really only little men and women, then it is fitting that they should be encouraged to take on roles appropriate to men and women and that childishness should be discouraged. But then, again, if boys and girls are only little men and women, then men and women are only big boys and girls. As Lewis Carroll (1832–98) puts it in the dedicatory poem to *Through the Looking Glass* (1871), 'We are but older children, dear.' There is, to the present day, an ambivalence in the adult–child relationship, which partly reflects a belief, encouraged by Christianity, in the value of innocence and in children as the carriers of this virtue. For many writers, the innocence of children is combined with wisdom. Children are as yet unspoiled by the ways of the world and are therefore able to understand and perceive more clearly than adults the most basic truths of nature and existence. The wise child, from whose innocent, but natural and/or virtuous, actions and words the adult protagonist derives much instruction, is a common character, especially in Romantic and Victorian literature. However, the notion that children are wise still remains in literature written for children today. No doubt this feature can encourage children to identify with the children they meet in books, and this may precisely support the books' socialising function.

Differentiation in literature for children often takes the form of an exaggeration of the difference in size between different groups, as, for example, in *The Borrowers* and in stories involving giants and fairies. Frequently, there is an inverse relationship between physical size and moral rectitude, though, as we see in the case of *The Borrowers*, for example, the matter need not be so clear-cut. Here, the differentiation between Borrowers and humans is, on the one hand, obscured by the fact that they live by very similar social codes, but is, on the other, reinforced by the emphasis on the difference between 'borrowing', which takes place between groups (though in the story only *from* humans *to* Borrowers), and *stealing* which takes place only *within* groups (though in this story only within the human group).

When the boy begins to provide the Borrowers with items from the household in return for being read to by Arrietty, disaster ensues in so far as it leads to the discovery and destruction by the housekeeper of the Borrowers' home beneath the kitchen. This disaster has been foretold through the adult Borrowers' anxious reaction when they discover that Arrietty has told the boy enough about her home for him to be able to discover where it is. So, sympathetic though the narration is to both groups, the idea that it is dangerous to attempt to cross from one to the other is strongly upheld, both implicitly and explicitly. The following exchange takes place between the boy and the housekeeper when the latter discovers the boy's involvement with the Borrowers:

'And you're in league with them!' She came across to him and, taking him by the upper arm, she jerked him to his feet. 'You know what they do with thieves?' she asked.

'No,' he said.

'They lock them up. That's what they do with thieves. And that's what's going to happen to you!'

'I'm not a thief,' cried the boy, his lips trembling. I'm a Borrower.'

'A what?' She swung him round by tightening the grip on his arm.

'A Borrower,' he repeated. There were tears on his eyelids; he hoped they would not fall.

'So that's what you call it!' she exclaimed (as he himself had done – so long ago, it seemed now – that day with Arrietty).

The boy's attempt at unification with the Borrowers fails, and was doomed from the start to fail, because it involves an attempt at redefinition which the Borrowers' own social code forbids. If you take from your own group you are stealing, so the boy cannot make himself a Borrower by transferring goods he has taken from his own group to the Borrowers. It is a child Borrower and a child human who attempt to cross the boundary between groups to the consternation of the adults. The message conveyed is that of the adults, that groups' boundaries cannot be crossed.

Both in *The Borrowers* and in books like Clive King's *Stig of the Dump* (1963) differentiation is also established between the inhabitants of different actual or metaphorical worlds, often with subsequent, often only temporary, association between the child and the inhabitant of the other world. This, in turn, reinforces the differentiation between the child and the adults who are generally barred from the other world unless given access to it by the child. In *The Borrowers* there is a variation on this theme, as the adult borrowers amuse themselves by appearing on the bed-cover of the bedridden 'Her', the boy's Great Aunt Sophy, when she is drunk. She, however, takes them as a figment of her Madeira-befuddled imagination. When the child provides other adults with access to the Borrowers, he does so by mistake and the ultimate result is that the Borrowers move out of the human household altogether.

It is interesting to compare *The Borrowers* with *Stig of the Dump*, since, in the latter, unification is achieved in the end by means of strong hints of historical continuity. This, in fact, finally counteracts the impression of differentiation with which the story began. Barney, Lou and their parents go picnicking on the North Downs, near where the children had helped Stig and his group to fit the last of four standing stones in place on the night when Barney and Lou had gone 'midsummer crazy' and found Stig among his own kind in the pit. The stones are still there, and Barney is able to transfer the knowledge he has gained from his secret association with Stig to his parents, who

> got into an argument about stone-ages and bronze-ages, and about how the stones had got there at all, until Barney said, without thinking, 'They had *flint* spears, and it was the heave-ho that did it.'

And everybody thought about this quite a lot, and had to admit that Barney was probably right, though they couldn't think how he knew.

(p. 159)

Of Stig it is said that

One report was that he'd been seen working at a garage by the main road. . . . And somebody else said he saw him in a back lane of that woody country at the top of the Downs. . . . It certainly sounded like Barney's friend Stig, but perhaps it was only a relative of his.

(*ibid.*)

In fact this novel instructs the child reader clearly, though subtly, in the inevitability of adult influence, and this counteracts its apparent differentiation between Barney and the adults. This differentiation is staged very early in the narration by Barney's referential, non-anaphoric use of 'they' in the remark (pp. 2–3 of the Sainsbury edition) 'They didn't let him have a bicycle.' This is indirect thought by Barney, and since no-one has been mentioned in the preceding text to whom 'they' can co-refer, 'they' cannot operate anaphorically in the text, but must refer out of the text to those characters in the fictional world who have power to bestow bicycles on children, that is, adults, probably Barney's parents. The differentiation from adults is also furthered by references to phenomena with expressions like 'what the grown-ups called a Sense of Humour' (p. 18) and 'what his Grandmother used to call hot-and-cold-all-over' (p. 27). Barney's attempt to identify with Stig is made clear both behaviourally, for example when Barney goes to a fancy-dress party dressed up as a cave man, and through indirect thought, like 'Stigs don't mind stings, he thought, so he'd better not' (p. 21). However, when in the company of Stig, Barney alternates between, on the one hand, identification as just illustrated coupled with admiration of Stig's own 'primeval' strength and cleverness, and, on the other hand, attempts at improving Stig's condition by providing him with materials for his house, and by speaking to him in the way adults speak to a child. For example:

'You want me to show you how to strike a match, Stig? Here, push the little drawer thing! That's right, but not too far. Take out a match. Now you better shut the box. Hold the match by the white end, not the black end, silly! Now rub it on the side of the box. No, the *side*. There!'

(p. 46)

In addition, the influence on him of adults is clear in examples like the following:

'Well, well,' said Barney. 'That's that!' It was a thing he had often heard his Grandfather say when he'd finished a job.

(p. 34)

'My grandfather always says wood warms you twice, once when you cut it and once when you burn it.'

(p. 39)

Finally, a passage like the following is the clearest possible indication, barring explicit declaration, that adults know best and give good advice, and that children understand this and only rebel for the sake of it, which is perhaps rather silly and childish:

Barney looked up at the wintry sky. Hunting people didn't take any notice of the weather, he thought. All the same, since nobody had told him he *ought* to, he decided to put on his rubber boots and mackintosh and sou'wester hat.

(p. 52)

On the whole, then, this novel employs strategies of unification. It sets up fragmentation only in order that unification may ensue. What it teaches is primarily the inevitability of development through history and through the life of the individual. Stig himself makes optimum use of the materials of 'civilisation', although the advantages of his own state are also heavily stressed. He will not, for example, kill a fox during the fox-hunting scene because foxes are inedible. Barney 'inherits' much of Stig's primeval wisdom and some of his skills but is as heavily dependent on and influenced by the wisdom of his contemporary elders.

Finally, fragmentation may take the form of *expurgation of the other*: creating an enemy within or without (Thompson, 1990: 65). In fiction, 'the other' can take many forms, from school bullies to witches, and tends, of course, to have those characteristics which the writer deems undesirable. It is common, particularly in fairy tales, to superimpose 'the other' upon a main character by magic, but this phenomenon can also be used more naturalistically in novels which begin by alienating the reader from the central character whose development towards reform is then traced. This serves the ideological purpose in so far as it unites reader and writer against the undesirable characteristics of 'the other' and enables the writer to demonstrate the beneficial effects of those modes of behaviour which the writer, and often the adult characters in the story, advocate. In other words, it unifies the 'good' child with 'good' adults against the common enemy, the 'bad' child and the 'bad' adult.

The Secret Garden works a variation of this pattern. The 'other' expurgated here is the self-absorbed adult who substitutes overindulgence for responsible, committed care for the child, which, therefore, becomes equally self-absorbed, and unhealthy in mind and body. This state of affairs is heavily signalled as unnatural, not least through the strong emphasis on nature as the force which saves the child – or which helps the child save herself and others. The overindulgence is committed by servants in order that the child should not disturb the parent. However, it is not the intention in the novel to undermine the social structure which supports differentiation between classes, or between rich and poor, or between master and servant; only the misuse of these perfectly proper social arrangements is criticised. The beginning of Mary's salvation is her removal from the, for her, unnatural Indian setting and her meeting with Martha, the maid who has been assigned the task of cleaning Mary's rooms and waiting on her 'a bit'. 'You are a strange servant', observes 'bad' Mary, and Martha explains that she would never have got an upstairs job 'if there was a grand missus at Misselthwaite' (p. 34). Martha could not have furthered the catharsis of Mary if she had been 'a well-trained fine young lady's-maid', who

> would have been more subservient and respectful and would have known that it was her business to brush hair, and button boots, and pick things up and lay them away. She was, however, only an untrained Yorkshire rustic who had been brought up in a moorland cottage with a swarm of little brothers and sisters who had never dreamed of doing anything but waiting on themselves and on the younger ones who were either babies in arms or just learning to totter about and tumble over things.
>
> (p. 38)

The satirical use in this passage of the expressions 'subservient', 'respectful' and 'only an untrained' is heavily underlined by the last four lines of the quotation where 'waiting on' is reserved for oneself and incapable infants. However, the 'other' expurgated in this novel is only that sector of the dominant class which retreats from responsibility and duty to indulge instead, in the case of Colin's father, in their own sorrow, or, in the case of Mary's mother, in artificial social amusements. Both restrain natural human creativity and independence, the 'freedom of manner' which Martha and her family display. It is 'nature' in all its Yorkshire splendour which conquers Mary's and her cousin Colin's helpless, hapless, sickly characteristics and helps their transformation to healthy, happy, self-reliant children, and which helps to place Colin and his father in a natural parent–child relationship. The presentation of the 'unnatural' and self-destructive use of power by that sector of the dominant class which is expurgated (by death or catharsis) merely highlights the harmonious manner in which representatives of the different classes can work together 'naturally' for the good of all.

The final mode of operation of ideology Thompson (1990: 65–6) discusses is *reification*. Relations of domination which are in effect transitory, historical states are presented as though they were timeless, natural and permanent. For example, *naturalisation* is often used, as in the example from *The Railway Children* quoted above, to justify male domination as the outcome of natural, physiological characteristics of males and females.

Second, *eternalisation* may be evoked to obscure the development of institutions, customs and tradition: 'that is how it has always been'. It can be difficult to distinguish this strategy from naturalisation, since it is often claimed that the reason why 'it has always been like that', and why history repeats itself, lies in human nature which, according to writers who employ this argument, is eternally and everywhere the same. However, in *The Secret Garden*, eternalisation plays an important part in differentiating between the British upper class as rulers in India, which is unnatural and transient in the novels' terms, and the British upper class as rulers in Yorkshire, which is traditional. Towards the end of the novel, Colin's father returns to Misselthwaite feeling

> that sense of the beauty of the land and sky and purple bloom of distance, and a warming of the heart at drawing nearer to the great old house which had held those of his blood for six hundred years.
>
> (pp. 320–1)

In contrast, the English are new arrivals in India, and Mary recalls these new masters' inability to alter true Indian tradition:

> If one told them to do a thing their ancestors had not done for a thousand years they gazed at one mildly and said, 'It is not the custom' and one knew that was the end of the matter.
>
> (pp. 37–8)

In *nominalisation*, or *grammatical metaphor* (Halliday, 1985: 321), actions, which would usually be described by a sentence like *We study ideology*, come to be referred to by a noun phrase like *the study of ideology*; that is, an activity has come to be presented as a 'thing' – it has become reified. Nominalisation can serve ideology in so far as it obviates the need to mention any agent of the action which has been reified; this, in turn, may facilitate naturalisation and eternalisation. For example, expressions like *low birth* and *high birth* can give the impression that the social hierarchy is as natural as the scales of temperature and size; expressions like *person whose parents were poor or common* and *person whose parents were rich or noble* are more likely to encourage questions about why one type of person should be more highly valued than another.

Passivisation, too, allows the agent who carried out an action to be left unmentioned, or to be mentioned after the affected entity has been introduced. So, instead of a sentence with the verb in the active voice, *the students study ideology*, we might see a sentence with the verb in the passive voice, *ideology is studied* (*by the students*). Passivisation also allows the focus of the sentence, the point at which the sentence takes off, so to speak, to be placed on the entity to which something is done, rather than on the doer of the action, by placing the affected entity at the beginning of the sentence, in *theme* position (Halliday, 1985: ch. 3). Passivisation is relatively rare in literature for children. This is partly because so much of this describes the actions of the characters (see chapter 3), but it may also be the result of the authors' implicit or explicit awareness that passivisation may cause comprehension difficulties for young readers (Perera, 1984: 8). Where passives do occur, they often focus attention on a main character, as in the opening sentence of *The Secret Garden*: 'When Mary Lennox was sent to Misselthwaite Manor . . .'. However, as well as focusing attention on Mary, this sentence highlights the inactivity of her early life, a function which most passives with Mary as the affected entity in subject position fulfil in the early parts of the book.

In this section we have discussed and briefly illustrated the modes and strategies of ideology highlighted by Thompson (1990), using examples from literature for children. In the following section, we discuss Hollindale's notion of 'levels' of realisation of ideology in children's literature, relating the two schemes to each other. Finally, we provide outline descriptions of those aspects of the language system in terms of which the more detailed textual analyses in later chapters are predominantly carried out.

IDEOLOGY IN CHILDREN'S LITERATURE

Interest in ideology in children's literature arises from a belief that children's literary texts are (Hunt, 1990: 2) 'culturally formative, and of massive importance educationally, intellectually, and socially. Perhaps more than any other texts, they reflect society as it wishes to be, as it wishes to be seen, and as it unconsciously reveals itself to be', at least to (predominantly middle-class) writers. Clearly, literature is not the only socialising agent in the life of children, even among the media. It is possible to argue, for example, that, today, the influence of books is vastly overshadowed by that of television. There is, however, a considerable degree of interaction between the two media. Many so-called children's literary classics are televised, and the resultant new book editions strongly suggest that viewing can encourage subsequent reading. Similarly, some television series for children are published in book form. There is, in any case, no doubt that for the reading child, books have a permanency not shared by television programmes, or even by films available on home video: the child can read and reread at its own speed in its own time and in its own private place. Furthermore, once it moves beyond the heavily illustrated picture book, the child is arguably more actively engaged in the reading process than in the process of viewing television or video, since the world of the book has to be created through the text alone; the child must form his/her own mental representation of characters, places and actions, and this suggests a higher degree of collaborative involvement with the medium than television viewing does.

It is clearly difficult to demonstrate that what children read or have read to them influences their subsequent general behaviour, beliefs and attitudes. However, the widespread urge towards preventing access by children to at least some modes of expression (pornography and violence), even among otherwise liberal adults, strongly suggests a 'folk-belief', pretheoretic and unproven though it may be, in a causal relationship, whether direct or indirect, between child 'input' and child 'output'. The very notions of socialisation and 'upbringing' embody this belief, and it finds a degree of support in studies which demonstrate, for example, that the structure and narrative techniques displayed in stories written by children mirror those of literature to which the children have been exposed (Steedman, 1982: 11).

Writers for children have clearly also *hoped* that their efforts would have some subsequent beneficial (in their view) effect on the child reader. Thus Sarah Fielding (1710–68) explains to the reader that 'the true Use of Books is to make you wiser and better' and that 'the design of the following Sheets is to prove to you that Pride, Stubbornness, Malice, Envy, and, in short, all manner of Wickedness, is the greatest Folly we can be possessed of' (1749; quoted in Hunt, 1990: 16, 17). Obviously, the purpose here is didactic, the ultimate goal being to ensure societal harmony: 'Certainly, Love and Affection for each other makes the Happiness of all Societies' (*ibid.*).

On the other hand, it has been feared that literature might have a detrimental effect, and that it should therefore not be left to the child to choose for itself which books to read. For example, Sarah Trimmer (1741–1810) advises that 'the utmost circumspection' is necessary in selecting books for a child to read, and 'children should not be permitted to make their own choice, or to read any books that may accidentally be thrown in their way, or offered for their perusal; but should be taught to consider it a *duty*, to consult their parents in this momentous concern' (1803/Hunt 1990: 18).

In contrast, Elizabeth Rigby (1844/Hunt 1990: 20) considered that the child should be left to 'forage for itself'. Rigby believed that children could not be damaged by reading anything which adults thought unsuitable, since they could not understand it; that they would, in any case, read the forbidden books sooner or later; and that the sooner they read them the better, since younger children were less likely to understand the evil in them.

It is not our intention to contribute to the censorship debate, but, rather, to raise awareness of the workings of ideology in literature for children. Childhood (as all of life) is a time for learning about a(n adult) world. Many writers have used writing by children as evidence of the steps children take in this learning process (see, for example, Steedman, 1982: 76). It is equally interesting and instructive to consider the devices through which adults try to facilitate it. For fiction written for children to have a didactic or socialising function, it is necessary that events and characters in it relate to the world of adults. As children use their writing to reorder their experience to fit adult expectations (Steedman, *ibid.*), so adult writers for children reorder and relexicalise their adult world to fit what they perceive to be the world of the child, or to fit what they think that world ought to be. As 'in play, children can control the adult world they represent to themselves' (*ibid.* 122), so in fiction written for children, adults can control the adult world they present to children.

This requires that the child learn how to read; not only, and not in the first instance, in the sense of relating the written word to the spoken, but in the sense of coming to understand how books work, that is, how books are structured and how they relate to concrete experience. In fulfilling this dual function, even books for very young children can simultaneously actively promote certain beliefs and certain forms of behaviour while discouraging others.

Consider Rod Campbell's *Dear Zoo* (1982; Puffin edition, 1984), which is a literary work for the 2–3-year-old, short enough for us to be able to consider it in its entirety:

[1] I wrote to the zoo to send me a pet. [2] They sent me an [flap with a picture of a box with the label 'very heavy' on it; flap lifts up to reveal an elephant]. [3] He was too big! [4] I sent him back. [5] So they sent me a [as before, though the box is labelled 'fragile'; giraffe]. [6] He was too tall! [7] I sent him back. [8] So they sent me a [lion]. [9] He was too fierce! [10] I sent him back. [11] So they sent me a [camel]. [12] He was too grumpy! [13] I sent him back. [14] So they sent me a [snake]. [15] He was too scary! [16] I sent him back. [17] So they sent me a [monkey]. [18] He was too naughty! [19] I sent him back. [20] So they sent me a [frog]. [21] He was too jumpy! [22] I sent him back. [23] So they thought very hard, and sent me a [puppy]. [24] He was perfect! [25] I kept him.

There is much to be learnt from this text. It displays a very common discourse structure with sentence 1 presenting a situation embodying a problem we might label 'pet-lack'. Sentence 2 presents an attempted solution to the lack-of-pet problem, sentence 3 a negative evaluation of the attempted solution and sentence 4 a reaction following from the negative evaluation. There are in all seven cycles like this before the solution in sentence 23, the positive evaluation of that solution in sentence 24 and the reaction following from the positive evaluation in sentence 25 (for a full exposition of the Problem–Solution and other discourse patterns, see Hoey, 1983). This is excellent preparation for future novel reading, since many novels are constructed around variations on this pattern.

By using pictures, the story mediates between language and the world. It helps the child to learn or be reassured about what kind of thing a word can be used to refer to. The use of flaps encourages interaction with the text. It is necessary, and exciting, for the child to lift the flap to see what animal has been sent, and to acquire or demonstrate its mastery of the skill of referring to animals with the appropriate nouns. This requires thought and response to the text and pictures, rather than just passive reception of the story, again something that will be required in the child's later reading life.

From the point of view of the study of ideology in children's literature, however, the most important feature of this book is the lexical choices and organisation it displays. From sentence 2 onward the text is organised in terms of repetition of three sentences, two of which display variation within the repeated sentence frame as shown below:

(I wrote to the zoo to send me a PET.)

	List 1	List 2	
They sent me a/an	elephant. He was too	big!	I sent him back.
	giraffe	tall	
	lion	fierce	
	camel	grumpy	
	snake	scary	
	monkey	naughty	
	frog	jumpy	
	PUPPY	PERFECT	I kept him

Each lexical item in list 1 above is a noun which can be used to refer to an animal, and each lexical item in list 2 is a property- or characteristic-adjective. 'He' in each sentence which contains an adjective co-refers to the animal mentioned in the preceding sentence, so the syntax relates the animals to the properties on a one-to-one basis: for each animal we are given one salient property. But since each property is modified by 'too' – 'he was too big, tall, etc.', and because we know that the narrator's desire is for a pet, we realise that the properties in question are inappropriate in a pet. A pet is a *domestic* animal, an animal fit to keep at home, and the only animal mentioned here as qualifying for pet status is a puppy. The puppy is the perfect pet (and rarely seen in zoos, of course, which may be why 'they' in the zoo have to think so hard before dispatching the puppy). All the other animals, in being sent back to the zoo, are being cast out from the field of pets, and from the home, because of the characteristics which are ascribed to them: being fierce, grumpy, naughty, and so on. The effort at socialisation is pleasantly veiled and distanced, but it is there nevertheless (along with the very obvious emphasis on maleness: all the animals are referred to by the masculine pronoun 'he').

If a zoologist were asked to list the most salient characteristic of types of animal, the second list in the figure above would presumably look rather different from Rod Campbell's, which takes account of a child's experience of animals and of types of behaviour, and which is guided by the socialising purpose of the book. It is because all writers, whether of fiction or not, have this power to order and classify to suit their purposes, that they can mobilise meaning to establish and sustain relationships of domination.

Hollindale (1988/Hunt 1992: 19–40) adopts the *Oxford English Dictionary*'s definition of *ideology* as a systematic scheme of ideas related to a class or group. In other words, he adopts the neutral conception of ideology referred to on page 42 above. Although we adopt a critical conception in this book, we can still usefully consider the three levels at which ideology is present in children's books which Hollindale (1988/Hunt 1992: 27–34) isolates.

The first is the level of 'intended surface ideology' where the effort at establishing and/or sustaining relationships of power is clearly realised in the narrative as a whole. In Thompson's terms (see page 47 above), the narrative as a whole constitutes narrativisation in the service of legitimisation of an actual or fictional (hoped for) state of affairs. Some writers make this explicit in extra-narrative statements such as prefaces or scholarly papers, and Hollindale's example is of this kind. However, it is equally possible to refer to one's purpose within the narrative itself, particularly when this takes the form of story-within-story. For example Harriet Louisa Childe-Pemberton explains in 'All my Doing; or, Red Riding-Hood Over Again' (1882/Zipes 1987: 211–48) to her listening niece:

> Thus you see it is sometimes possible to be so heedless and silly as to cause the deaths of other people, and that there may be more in the story of Red Riding-Hood than is to be seen at first sight. . . . Ah! you fancy, perhaps, as I did, that little things have no consequences. Never think it! The slightest word has an echo far beyond what you can hear; the smallest deed casts a shadow broader than you can see.
>
> And of all sad words, none so sad as the wail, Too late! Of all bitter memories, none so bitter as the thought, It never need have been!
>
> (Zipes, 1987: 247–8)

Hollindale's second category of ideological content in children's fiction consists of the writer's inexplicit, and possibly subconscious, assumptions. On the importance of these, Hollindale comments:

The working of ideology at this level is not incidental or unimportant. It might seem that values whose presence can only be convincingly demonstrated by an adult with some training in critical skills are unlikely to carry much potency with children. More probably the reverse is true: the values at stake are usually those which are taken for granted by the writer, and reflect the writer's integration in a society which unthinkingly accepts them. . . . Unexamined, passive values are widely *shared* values, and we should not underestimate the powers of reinforcement vested in quiescent and unconscious ideology.

(1988/Hunt, 1992: 30)

Hollindale (*ibid.* 27) provides an interesting reflection of his own integration into a society in which many unquestioningly accept that 'the writer' is male, when he quiescently reinforces this belief in explaining that a story may express 'the explicit social, political or moral beliefs of the individual writer, and his wish to recommend them to children through the story'. As Hollindale further explains, passive ideology may be in evidence in works which explicitly distance themselves from the asymmetrical relationships of power which the passive ideology sustains (*ibid.* 31). For example, although Clive Staples Lewis (1898–1963) is generally scrupulously careful to include among his main characters equal numbers of males and females, there are times when his females become curiously invisible linguistically speaking. In chapter 9 of his first (in reading order) Narnian chronicle, *The Magician's Nephew* (Bodley Head, 1955; Lions edition, 1990, pp. 104–5), the boy Digory sets off to speak to Aslan. Polly, the girl, 'waited for a moment and then went after him'. Digory's uncle 'followed the children'. There follows a lengthy description of the effect of Aslan's song on Digory, ending 'It made Digory hot and red in the face', and immediately followed by a passage from which any consciousness of the previously asserted presence of Polly is conspicuously absent:

> It had some effect on Uncle Andrew, for Digory could hear him saying, 'A spirited gel [referring to the witch, not Polly], sir. It's a pity about her temper, but a dem fine woman all the same, a dem fine woman.' But what the song did to the two humans . . .
>
> (Lions edition, p. 105)

The third way in which ideology works in children's literature is in fixing the limits of expression. Hollindale (Hunt, 1990: 32) quotes Waller (1986: 10): 'When a text is written, ideology works to make some things more natural to write; when a text is read, it works . . . to force language into conveying only those meanings reinforced by the dominant forces of our society.' Chomsky (1979: 38–9) notes that in democracies, where everyone is permitted to say what they like, and dissidence is encouraged, the 'propaganda system' may in fact work more effectively than the propaganda system in totalitarian states which employs clear enunciation of official doctrine. According to Chomsky, the system in a democracy attempts to 'fix the limits of possible thought: supporters of official doctrine at one end, and the critics . . . at the other' (quoted in Chilton, 1982: 94). In other words, the dominant group not only defines its own preferred modes of thought and expression, but also those of opponents. It is the dominant group, with access to the media of expression, which gets to define the framework within which discussion can take place; it is 'the writer of the story' who gets to select its metaphors and other forms of symbolic expression. This can mean that certain thoughts are, if not unthinkable, then at least less likely to occur to people in certain historical periods than in others: writers and thinkers are limited to a significant degree by the theoretical frameworks and generally established modes of reasoning prevalent in their culture at their time. These limitations are reflected in the modes of expression and in the vocabulary writers have at their disposal.

Stories which share a general theme but which are temporally distant from each other provide interesting illustrations of this phenomenon. Consider Edith Nesbit's 'The Last of the Dragons' (*c*.1900) and Martin Baynton's *Jane and the Dragon* (1988). Both tales are set in the past relative to the time of writing, both employ role reversal (as compared with the traditional tales of males rescuing females from dragons) and both deny the stereotype of the fierce dragon in favour of a dragon which just wants to be loved, and, once loved, finds useful employment (though Baynton's dragon has to wait for this until the sequel, *The Dragon's Purpose* (1990)). Both heroines object to the roles assigned to them by tradition. Nesbit's princess wonders whether it might not be possible to tie up 'one of the silly little princes for the dragon to look at – and then *I* could go and kill the dragon and rescue the prince', but has to be content with plotting an elaborate scheme with the prince during which the princess 'began to like him a little' (Zipes, 1987: 354). The two are married once they have brought the gentle dragon home to the palace.

Baynton's prince's main contribution to the story lies in being abducted by the dragon so that Jane can go and fight the dragon, realise his gentleness and free the prince. There is no wedding at the end, only a ball during which Jane dances with the jester who lent her his armour (see also Robert Munsch's *The Paperbag Princess* (1980) in which a planned marriage does not take place because the princess who has freed the prince by outwitting the dragon realises that the prince is 'a toad'). In 1900, the marriage was still an important aspect of the happy ending; by the 1980s it was no longer necessary or necessarily desirable.

IDEOLOGY AND LINGUISTIC CATEGORIES

In the preceding section, we have discussed Hollindale's three 'levels' of realisation of ideology, and in the section preceding that, we outlined Thompson's (1990) general modes of operation of ideology and the strategies typically associated with the general modes. Thompson's strategies may operate at each of Hollindale's levels, of (i) intended, surface ideology, (ii) implicit ideology, and (iii) boundaries of possible thought and expression.

Thompson explicitly emphasises the role of language in the creation and maintenance of relations of power. Hollindale's discussion, too, touches on the role language plays in the socialising function of literature for children. Yet neither adopts what one could call an explicitly linguistic perspective. Once such a perspective is adopted, it seems necessary to add a 'level' of operation of ideology which is superimposed upon each of Hollindale's levels, and through which each of Thompson's strategies may be realised, namely the level of selection of linguistic expression. It is clear that a writer's linguistic choices can aid the creation and maintenance of relations of power. This is so whether the writer intends his/her linguistic choices to function ideologically or whether they merely reflect implicit ideology. Furthermore, linguistic choices have to be made whether or not the writer gives vent to intended, surface ideology.

We have indicated that the strategies Thompson lists are realised through stretches of discourse of varying lengths, but that the smallest individually ideologically 'effective' unit might be the word in the case of some strategies and the clause in the case of other strategies. In any work, the overall impression one gets from reading is obviously a compendium of many 'small experiences' of individual items of language and of linguistic patterning, and a thorough stylistic description of any novel, or even a short story, bringing together the impressions created through the interrelationships between the patterning perceived at each of the linguistic levels of sound, structure and meaning, would fill a book. Since our purpose here is less to provide full interpretations of complete novels than to highlight ideology in children's literature in general, we confine ourselves in the main to clausal and lexical (word-rank) analyses. We adopt a Hallidayan framework for clausal analyses, and a neo-Firthian framework for the analysis of collocation, the study of 'the company words keep'. While we do not in any sense purport to present a complete account of these frameworks – an aim that would be well beyond the scope of this book – we believe that a brief exposition of the frameworks on which we rely will assist readers in following our subsequent analyses.

Collocation

The notion of collocation derives from Firth (1957a; 1957b) and has been further refined and developed by, among others, Halliday (1966) and J. Sinclair (1966; 1987a; 1987b; 1991). The notion relates to the tendency of certain words in spoken and written texts to appear in the vicinity of certain other words. In a collocation-orientated search through one or any number of texts for a particular word (or expression), the word one searches for is called the 'node', and the words (or expressions) which are shown to have a tendency to appear in its vicinity are called the 'collocates' of the node.

Some nodes are very strongly related to their collocates. For example, it is unlikely that *kith* and *fro* will occur without *and kin* and *to and*, respectively. *Blond* relates somewhat less strongly to words like *hair*, *tresses* and *wig*, but is nevertheless unlikely to occur outside contexts involving hair or persons. Normally we would not, for example, describe a car as blond, no matter how closely its colour might resemble the colour of our neighbour's hair. So what is at issue here is not so much what the world is like: the car may in reality be the same colour as the hair. The fact that we call the hair blond and not the car is a linguistic fact. Similarly, it is a linguistic fact that we normally say of brains and eggs that they are addled, whereas we normally say of butter and bacon that they are rancid.

These collocational relationships are firmly established. Others are less restricted. The node *pretty*, for example, can occur in the vicinity of very many terms and expressions. Nevertheless, its use tends to be restricted to females and small phenomena, and this tendency of use begins to affect what we might refer to as the meaning of the term *pretty*: although we might not wish to say that *pretty* exactly *means* either 'small' or 'feminine', we might feel that it strongly *suggests* smallness or femininity.

Words' tendencies to call certain associations to mind has been named by Louw (1993: 158, quoting personal communication with J. Sinclair in 1988) their 'semantic prosodies'. Semantic prosodies can be explicated by means of searching texts for collocates for the word whose semantic prosody one is interested in. For example, Louw demonstrates that the phrasal verb *set in* tends to occur with terms that refer to unpleasant phenomena such as death and *rigor mortis*, and suggests that this shows that its semantic prosody is negative: it connotes unpleasantness. It would not be unreasonable to suggest that in the normal course of events semantic prosodies are also learnt collocationally, so to speak. A child is unlikely to be explicitly told only to use the expression *set in* when something unpleasant is being discussed; s/he is more likely to gain this impression through exposure to use, and to store it as part of a developing base of implicit knowledge about the language system. Similarly, a semantic prosody which is fairly firmly fixed to an expression can be 'transferred' to other terms with which the expression co-occurs. For example, if someone says of a man that he is pretty, the 'small and feminine' prosody of *pretty* is very likely to be transferred to *man*, and to override the everyday-use prosody of *man*, which is probably still for most people 'fairly large and masculine'.

The members of any linguistic community have in common vast quantities of implicit knowledge about collocational relationships and the semantic prosodies of terms and expressions, and writers, including, of course, writers of literature, as well as members of various pressure groups, may exploit this knowledge implicitly or explicitly. From time to time we are made aware that some of our linguistic habits perpetuate stereotypes which may be damaging to some groups in society. For example, if the semantic prosody of *black* is negative, as its tendency to occur in expressions like *black magic*, *black Wednesday*, *the black sheep of the family* and so on suggests, then this prosody may spill over onto the person referred to in expressions like *black man/woman/boy/girl*. This particular phenomenon was actively combated through the 'Black is Beautiful' slogan used by campaigners for racial equality in the 1970s and 1980s – a slogan which itself manipulates collocation and whose success testifies to the effectiveness of such manipulation. Through frequent collocation with the positively loaded term *beautiful*, any negative connotations of *black* are overridden.

The phenomenon of collocation, then, allows writers, without explicit statement, to encourage certain reader reactions to characters and phenomena in the fictional worlds of realistic novels, and it allows them, further, to encourage associations between phenomena in the fictional world and those of the readers' extra-literary experience. The latter is particularly important in fantasy fiction if the fantastic world is to be of any consequence, or even comprehensible, for the reader.

A typical outcome of studies of collocation is a set of 'concordance lines' in which the node is displayed centrally with about four words either side of the node. For example, the concordance lines for the word *dragon* in Baynton (1988) (A below) and Baynton (1990) (B below) would look something like this (T stands for title):

A

```
T                        Jane and the   dragon
 1 day, an enormous green dragon    came and stole the Prince
 2   alloped away after the dragon.   Jane followed the dragon
 3 gon. Jane followed the  dragon    to his mountain lair. 'Re
 4   er sternest voice. The dragon    laughed. 'Make me!' he ro
 5   could have stabbed the dragon,   but she did not. Twice th
 6   she did not. Twice the dragon    could have toasted her wi
 7   e killed me,' said the dragon.   'You could have killed me
 8   ng people,' sighed the dragon.   'Then why did you steal t
 9   asy for you,' said the dragon,   'you're a knight and peop
10   ok off her helmet. The dragon    was amazed. 'You're just
11    be loved,' sobbed the dragon,   and he covered his face w
12   , thank you,' said the dragon,   and he sobbed all the lou
13   sometimes?' asked the  dragon.   'Every Saturday,' Jane pr
14   go.' And she gave the  dragon    a hug and another kiss. I
```

B

```
T                        The   dragon's purpose
 1 ntment to keep. With a  dragon.   Jane was a knight. Not a
 2   son from a giant green dragon.   Jane had not killed the d
 3   ane had not killed the dragon.   She had made friends with
 4   urday. The ride to the dragon's  mountain was hot and dus
 5   t when she came to the dragon's  cave, Jane found a new s
 6   e me?' asked Jane. The dragon    smiled and wiped his eyes
 7   ause I'm a giant green dragon.   I was born to scare peopl
 8    start crying too.' The dragon    brightened up at once. He
 9   was worried about the  dragon    and needed time to think.
10   told him all about the dragon's  empty life. 'He needs a
11   all about the unhappy  dragon.   The jester listened caref
```

12	d shook his head. Your	dragon	was born to scare people.
13	nk of so many jobs the	dragon	might do. Yet none of the
14	ature of a giant green	dragon.	The other knights were bu
15	roar, the giant green	dragon	burst from his hiding pla
16	lambered up beside the	dragon.	'How do you feel now?' sh
17	'Better,' laughed the	dragon,	'much, much better.' The
18	uch, much better.' The	dragon	won first prize. And when
19	ride on his back. The	dragon	agreed, though his heart
20	ne. 'I'm a giant green	dragon	born to scare people.' 'A
21	a moment,' sighed the	dragon,	'and it was a sham; a pie
22	about was the unhappy	dragon.	Each evening she walked t
23	d stared across to the	dragon's	mountain. Then, late one
24	y purpose.' It was the	dragon.	'Climb up, climb up,' he
25	how you.' Jane and the	dragon	flew to a distant cloud.
26	o a distant cloud. The	dragon	beat his wings and drove
27	ee that!' bellowed the	dragon.	'I scared the rain right
28	it! I'm a giant green	dragon	born to scare rainclouds.

From lines like these, the collocates for a given node, within a given text or set of texts, can be established.

The lines above give *green*, with seven occurrences, and *giant*, with six, as the most common adjectival collocates of *dragon* in this set of texts, followed by *unhappy*, with two occurrences, and *enormous* with one. Among these, *unhappy* stands out against the rest, in so far as it ascribes an emotion to the dragon while the rest ascribe physical features – colour and size in equal proportions. It may also conflict with our expectations of dragons, whereas the other adjectives may not.

Of the verbal groups which function as Predicators with the dragon as Subject (see below), twelve ascribe a physical action to the dragon, and two, *could have toasted* and *might do*, ascribe to him potential physical action. Of the actions ascribed, however, only four are actions which directly affect an entity other than the dragon. Eleven ascribe to him speech action. Of these, three are the neutral *said*, one is the interactive *asked* and one the interactive *agreed*; two are *sighed*, two are *sobbed*, one is *laughed*, and one is *bellowed*; that is, there are three neutral speech actions, two explicitly interactive speech actions, one which indicates loudness, and five which indicate emotion (*laughed*, and *sighed* and *sobbed* twice each). There are, further, three instances of the verb *to be*, and one instance of the verb *feel*.

An exercise such as that just performed can show how the language of the parts of a text which deal with a given phenomenon may lead the reader to form an impression of the phenomenon. In the case above, for example, we can see why the dragon may strike readers as a fairly emotional creature who is more concerned to affect others through speech than through physical action. In all probability, this will conflict with many people's dragon stereotype.

Naturally, concordance lines can only be used as part of an interpretative effort, and it is necessary, if one wants to make any strong claims concerning effect, to consider substantially more text than that provided in them. Nevertheless, sets of concordance lines can serve as useful starting points for further textual searches, or as checks on claims one might wish to make. If the search is performed by computer it can, in addition, be carried out quite fast, and with a higher degree of accuracy than most human readers can achieve, particularly where a number of long texts are concerned.

The clause

The clause embodies three so-called linguistic systems: the mood system, the system of Theme and Rheme, and the transitivity system. Each system can be considered to perform a particular function. The mood system indicates interpersonal relationships and interaction; the system of Theme and Rheme indicates which aspects of actions, events, participants and circumstances are in focus; and the transitivity system allows for the representation of events. Each system is complex, and we provide only the most basic outline. For further information, consult Halliday (1985, chs 3, 4 and 5).

Mood

The mood system is realised grammatically by the positioning relative to each other of Subject (S) and Predicator (P). Consider part of concordance line A7 above, 'You could have killed me'. In it, the Subject, *You*, comes before the Predicator, *could have killed*:

You could have killed me
  S   P

The order, S followed by P, indicates the Declarative mood, the mood standardly used to make statements.

In line A4 above, we find 'Make me'. This consists of a Predicator, *Make* and an Object, *me*, but there is no Subject. The absence of S indicates that the mood is Imperative, the mood standardly used to issue commands or encourage people to do something (*have a biscuit*; *do sit down*).

In line A8, we find 'Then why did you steal t'. The structure here is more complex; the Subject *you* divides the Predicator *did steal*:

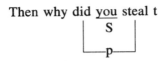

This configuration of S and P indicates that the mood is Interrogative, the mood standardly used for asking questions.

Mood, then, is the grammatical notion that corresponds to the use-orientated notion of clause or sentence action. It is at least partly by using different moods that we seek to affect each other in different ways through language, and it is for this reason that linguists with an interest in the functions of language claim an interpersonal function for the system of mood. In interpersonal relationships, roles are often distributed in such a way that certain persons have, or claim for themselves, the right, duty or need to issue commands or encouragements to action, to ask questions for others to answer, or to make statements and provide information. Some roles are of a more permanent nature than others, of course, and everyone has many different roles to perform. Nevertheless, the distribution of questions, commands and statements among the participants in linguistic interactions, including the characters in fiction, can reveal a good deal about the relationships between them.

Theme and Rheme

The first element of a clause of English, regardless of its grammatical category, is called its Theme, and the rest of the clause is called the Rheme. So in the opening clause of Burnett (1911): 'When Mary Lennox was sent to Misselthwaite Manor', *When*, which is a grammatical Adjunct (A), is Theme and the rest is Rheme:

When	Mary Lennox	was sent	to Misselthwaite Manor
A	S	P	A
Theme		Rheme	

As the example shows, the Theme need not coincide with the grammatical Subject. The theme serves as the point of departure for the message of the clause; it shows what the clause is about (Halliday, 1985: 38), and is, for that reason, sometimes called the 'psychological subject'.

However, Theme selection also has an explicitly textual function in so far as it often helps readers to perceive the coherence of the text and the structure of the narrative. For example, the focus in the clause just quoted is on the time at which Mary was sent to where the main action of the story is to take place, and it paves the way for the subsequent description of her as she was before she got there. Chapter 2 continues with this description, and begins with 'Mary', which is also Subject, as Theme: 'Mary had liked to look at her mother from a distance.' Later in the chapter, Mary begins her journey, which continues (and ends) in chapter 3, which again begins with an expression referring to Mary as Theme: 'She slept a long time.' By chapter 4, however, Mary has arrived, and her new life is about to begin. *When* is thematised again: 'When she opened her eyes in the morning.' Temporal themes recur as first Themes in the following three chapters: 'At first each day which passed by for Mary Lennox was exactly like the others'; 'The next day the rain poured down in torrents again'; and 'Two days after this, when Mary opened her eyes . . .'. At this point, Mary is about to find the key to the garden, and the focus shifts from 'the time of waiting' to interaction between Mary, the garden and the friends with whom she shares it, the weather and nature.

Of course, thematisation also functions to focus aspects of clauses within chapters, and to relate to each other different parts of chapters in particular ways. The novel ends:

> 'Look here,' he said, '. . . Look what's coming across th' grass.'
>
> When Mrs Medlock looked she threw up her hands and gave a little shriek, and every man and woman servant within hearing bolted across the servants' hall and stood looking through the window with their eyes almost starting out of their heads.
>
> Across the lawn came the Master of Misselthwaite, . . . and by his side . . . walked . . . Master Colin!

Here, the thematisation of the Adjunct *across the lawn* clearly links the final paragraph to the first in the quotation because it repeats (with the rephrasal: grass – lawn) the expression which occurred just before the intervening paragraph. Had the final paragraph begun 'The Master of Misselthwaite came across the lawn', the effect would have been quite different; it would not, for example, have been so immediately obvious that this was the sight that had caused Mrs Medlock's reaction.

Thematisation can, in addition, be a powerful tool for reinforcing a writer's explicit message. Consider, for example, the first two-thirds of the opening paragraph of the final chapter of *The Secret Garden* (Themes in the main clauses are italicised):

> *In each century since the beginning of the world* wonderful things have been discovered. *In the last century* more amazing things were found out than in any century before. *In this new century* hundreds of things still more astounding will be brought to light. *At first* people refuse to believe that a strange new thing can be done, *then* they begin to hope it can't be done, *then* they see it can be done – *then* it is done *and* all the world wonders why it was not done centuries ago. *One of the new things people began to find out in the last century* was that thoughts . . . are as powerful as electric batteries.

In this passage, Burnett is eternalising scientific endeavour and development, and describing the gradual acceptance of new ideas, before homing in on one particular new idea: that thoughts are as powerful as electric batteries. She reinforces the communication of the constant nature of the quest for knowledge by thematising first all the past, then the immediate past, and then the time of writing and its immediate future; in other words, she moves from the general to the particular, making the particular an example of the general, a pattern which is clearly signalled in the selection of Themes. She emphasises the historical nature of the process of acceptance of a new concept through thematisation of *At first*, *then, then* and the final *and* which introduces the result of acceptance.

It is important for her to establish her message firmly in the reader's mind here, because, in 1911, when the book was written, psychology was a relatively young science, and Burnett is about to make a strong claim about the effect of the mental lives of Mary and Colin on their physical condition:

> So long as Mistress Mary's mood was full of disagreeable thoughts . . . she was a yellow-faced, sickly, bored, and wretched child. . . . When her mind gradually filled itself with robins . . . there was no room left for the disagreeable thoughts which affected her liver and her digestion and made her yellow and tired.
>
> So long as Colin shut himself up in his room and thought only of his fears . . . he was a hysterical, half-crazy little hypochondriac. . . . When new, beautiful thoughts began to push out the old,

hideous ones, life began to come back to him, his blood ran healthily through his veins, and strength poured into him like a flood.

Burnett's claim is staged as *one of the new things people began to find out in the last century*, and which will be brought fully to light *in this new century*. Any doubts about the validity of her claim have been effectively pre-empted through the prior description of the general acceptance of new claims, and the reader should be prepared to accept that what happened to Mary and Colin 'is done', and to wonder 'why it was not done centuries ago'.

Transitivity

Through the system of transitivity, the clause presents the processes which take place in the (fictional) world, the participants in them and the circumstances attendant on them. There are three types types of basic process: Material, Mental and Relational.

Material processes are processes of doing. They require a participant who does the deed, and that participant is called an Actor. Some Material processes affect another participant, called the Goal. In the clause from Baynton (1988), 'Then why did you steal the Prince', the Material process of stealing is represented by the grammatical Predicator *did steal*, the Actor (who is the addressee, the dragon) by the grammatical Subject *you*, and the Goal by the grammatical Object (O), *the Prince*:

Then	why	did	you	steal	the Prince
A	A	P-	S	-P	O
THEME	RHEME				
	ACTOR				GOAL
	PROCESS				

Here, the grammatical Subject is not identical with the Theme, or psychological subject. It coincides, however, with the Actor. Compare the opening clause of *The Secret Garden*:

When	Mary Lennox	was sent to	Misselthwaite Manor
A	S	P	A
THEME	RHEME		
	GOAL	PROCESS	

Here, the unmentioned Agent obviously does not coincide with the grammatical Subject, Mary Lennox. Compare, now, two invented elaborations of this clause:

When	Mary Lennox	was sent	to MM	by her guardian
A	S	P	A	A

THEME	RHEME			
	GOAL	PROCESS	ACTOR	

When	her guardian	sent	Mary Lennox	to MM
A	S	P	O	A

THEME	RHEME			
	ACTOR	PROCESS	GOAL	

These two examples show that the roles specified by the transitivity system remain stable under variation in the grammatical functions of clause parts. They also remain stable under variation in Theme selection, as the following invented example demonstrates:

Her guardian	sent	Mary Lennox	to MM
S	P	O	A

THEME	RHEME		
ACTOR	PROCESS	GOAL	

Because the participant roles remain stable under varied classification of clause parts in terms of the other two clause systems, these roles are sometimes referred to as 'logical subject and object'. The 'logical' roles are the roles which the participants are presented as performing in the (fictional) world, so the transitivity system is arguably the system of the clause which is closest to 'real life'. It represents 'who does what to whom', and its function may therefore be thought of as representational.

Mental processes are processes of sensing, and their participants are Senser and an optional Phenomenon. The Senser is 'a conscious being that is feeling, thinking or seeing. The Phenomenon is that which is "sensed" – felt, thought or seen' (Halliday, 1985: 111). In the clause, 'So long as Colin . . . thought only of his fears', *Colin* is Senser and *his fears* is Phenomenon.

Relational processes are processes of being. They have Carriers and Attributes as participants. In the clause from the opening paragraph of *The Secret Garden*, 'she was the most disagreeable-looking child ever seen', *She*, which refers to Mary Lennox, is the Carrier of the Attribute *the most disagreeable child ever seen,* and in the clause a little further on in the text, 'Her hair was yellow', *her hair* is the Carrier of the Attribute *yellow.*

The transitivity system, then, represents processes and participants, and we have pointed out that participant roles remain stable under variation in the two other systems of the clause. However, the role of an individual may vary with variations in process. For example, Mary Lennox, who, in the first example of a process of Being given above, is assigned the role of Carrier, is in the opening clause of the novel assigned the role of Goal, and in the initial clause of chapter 12 'Mary ran so fast . . .' she is assigned the role of Actor. All that actually remains stable, therefore, is the referent of a given expression, the entity in the world to which the expression refers; in clauses, this entity can be represented in a variety of guises, and the writer's selection of processes for a participant to engage in may form an important element of the narration. In *The Secret Garden*, for example, the development of Mary Lennox from inactivity to action is traceable through a shift in role assignment tendencies. Compare, for example, the proportions in which types of role are assigned to Mary in the first chapter, which introduces Mary in India (table 2.1), and in the eighth chapter in which Mary finds the door to the secret garden (table 2.2). Analyses like

Table 2.1 Chapter 1, Instances of role assignment to Mary: 144

Role	Number	% of total
Actor	54	37.5
Goal	35	24.3
Senser	29	20.1
Carrier	20	13.8
Attribute	6	4.1

Actor and Goal relate 3:2

Table 2.2 Chapter 8, instances of role assignment to Mary: 200

Role	Number	% of total
Actor	125	62.5
Goal	24	12
Senser	26	13
Carrier	23	11.5
Attribute	2	1

Actor and Goal relate 5:1

these can help to account for the impression one might get of Mary as a far more active person towards the end of the book than she was at the beginning. Narration obviously has to be carried out by means of language, and linguistic analyses can be a powerful means of support for textual interpretation.

3 Traditional juvenile fiction

INTRODUCTION

In chapter 1 we saw how modern children's fiction has its roots in the nineteenth century and how the first major tradition to produce entertaining narratives for young readers was that which is characterised by the adventure story and the school story. In many respects the evolution of the former is a continuation of the tradition that had already been well established by Sir Walter Scott. From the mid nineteenth century adventure stories were being written specifically for juveniles as well as adults. The narratives of the traditional adventure story writers might well be regarded as the nineteenth-century boys' equivalent of what Nash (1990: 56) calls the 'action-book'. Nash cites, amongst others, Frederick Forsyth, Robert Ludlum and Wilbur Smith. All of these writers were named in Knowles's 1989–90 survey and they are the natural successors of John Buchan, Sapper and Dornford Yates and thus of Henty and W.E. Johns. The adventure story, with additional violence and now sex, is alive and well for the adult (and adolescent) reader.

We do not, on linguistic grounds, as we pointed out in chapter 1, differentiate between the adventure and school narratives in terms of genre. There are, of course, differences of setting but we prefer to consider them as complementary wings. Our genre of traditional juvenile fiction, then, is made up of two sub-genres which are similar in linguistic form. The school and adventure stories generate a class of works which can be considered in terms of a common authorship as regards point of view and audience. *Tom Brown's Schooldays* may be set in Rugby School and *The Coral Island* in the South Seas but the authors will not be dissimilar in how they represent God and country, for example, and they will be read by the same boys (and girls). The genre, therefore, enscribes a set of institutions; gender, friendship, family, religion, race; and it is these which allow the authors to provide an ideological view of the world

Of the two wings of the genre the adventure story is best exemplified in the first half of the century in the works of R.M. Ballantyne, W.H.G. Kingston and Captain Marryat. Thomas Hughes and his imitators, Talbot Baines Reed being the best known, represent the other wing. We shall refer to all the writers listed above though more extensively to *Tom Brown's Schooldays* and *The Coral Island*. These two are the best known of the Victorian pre-Henty classics having been published well into the twentieth century. We shall also draw upon G.A. Henty's work as indicative of popular late-nineteenth-century juvenile reading matter. Although he did not figure highly in Salmon's poll he was well known and popular as a story-writer in *The Boys' Own Paper* and *The Union Jack*. Salmon's survey was probably too early for a major response to Henty's books as the vast majority of these were published between 1884 and 1906. He was, nevertheless, extremely popular and influential as a writer and purveyor of ideology. The narratives throughout the ninetenth century are simple and while they are more entertaining than earlier books for children, preaching of one sort or another is still an authorial prerogative.

The defining institutions of the genre in its traditional forms are, in general terms, relatively straightforward. These institutions provide the means of identifying and classifying the genre and assist in providing a framework for linguistic description. Hodge (1990: 21) writes of domains which, he says, are 'categories of place associated with kinds of meaning and kinds of semiotic agent'. These institutions are not the same as Hodge's domains but, like them, they are part of a system of control because through them ideologies or power relations can be articulated. Thus, the importance of the representation of the family, for example, in traditional juvenile fiction when we recall its role as an agency of power in which men, women and children formed a strictly hierarchical grouping:

> Girls were taught to be gentler than boys and the literature written to assist this teaching was different in its tone and content. Charlotte Yonge celebrated the family, its place in cherishing children and the need for girls to adapt to the needs of their family, even to the extent on occasion of marrying against their wishes. W.H.G. Kingston told of boys leaving the family to make their way in the world at large, albeit in a Christian way and eventually to return home to a loving and supportive mother or wife.
>
> (Musgrave, 1985: 41)

FAMILY

The family was perceived as being a bastion of Victorian society and rooted in Christian values. Whatever the truth concerning attitudes and behaviour in the 'real world' the family was sacrosanct as an institution. As we saw in chapter 1 Marryat changed radically his style of writing for children when he produced *Masterman Ready*. In this 'classic' nineteenth-century family adventure story gone are the jokes and racy style that mark the discourse of *Mr. Midshipman Easy*. One particularly noticeable difference is in the focus on religion as exemplified in the frequencies of the lexical items below:

Victorian corpus	*Masterman Ready*
(760,000 words)	(120,000 words)
God 193 occurrences	God 82 occurrences
Providence 26 occurrences	Providence 9 occurrences
Almighty 26 occurrences	Almighty 21 occurrences

The family can be viewed as a social agency which taught and supported moral values. This was not exclusively a middle-class phenomenon as the 'respectable' working class were equally adamant in their adherence to this concept of the family. The texts in our corpus have middle-class heroes but glimpses of the type of working-class background noted above confirm this. 'The Victorian family was, therefore, a social and educational institution of prime moral importance' (Musgrave, 1985: 41).

Fathers and mothers

The young hero's father does not appear at regular intervals throughout every narrative. Nevertheless his influence is never in doubt. It is not surprising, therefore, that, after *and* the two most frequent items collocating with *father* in approximately 760,000 running words are *my* and *his*. These pronominal references reflect, of course, whether the narrative is first person or third person. Furthermore, the most frequent lexical verb is *said* and there is a high frequency amongst lexical items of the item *words*. Often, but particularly in times of great difficulty, the young hero will remember his father's *words* and the recollection of that *wisdom* will give him the *courage* to continue. In some narratives the direct speech of the *father* has an important place early in the narrative and subsequently at the end. Kingston's *Peter the Whaler* provides an excellent example. In the first extract, part of a much longer monologue, Peter's father is warning him of the consequences of poaching.

> 'Think, Peter, of the **grief** and **anguish** it would cause your poor mother and me to see you **suffer** so **dreadful** a **disgrace** – to feel that you merited it. Think of the **shame** it would bring on the name of our family. People would point at your sisters, and say. 'Their brother is a **convict**!'
>
> (1851/1909: 9)

The set *grief, anguish, suffer, dreadful, disgrace, shame, convict* highlighted above may represent a style which is melodramatic by contemporary standards of children's writing but these are significant lexical items. They are specific to the genre in that they exemplify excedingly well the attitude of and effect on the family if the code is broken. They are to be found in many of our Victorian narratives usually in didactic passages uttered by a real or surrogate father (see the following section) whom we can assume represents authorial voice and the voice of duty.

Peter has to leave home because of his lawlessness. After a series of adventures he returns home. The book concludes with the following interaction between Peter and his father.

> 'Well, Peter,' said my father, after I had been washed and clothed, and put on once more the appearance of a gentleman, 'You have come back, my lad, *poorer* than you went away, I fear' . . .
>
> 'No, father,' I answered, 'I have come back *infinitely richer*. I have **learned** to **fear** God, to **worship Him** in **His works** and to trust to **His infinite mercy**. I have also **learned** to **know myself**, and to **take advice** and **counsel** from my **superiors** in **wisdom** and **goodness**.'
>
> 'Then,' said my father, 'I am indeed **content** and I trust others may take a needful **lesson** from the adventures of Peter the Whaler.'
>
> (p. 318)

The repetition of *learned* and his father's use of *lesson* underline the role of the family as a controlling institution. There will be no *shame*, *anguish* or *grief* brought upon the *family*. They may rest *content*, Peter may now rejoin them. As he is about to marry the daughter of his captain, he will no doubt extend and reinforce the institution in his turn.

The point that is illustrated by these exchanges is that the family is important in upholding relations of domination. If you try to disturb the social structure which supports these relations you bring disgrace on your family. Therefore you do not disturb them, or, if you do, you eventually return to the fold a *sadder* and a *wiser*, or *infinitely richer* young man. The use of *rich* as a near synonym of wise is interesting because often the young hero did go away and acquire material wealth but Kingston is able to moralise that worldy goods are less important than the fact that a lesson has been learned. The inference is that Peter is still young enough to prosper and no doubt will do so as a just reward for being a reformed character and having acquired the Victorian virtues of duty and obedience.

The role of the mother is interesting in that she engages in inter-action much less than the father. Yet the lemma *mother* is almost as frequent (311 occurrences) as *father* (336 occurrences). After *father*, the most frequent lexical item to collocate with *mother* is *poor*. The nominal group *poor mother* either indicates an appeal made to the young hero by his father or some other substitute or a memory of how youth and rashness caused hurt to this venerated symbol of the institution. *Mother* occurs frequently in the young hero's mind at moments of great peril as this extract from one of the popular writers of the genre, Gordon Stables, illustrates:

> Such a night as this leads to thought, and, as the boy lingered here for a few minutes, gazing down into the **terribly, deep-like, black** and **rushing** water, it seemed to carry his mind far away south to the **bonnie land** where his **mother** lived, and his **dear little sister** and **sweetheart cousin.**
>
> (1901: 90)

The perils of nature as represented by the first group of highlighted items are offset by the memory of *home* which is the superordinate for 'femaleness' in all its positive attribution. However, these mem-ories are not allowed to persist for too long as this would, no doubt, be detrimental to the essential 'maleness' of the young hero. The author restores him to the 'real world', the world of masculine activity and the *mother*, *sister* and *cousin* fade from memory. They have served their purpose: "'Ah, well!" he sighed "Years must elapse before then, and till then I have my *just duty* to do"' (91). Again the notion of reward is implied. In this example the assumption is that the hero's eventual return to the beloved family can be seen as a reward for doing one's 'just duty' in upholding the social order as enshrined in the pax Brittanica.

Surrogates

In the texts typical of the genre the young hero is, of course, not at home with the family for much of the narrative. Either he is at school or out in the world away from England. However, the moral training commenced within *the family* is continued by surrogate institutions such as school, regiment or ship. Thus, the headmaster, colonel or captain may assume the role of 'father'. The description of such characters often concentrates on physical attributes and we shall see this again in the institution of friendship when companions, comrades and friends are described for the reader. Note this portrayal of Doctor Arnold, the headmaster, as Tom Brown hears his first sermon from him in the chapel at Rugby and how the inclusive relations of the italicised headwords and the sets formed by their modifiers represent this surrogate father:

> the **tall**, **gallant** *form*, the **kindling** *eye*, the *voice*, now **soft** as the low notes of a flute, now **clear** and **stirring** as the call of a light infantry bugle . . .
>
> (Hughes, 1857/1880: 140)

And, at the end, Tom having overcome his moral weaknesses thanks to the Doctor returns to Rugby upon hearing of Arnold's death. The concluding passage encapsulates neatly the concept of the family as a defining institution and its role as a controlling agent. It does so firstly (see fig. 3.1) through its use of lexical specificity in its assigning of attributes to gender and secondly (see fig. 3.2) in an overall inclusive relationship where these attributes are seen in a kind of asymmetrical synonymy (see Carter, 1987: 20–1) in which the meaning of the specific items are subsumed within the item *Him* thus inextricably linking the institutions of family, gender and religion:

> For it is only through our **mysterious human relationships**, through **the love and tenderness and purity of mothers, and sisters, and wives** through **the strength and courage and wisdom of fathers, and brothers, and teachers**, that we can come to the knowledge of **Him**, in whom alone **the love, and the tenderness, and the purity, and the strength, and the courage, and the wisdom** dwell forever and ever in perfect fulness.
>
> (p. 376)

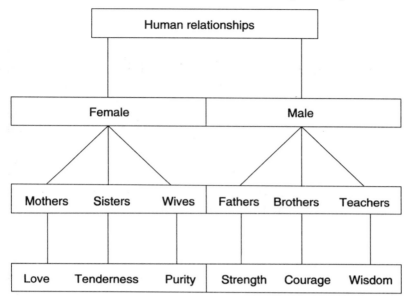

Figure 3.1   Lexical specificity and the representation of gender

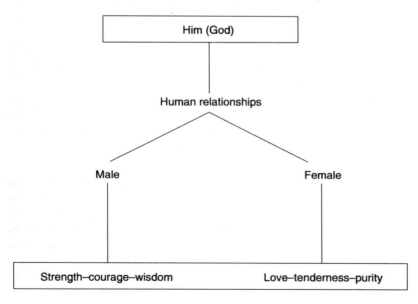

Figure 3.2   Inclusive relations of religion, family and gender

GENDER: THE YOUNG HERO

Central to the genre is a hero who overcomes many trials often in strange surroundings. The institution of gender emphasises the 'maleness' of the world in which the narrative occurs. The hero is essentially a man of action, usually a young man in his early twenties (in the school stories they were obviously a few years younger). The genre here is very much concerned with how 'maleness' is to be represented to the reader in the real world. There is a view of Ballantyne's, Hughes's, Kingston's and Marryat's heroes which is almost anti-intellectual. Consider Tom Brown, for example, or any of Henty's heroes in the later works. Squire Brown's meditations on Tom's departure for Rugby sum up well this particular dimension of traditional, juvenile fiction and allow authorial voice to present its model youth to the young reader in a series of questions and answers:

> Shall I go into the sort of temptations he'll meet with? No, I can't do that. Never do for an old fellow like me to go into such things with a boy. He won't understand me. Do him more harm than good, ten to one. Shall I tell him to mind his work, and say he's sent to school to make himself a good scholar? Well, but he isn't sent to school for that – at any rate, not for that mainly. I don't care a straw for Greek particles, or the digamma, no more does his mother. What is he sent to school for? Well, partly because he wanted to go. If he'll only turn out a *brave*, *helpful*, *truth-telling* **Englishman**, and a **gentleman** and a **Christian**, that's all I want.
>
> (p. 72)

The squire's deliberations pick up on a number of institutions but for the moment it is worth noting how they articulate the moral qualities Thomas Hughes sees as essential for the young English boy: courage and Christianity. They are qualities, however, where the inference to be drawn from the squire's discourse is that to be physical rather than intellectual is desirable for that boy. With the representation of the young hero in these narratives stress was very much on the physical and there were straightforward choices presented by authors between right and wrong. Complex mental activity was not the order of the day. The italicised and highlighted lexical items in the three co-ordinated nominal groups in the final sentence are particularly significant and we shall return to them a little later.

The heroes of the genre were 'manly' boys and, particularly in the work of G.A. Henty and his successors in the late nineteenth century, were the epitome of all that was seen as good in the British Empire.

This was true of both types of text as Avery points out: 'It was the manly hero with his "frank, open face" who mattered in school fiction too' (1965: 145). Barbara Wall (1991: 66) has shown how writers of adventure stories were concerned with 'the preparation of a stereotypic adolescent "British boy" to take his place in the world of action'. The two extracts below illustrate this point. The first is from a school story by W.H.G. Kingston, *Ernest Bracebridge*, first published in 1860. It describes the hero on his first day at school.

> An unprejudiced person would certainly not have designated him as a **muff**. He was an *active*, *well-built* boy, of between twelve and thirteen years old. He had light-brown hair, curling slightly, with a *fair* complexion and a good colour. His **mouth** showed a good deal of *firmness*, and he had *clear honest* eyes, with no little amount of *humour* in them.
>
> (Kingston, 1860: 17–18)

The second is from Ballantyne's *The Coral Island*. This story is narrated in the first person by Ralph Rover and below he describes Jack Martin, one of the two companions with whom he is ship-wrecked on a South Sea island.

> Jack Martin was a *tall*, *strapping*, *broad-shouldered* youth of eighteen, with a *handsome*, *good-humoured*, *firm* **face**. He had a good education, was clever and *hearty* and *lion-like* in his actions, but *mild* and *quiet* in his disposition.
>
> (Ballantyne, 1858/1966: 11)

The italicised items lexically signify the essence of 'maleness' in the genre: *active*, *well built*, *tall*, *strapping*, *broad shouldered*, *handsome*, *brave*. These all serve to represent to the reader the physical description of the ideal hero. The physical is linked to the desired qualities of character with the selection of *clear* and *honest* to describe Ernest's eyes and *firmness* his mouth. *Firm* is a key lexical item in these texts and we note it again in the description of Jack's face in the second extract. The representation of positive maleness in many of the Victorian narratives strongly connects the active and physical to either the superordinate *face* or its co-meronyms *eyes* or *mouth*, wherein, according to the authors, can be detected evidence of the young hero's superior moral qualities to match his physical attractiveness. The two are inseparable and characterise the idealised male as opposed to the '*muff*'; this latter item is very much culturally and historically bound and now redundant.

It is also interesting to note the antonymy in the second extract,

Figure 3.3   Positive oppositeness and the young hero

where the hero is described as '*clever* and *hearty* and *lion-like* in his *actions*, but *mild* and *quiet* in his *disposition*'. This is *positive oppositeness*, however, where the highlighted adjectives represent all that is desirable in the author's description of the ideal young nineteenth-century male and an illustration of how the mental (but not intellectual) and the physical are complemented in his depiction of that ideal. Note how cleverness is a physical attribute rather than one with intellectual pretensions in figure 3.3.

Disposition is a good example of a word unlikely to be found in a modern children's novel. Nowadays such an item would be regarded as somewhat formal, if not old fashioned, for such a context. The *Oxford English Dictionary (OED)* (1972: 493) gives it as 'a natural tendency or bent of mind especially in relation to moral or social qualities' or 'the state or quality of being disposed to do something'. Cobuild (1987: 407), defining it in the context of modern usage, notes that it is a rather formal word indicating the way that (someone) tends to behave or feel or 'their desire to do something at a particular time'. Thus, the lexical sets above would indicate the author's wish to impress upon his readers the 'all-roundedness' of the ideal male.

Hearty is particularly interesting as a significant lexical item. In its contemporary usage the word would indicate a quality that is, perhaps, not universally aspired to, with its connotations of loudness and overindulgence. Certainly usage would be unlikely to give *hearty* and *mild* as familiar collocates of the central male character. There is much *hearty* eating and giving of handshakes in the texts and, of course, *hearty* cheering where *British* is also an adjacent collocate and this seems to give an extra dimension to the evaluation as in:

> then he heard in another minute that true **hearty British cheer** which has so often struck terror . . .
>
> (Kingston, 1873/1909: 180)

> and then rose above the din of battle three **hearty British cheers**.
>
> (*ibid.* 243)

As these stories were written for adolescent boys, girls were not well served in the narratives. The representation of adolescent females in the genre is minimal and tended to be located on descriptions of mothers and sisters, as we saw in our consideration of the institution of family. It is interesting that Salmon in his *Juvenile Literature as it is* comments that 'the whole body of successful boys' literature cannot be more concisely described than as a vast system of hero-worship' (1888: 217).

Maleness and the school story

The young hero is represented not only through careful lexical selection but in the representation of what he does. In *Tom Brown's Schooldays* the very physical nature of processes attached to male central characters is well illustrated below:

> [1] Boys will quarrel and when they quarrel will sometimes fight. [2] Fighting with fists is the natural and English way for English boys to settle their quarrels. [3] What substitute for it is there, or ever was there amongst any nation under the sun? [4] What would you like to see in its place?
>
> (Hughes, 1857/1880: 299)

These clause complexes are typical of Hughes at his most didactic and provide interesting lexical choices that we shall consider a little later. As well as significant lexical selection Halliday's interpersonal function plays an important role here. The rhetorical structure of the extract allows two statements followed by two questions. Together with the accompanying modality a very strong signal of authorial attitude is delivered to the reader. By means of modality the writer can either comment directly or intervene through his characters in a speech event and thus evaluate an interpretation of reality. For the moment, however, let us take note of the transitivity features of the extract.

In clause complex 1 above we are told that boys will *quarrel* and (sometimes) *fight*. This is the reality for *all* boys. In Hallidayan terms boys are the Actors – the 'doers'. In this instance they will 'fight' a *material* process, a process of 'doing'. Quarrel is a *verbal* process and here the participant who communicates is a *sayer*. *Quarrelling* is, of course, a very physical verbal activity and in this instance we subsume the two grammatical subjects within the participant *agent*. We shall refer to the processes for the moment as *active* (not to be confused with active voice). We are not informed of other participants but it is reasonable to assume that boys will quarrel and fight with other boys even if these inherent participants have not been actualised. For these participants we will use the term *affected*. Thus, clause complex 1 can be represented as shown below:

Boys	will quarrel and when they	
{Agents + Affected}	{Process: Active}	{Agents + Affected}
quarrel	will sometimes	fight
{Process: Active}	{Circumstance}	{Process: Active}

Clause complex 1 allows the fronting of *Fighting with fists* in clause complex 2 and as Theme it is the 'point of departure of the message' (see above, chapter 2). In terms of transitivity a *relational* process is being represented here. As we saw in the previous chapter, that is a process where one participant (the Carrier) *is* in some way the other participant (the Attribute). Furthermore, in this particular instance the participants can reverse roles as the *attribute* has an *identifying* function (see Halliday, 1985: 114–16) as illustrated below:

{Carrier}	{Process: Relational}	{Attribute}
Fighting with fists	is	the natural and English way

Thus:

The natural and English way is	fighting with fists

A very strong ideological statement is being made through this representation of the relationship between entities. *Fighting with fists* is being evaluated as *the natural and English way*. Lexical selection heightens this by the co-ordination of *natural* and *English*.

The extract concludes in typical Hughes didactic style with two rhetorical questions. The answer has already been provided in clause complex 2. Overall, the reader has been presented with a *fait accompli* which we can summarise thus:

> Boys will quarrel. Boys will sometimes fight. English boys will fight with their fists. This is the natural way. This is the English way. No other nation can provide a substitute.

Hughes here is clearly engaged in naturalisation. This is a strategy which serves the mode of ideology which Thompson (1990) refers to as reification, as discussed in chapter 2. What Hughes is doing by adopting this strategy is justifying the domination of others by the English by appealing to the English way as the 'natural way'.

Maleness and the adventure story

Ballantyne too saw this physical demonstration of the young hero as a necessary attribute of maleness. In *The Gorilla Hunters* (the sequel to *The Coral Island*) he railed against what he called the *muff* or boy of timid disposition:

> himself unable to act in the common emergencies of life; to protect a lady from insolence; to guard his home from robbery; or to save his own child should it chance to fall into the water.
>
> (cited by Carpenter and Prichard, 1984: 7)

Ballantyne is just as attitudinal as Hughes in his transmitting of his message that to be physical is to be positive under certain conditions. The modality of the clause complex is, in fact, a condition: that is, if a boy is passive he will be a failure as a man. This is not possibility being expressed but a very high degree of certainty. The domination of the strong male is thus legitimised through rationalisation.

In the last decades of the century Henty, the most prolific of all the writers for boys, placed strong emphasis on the physical in his books. His heroes proved themselves by force of arms before returning to England while weak characters were failures who died or were disgraced. G. Manville Fenn, a contemporary writer of books for boys and Henty's biographer, comments:

> Henty wanted his boys to be bold, straightforward, and ready to play a young man's part, not to be *milksops*. He had a horror of a lad who displayed any weak emotion and shrank from shedding blood, or winced at any encounter.
>
> (Fenn, 1907: 333)

We can regard Fenn's, and presumably Henty's, *milksop* as being synonymous with Kingston's and Ballantyne's *muff*. Henty, however, carried the additional ideology of British imperialism with him in his narratives. This added a new dimension to the concept of 'maleness'. With the earlier writers the message of imperialism is not so developed and action is often realised through verbal processes on behalf of the main participants.

In *The Coral Island*, a first-person narrative of around 90,000 words, the most frequent transitivity patterns are concerned with verbal processes. There are three main characters: Ralph, Jack and Peterkin, with Ralph as narrator. In each case where *Jack* and *Peterkin* occurred as nodal items two of the three most frequent process collocates were verbs of saying. Where *I* (for Ralph) occurred the lemma *say* was, not surprisingly, the second most frequent collocate. The pattern *I have/had*, *I said*, *I saw* would be typical of this type of first-person narrative. The patterns are summarised below with the numeral referring to the number of occurrences of nodal item or collocate:

Nodal item		Collocate I		Collocate II		Collocate III	
I	953	have	125	say	124	saw	40
Jack	546	say	115	cry	39	be	36
Peterkin	478	say	114	cry	53	be	47

Where *Ralph* (112 occurrences) is node (usually the addressee) the most frequent process collocate is *say* (24 occurrences) and after *see* (9 occurrences) and *be* (9 occurrences) we have *replied* and *exclaimed* with three occurrences each. Thus, overall, the young hero is very much a *sayer*. A considerable proportion of the 'saying' is in direct speech and *saying* is, in one sense, an extension in these narratives of *doing*. Very often *say* is used to frame a question or an imperative requiring an active or material process such as one of movement in response. This is frequently signalled by an '*I say* + Christian name' opening move. Typical examples from *The Coral Island* are listed below:

'**I say, Jack**, how does it happen that you seem to be up to everything?' (p. 21)
'**I say, Jack**, you're a Briton – the best fellow I ever met in my life.' (p. 22)

'**I say, Jack**, I'm sorry to say I must apply to you for another strip of handkerchief.' (p. 45)
'**I say Ralph**, what's that in the water? Is it a shark?' (p. 50)
'**I say, Jack**,' cried Peterkin, waving his hand. 'Come here, . . .' (p. 64)
'**I say, Ralph**, look here. There's one of your crabs up to something uncommon.' (p. 65)
'**I say, Peterkin**,' cried Jack, in a hoarse whisper. (p. 75)
'**I say, Ralph**, do leave just one little slice of that yam.' (p. 175)

Often the use of *say* allows the introduction of other verbs of communication, some of which may have other, connotative meanings which can really only be interpreted by using *say* as the core item. Thus we have *acknowledged, continued, cried, ejaculated exclaimed, inquired, promised, remarked, replied, retorted*. All of these verbal processes are contained in paratactically projected locutions, that is, direct statements or direct directives where the exact words of the *sayer* are quoted. In addition, nominalisations are sometimes used to interpret the core item *say* as in 'we were attracted by an **exclamation** from Peterkin. "I say, Jack," said he, "here is something that will be of use"'(62). Peterkin does a lot of *crying, exclaiming* and *retorting* in the narrative. He is the youngest of the three central characters and is represented as the most excitable in emotion and reckless in behaviour. Indeed, as Carpenter and Prichard point out, the characterisation of Peterkin represents a boy who is 'almost effeminate' (1984: 131). Thus, in one sense, degrees of 'maleness' or a cline of 'maleness' is presented to the reader. Peterkin is allowed to be frivolous because of his youth but the ideal to be aspired to is that of Jack. We shall consider this further when we investigate the institution of friendship.

COMPANIONS/COMRADES/FRIENDS

In the genre of traditional juvenile fiction this institution is of central importance. In fact it still is, as we shall see in chapter 4. The linguistic representation of friendship/companionship/comradeship in the traditional juvenile texts, however, is not one that would always be easily understood by the contemporary reader. Consider the following extract describing reconciliation after a quarrel from Talbot Baines Reed's *The Fifth Form at St. Dominic's*, published in 1887:

Oh! the happiness of that precious quarter of an hour, when the veil that has divided two **faithful friends** is suddenly dashed aside, and

they rush one to the other, calling themselves every imaginable
bad name in the dictionary, insisting to the verge of quarrelling
that it was all their fault, and no fault of the other, far too
rapturous to talk ordinary common sense.

(Reed, 1887: 247)

Representation of friendship here is reminiscent of the school story as
written for girls and best known in the works of Angela Brazil (see
Cadogan and Craig, 1976). The style is, by contemporary standards,
florid and one could speculate on the reactions of a modern reader
accustomed to, for example, the characterisation and situations contained in the *Grange Hill* television series coming across the word
rapturous in that context. Furthermore, the collocation *faithful friend*
is much more likely to be associated with *Lassie*, for example, than a
relationship with a schoolfriend in a modern story.

In some of the early texts the 'hero' or central role is shared
amongst friends. The number three appears to be significant as in
The Three Midshipmen or *The Coral Island* though often one of the
three is cast as leader. John Rowe Townsend (1965: 46) tells us that
threesomes in the classic adventure story such as *The Coral Island*
allow 'its members to provide a three-cornered contrast in character
and approach to life, and distinguish themselves clearly from each
other without calling for any outstanding subtlety'. Linguistically, the
author in his comparing and contrasting permits us to consider
matching relations (see Hoey: 1983). Jack, for example, we have
already seen as characterised by significant lexical items emphasising both his physical and emotional maturity. By contrast we have
Peterkin, who is much younger, more impetuous and generally less
mature: 'My other companion was Peterkin Gay. He was **little, quick,
funny, decidedly mischievous**, and about fourteen years old' (Ballantyne, 1858: 11–12). Jack also often calms Peterkin, who tends to
be excitable in his conversation and behaviour. There are quite long
stretches of discourse referred to as Peterkin '*running on*' and several
occasions where he bursts into '*floods of tears*'. Jack, on the other
hand, will speak 'in a *grave* tone' which reinforces the representation
of maturity. Jack is the leader in active terms. He often speaks in
imperatives and makes the decisions when danger threatens. Ralph,
the narrator, is by contrast a character with an enquiring mind who
often 'fell into fits of *abstraction*'. Together all three can be regarded
as a composite male, each individual providing different attributes.
There are similarities as well as differences where the characters
share something. One of the most noticeable of shared attributes is

the ability to behave or speak *tenderly*. Thus, we have 'Peterkin on his knees by my side *tenderly* bathing my temples with water,' (p. 15) and eighteen lines later ' "Speak to us, my dear Ralph," whispered Jack **tenderly**.' Overall in the Victorian corpus there were 29 instances of the lemma *tender*. Twelve of these were used to represent male behaviour or a perceived male attribute as in this example from *The Three Midshipmen*: 'Who could wish for a more *tender*, **gentle** nurse than a true-hearted British sailor can make' (Kingston, 1873: 315).

In the representation of friendship today *tenderly* would not be a significant lexical item where male characters are the focus of the narrative. What this illustrates is that it was possible for some males to be *gentle* and *tender* within a particular context such as the battlefield or a situation of extreme danger where only males are present. Perhaps it was permissible for male Actors to behave *tenderly* and the item has undergone a type of semantic derogation. Certainly, in the modern fiction corpus we could only find ten occurrences of the lemma *tender*. Of these, six were concerned with the notion of *gentleness*. All except one had female actors and all of these were ministering to males. Lexical relations play a significant role in interpreting the discourse and semantic changes in current usage are reflected in different or changed collocational patterns.

Friendship and collocation

In the institution of gender the name of the young hero or the first-person pronoun provided the nodal items for discussion. With friendship, the focus is on the items *friend, companion, comrade* and the significant collocates obtained from the data. Amongst the most frequent of the collocates three natural sets appeared to establish themselves.

1 trust, true, constant, faithful, firm
2 brave, gallant, stout
3 duty, service

All of these items may be regarded as significant when we consider the traditional writers' view of the world. These sets contain words that are marked in terms of contemporary usage. In set 2, for example, while all items will be recognisable to the young reader (though *stout* in the context of courage is likely to be highly marked) *brave* can be considered the core word. We need *brave* to interpret the other two

items. Constraints imposed by space do not allow detailed consideration of all these sets but it is of interest to pursue set 2 a little further.

Bravery is positive

It is very obvious from the concordance lines that, not surprisingly,
bravery was a very positive condition. It was often co-ordinated with
another item thus generating a whole new lexical set as well as
appearing with its near synonym *gallant* as in the examples below:

'in his youth proved himself a **brave and able** soldier, but . . . who
. . .' (Henty, 1886: 191)
'was a good specimen. He was **brave and dashing** to a fault . . .'
(Stables, 1901: 172)
'idea seized him that Murray, his **brave and noble** friend had . . .'
(Kingston, 1873/1909: 244)
'It was terrible! No wonder that **brave and hardy** British seaman
. . .' (Stables: 285)
'from Herbert G. himself, the **brave and gallant** commander,
downwards . . .' (*ibid*. 2)

Along with the representation of bravery as a positive virtue there is a
high frequency of accompanying statements of some dire circumstance. Thus:

'The **brave fellows** little knew the terrible trap prepared for them
. . .' (Kingston, 1873/1909: 191)
'"Those are **brave fellows**," cried Jack; "we must try and save
their lives . . ."' (Kingston 1851/1990: 345)
'"We shall lose some other **brave fellows**," he exclaimed aloud
. . .' (*ibid*. 146)

The association of bravery with calamity might well be interpreted as
ideological. The author's message to the implied reader here seems to
be that in being trained for Empire it is seen as necessary to assert the
positive (i.e. bravery, gallantry, nobleness) when suffering is mentioned. Duty and service bring pain as well as reward and that pain
has to be endured with fortitude.

Collocates of collocates

Halliday's (1966) paper 'Lexis as a Linguistic Level' is seminal in the
study of vocabulary with its focus on how collocation can be used to
generate lexical sets. We have already seen a small example of this in

operation in the previous section. Here we wish to consider collocates of collocates, as thirty years on from that paper we have available the insights of corpus-based, computer-aided techniques which permit the speedy and precise investigations of language patterns in text. From the concordance lines obtained for our lexical set 2 above – *brave, gallant, stout* – it was immediately noticeable that there was a high frequency of occurrence of the item *fellow*.

There turned out to be 588 occurrences of *fellow* in the Victorian corpus of approximately 760,000 words . The item was then checked against the *Oxford English Dictionary* so that an impression of its usage in Victorian contexts might be gained. *OED* had 6.5 columns for *fellow*. Amongst the contextualised nineteenth-century entries were the synonyms *companions, associates, comrades*. Furthermore, we are informed that it is often used with *good* and *jolly* as in *good* and *jolly fellows* are *agreeable* and *pleasant companions*.

Additional information given was that *fellow* was a familiar synonym for *man* and that it was commonly used with the following qualifying adjectives: *good, bad, brave, clever, foolish, old, young*. Phrases like 'what *a poor fellow*' were often used exclamatorily as an expression of pity and '*My dear fellow*' was common in familiar address and a context was provided from Marryat's *Mr. Midshipman Easy*. Mention was also made of the item as a customary title of address to a servant 'or other person of humble station' (*OED*, 1971: 980) and that it was applied by schoolboys to themselves and to each other. All of these combinations occur frequently in the Victorian corpus with the following items being the most frequent collocations generated:

Item	*Number of occurrences*
poor	71
old	41
little	28
good	28
young	25
dear	16
big	13
black	13

It is clear that here is an item which had some considerable cultural significance in the nineteenth century and we thought it interesting to compare with late-twentieth-century usage. We could only find 24 occurrences of *fellow* in the modern fiction corpus. The most frequent collocates in –1 position (one word to the left of *fellow*) are:

little   4 occurences
young   4 occurences

There was one occurrence of *poor* in −2 position (two words to the left of *fellow*) as in: *poor, little fellow*. Furthermore, in one of the occurrences of *young fellow* the combination was in spoken English where the reference was to a possible boyfriend. It is in informal spoken contexts that the item is probably most frequent in contemporary usage, where it means boyfriend or lover. We found one instance of *stout fellow* but this was in a speech made by a Polish general in Robert Westall's *The Machine Gunners* and is part of a caricature. *Fellow* as a nodal item in the modern corpus did not generate anything like the frequency or range of collocates that it did in nineteenth-century boys' books. In addition, when we referred to the COBUILD dictionary *fellow* was given as 'rather old-fashioned English' when used in expressions such as *my dear fellow* (1987: 526).

Other COBUILD information was also interesting. The extra column which provides additional semantic information on entries gave *comrade* as a synoym of *fellow* in the sense of one who shares an activity with you and *associate* was given as a superordinate. The entry for *comrade* listed *friend* and *companion* especially in terms of sharing difficulties or dangers and importantly noted that, like *fellow*, it is 'a rather old fashioned word' (*ibid*. 287). So, while there are links with past usage, *fellow* is an item which does not translate easily into contemporary usage, being now very restricted in range and context. In the Victorian context, however, we can, via our consideration of collocates of collocates, add this item to our original set of nodal items (see above). So along with *friends*, *companions* and *comrades*, *fellows* were *brave*, *gallant* and *stout* in their endeavours and also generated another wider set of evaluative moderation as we noted earlier. It is one of these that we now consider.

Poor fellows

The function of the word *brave* as a signal of suffering has already been commented upon. Suffering is also very frequently signalled where the nodal item is modified by *poor*. We have seen that *poor* is the most frequent collocate of *fellow* in the Victorian corpus, with 71 occurrences both in direct and indirect speech. Indeed, the *poor fellow* collocation is so frequent as a very strong indication of impending calamity that we treat it as a fixed item in that context.

Table 3.1 Poor fellow and collocations

1	2	3
die ×2	groans ×2	steal out
shot ×2	crying ×2	leave alone
hit ×3	bleeding	hopelessness
never spoke again	blown off	dreadfully
is fast enough (dead)	ill-treating	escaped (from one
lost ×2	wounding	danger to another)
sunk ×2	washed off	low spirited
torn from (killed)	maimed	homesick
spring up (having been shot)	wounded	left abandoned
burying	racked	clinging
covered up (a body)	pain	compelled
nothing to be done	wounds	fear
sink under	groans	distress
lay (in death)	cries (of agony)	fate (of poor fellows)
gone	bound up	lose heart
never to rise again	agony	
fallen	fever	
killed outright ×3		
killed		
slaughtering ×2		
stark		
cold		
dead ×3		

The concordances were examined for lexical sets generated by process and circumstance where *poor fellow* was the only actualised participant as in 'two *poor fellows* died on board' or where there were other actualised participants.

There is a total of 116 lexical items generated by the collocation *poor fellow* as outlined above. These are presented in sets in table 3.1. Items specifically referring to the processes of dying or being killed are listed in column 1. They include verbs and other words to be found in the semantic field of death. Items which refer to other physically unpleasant processes are listed in column 2. Items which carry additional connotations of suffering are listed in column 3.

Of the items left after our categorisation of the above lexical information the following are significant: *saved, lifted (to safety), hold, tend, lives* x2, *survivors, God, prayers* x2, *water* x3, *cooling, beverage, fate.* All these items could well be evaluated as positive. Indeed, they appear to fall into three naturally occurring lexical sets.

(a) saved, lifted, hold, tend, lives, survivors
(b) God, prayers
(c) water, cooling, beverage

These three sets are antonymous to the items categorised in table 3.1. As positive evaluation they are far outnumbered by lexical signals of negative attribution. It would seem, therefore, that in Victorian usage *poor* as a modifier of *fellow* was certainly an expression of pity but within the context of literature written for children as manifested in our traditional fiction corpus this was most often associated with death.

Comparison with COBUILD

These lexical sets all arose from our consideration of the institution of friendship where *fellow* asserted itself to be a culturally significant item. We have already noted its infrequent usage in modern children's literature. A final useful point of comparison can be made with contemporary usage as contained in the COBUILD Bank of English corpus.

There are 9,520 concordance lines containing *fellow* in the COBUILD corpus. *Poor* occurs 22,293 times in 167 million words and collocates with *fellow* on 57 occasions in −1 position. Of the occurrences of *poor fellow* 19 are from the British books section of the COBUILD corpus which accounts for 23 million words. Overall, *poor* does not appear in the list containing the 22 most frequent collocates of *fellow*.

Our lexical analysis of the institute of friendship has been largely based upon collocational patterns as shown by the corpus. The emergence of *fellow* as a key item is a good example of how, in a relatively short space of time, a word can cease to be culturally significant. In the traditional juvenile story *fellow* can be seen, it has been suggested, as a synonym for *friend, companion, comrade*. Perhaps it is better considered as a general word or superordinate within which specific degrees of *friendship* are included and which reflect social intimacy, class and ethnic diversity and the attitudes expressed towards them.

Other considerations

There are other considerations as regards this institution which mark it off from contemporary representation. The interpersonal function of language in terms of forms of address, for example, is one. Briefly, in one text, *The Coral Island*, we observe how the three friends refer to each other in interaction. They frequently used the form *my dear* either on its own or to preface *boy*, *comrade*, *fellow*, *friend* or a specific Christian name.

Occasionally the *friend* of the hero allowed the inclusion of a female. This could be the sister of the hero or the *friend* whose role meant that one or other of the males could marry her and thus still be close to the *companion* of his adventures. Alternatively it could be someone rescued by the hero who is then allowed to become his wife. Sometimes a mother might be included as in *Tom Brown's Schooldays* where the mother of the hero's friend exercises a benign influence over Tom. This would have the desired effect on a character who might have erred from the straight and narrow. It is, perhaps, of interest to note that G.A. Henty prided himself on the fact that love interest was not a facet of his writing and 'his heroes are all cast in the same mould: they are straightforward, extroverted young philistines' (Townsend 1965: 47). Henty also provides examples of that other kind of *companion* 'a faithful attendant of lower rank who follows him [the hero] through thick and thin' (Townsend, 1965: 48).

Wall (1991: 67) makes the point that the nineteenth-century authors were writing for adolescents and 'celebrated the fantasies of adolescence, and for this reason maintained an attraction for an adult readership as well'. She addresses the narrative structure of the genre and the stereotypical *hero/friend* combination. When she focuses on what she calls 'male voices' she makes the point that the 'manly voice' was one about which there is very little to say, as the voices and personalities of the narrators of these stories were so interchangeable. In terms of narrative structure she might well be correct but we would maintain that a linguistic analysis of these texts yields much of interest in the representation of the *hero/friend* and the aspirations to which the various writers believed he/they ought to aspire as they made their way in the world: the social organisation, in other words, they presented to their readers.

Nicholas Tucker (1989: 147) also draws attention to the character and role of the *companion* in the genre. He makes the point that the friend can occasionally be an adult, a parent or indeed both parents. In the nineteenth century he cites *Masterman Ready* as the best-known English example. Marryat's story differs somewhat from the others in that we have a family adventure. The essential ingredients are there, however, even if the young man hero is not. The institution of friendship allows the inclusion, or arguably intrusion, of the institution of family:

the nineteenth century, with its lingering belief that children should principally follow in their parents' footsteps, could still get away with family adventure stories where father himself is the key figure giving out orders while confidently expecting general submission; thus the idealized (*companions*) parents in *The Swiss Family Robinson* or *Masterman Ready*.

(N. Tucker, 1989: 142)

Finally, the *companion* has persisted well into the twentieth century and across a variety of genres. The instructional and authoritarian 'voice' of Marryat may have changed as Tucker claims. He comments on *companions* such as Gandalf in *The Hobbit* and grandmothers in Dahl's works who 'combine the virtues of experience with fewer of the disadvantages of still belonging to the normal adult authoritarian establishment' (*ibid.* 145). There are some survivors of the parent (and surrogate parent) *companion*, though, as we shall see in chapter 4, when we discuss what Tucker refers to as 'rogue parents' or 'parent substitutes'.

RACE

Race as an issue and attendant racism is not new. It existed 100 years ago as it does now. In the eighteenth century in *Robinson Crusoe*, the progenitor of adventure fiction, racism and friendship were personified in the character of Man Friday. What is different is there was no mass challenge to racism. When issues are challenged relationships of domination emerge, they are clearly identifiable. In traditional juvenile fiction racial issues are not universally challenged and would appear to have a two-fold manifestation in texts: First, the concern is with a concept of 'Englishness' or 'Britishness' and, second, with the representation of non-English peoples.

'Englishness'

In many of the books in the corpus there is presented a concept of 'Englishness' which runs throughout each narrative, being reinforced at regular intervals almost like a refrain. This is well illustrated in *Tom Brown's Schooldays* where 'English' as an item is placed in a paradigm so that it becomes the only logical selection within the reality presented by Hughes. Thus, when the author states early on that 'the object of all schools is not to ram Latin and Greek into boys, but to make them good *English* boys, good future citizens' (Hughes,

1857/1880: 62) we have *English* as a modifier carrying an evaluation for which there cannot be any substitute. There is, straightaway, an inference that *good, future, citizens* cannot be other than *good, English, boys*. We could not, for example, replace *English* by *Italian* or *Danish* or *Irish*. Twelve pages further on we are told that: 'If he'll only turn out a brave, helpful, truth-telling Englishman, and a gentleman and a Christian, that's all I want' (*ibid.* 74) the inference is that without the attributes manifested in the set *brave, helpful, truth-telling* he cannot be a 'proper' Englishman.

There are several examples of this notion of 'Englishness' in *Tom Brown's Schooldays* but two other references will suffice to illustrate the point further. One is from early in the narrative as Tom travels to Rugby School. It follows the story-telling of the coach guard who has been recounting an incident where Rugby boys had fought a running battle with Irish labourers. Here authorial comment again reiterates the nature of 'Englishness':

> It's very odd how almost all **English** boys love danger; you can get ten to join a game, or climb a tree, or swim a stream when there's a chance of breaking their limbs or getting drowned, for one who'll stay on level ground or in his depth or play quoits or bowls.
>
> (pp. 84–5)

What the reader is receiving here is the message that it is only true English boys who will be participants in the most active of situations. Gender and race are complementary.

The other example we have already discussed in terms of transitivity earlier in the chapter but note again clause complex 2:

> Fighting with fists is the **natural** and **English** way for **English** boys to settle their quarrels.

The inference here is that any other means of settling disputes is *unnatural* and therefore '*un-English*'. This is reinforced by the two rhetorical questions which conclude the extract.

Overall, Hughes appears to be listing classificatory attributes which represent the idealised English youth. He seems to be presenting an ethic of 'Englishness' which, in fact, would be at odds with his hero Arnold, who, as we saw in chapter 1, he understood imperfectly. Arnold was not a 'muscular Christian'. Nor have we quite reached the jingoistic years of high empire. Hughes is more nationalistic than imperialistic, but we see, none the less, that 'British society, and the building of the Empire, required team-spirit more than individual virtue, and Hughes's misinterpretation helped the Arnold revolution to find its way into a new channel' (Townsend, 1965: 58).

Carpenter and Prichard (1984: 6) claim that the early writers in the genre made no special virtue of being white and British. There is, none the less, a feeling that to be English is to be in some way special. Certainly, as the century progressed the notion of 'British-ness' as distinct from 'Englishness' appeared more frequently in aggressive contexts. The Victorian corpus gives 256 occurrences of *English* and 254 occurrences of *British*. Interestingly, the five most frequent lexical items collocating with *English* are *good*, *words*, *spoke*, *boys*, *seamen* as compared to *seamen*, *troops*, *force*, *Government*, *sailors* as the most frequent lexical collocates of *British*. Thus, in the latter instance we have five types of participant capable of initiating very active processes and being powerful actors in a situation.

It is G.A. Henty more than any other writer who transforms the nationalism of earlier writers into the imperialism of the type which Marcus Crouch called 'as simple as a child's faith in God, or father or Santa Claus' (1962, cited by Leeson, 1985: 99). Henty, however, was not without his critics even then. Leeson (1985: 99) notes the comments of a Dutchman writing in May 1908 in the boys' magazine *The Captain*. He commented that, thanks to Henty and his imitators:

> the young Englishman came to believe that he was equal to two or more Frenchmen, about four Germans, an indefinite number of Russians and any 'quantity you care to mention of the remaining scum of the earth'.

Whatever the criticism there were plenty of writers in the Henty mould. W.E. Johns in an interview with Geoffrey Trease in 1948 was asked why he wrote for children. He said that part of the reason was entertainment but that he also wrote to '*teach sportsmanship according to the British idea. . . . I teach that decent behaviour wins as a natural order of things. I teach the spirit of team-work, loyalty to the Crown, the Empire* and to *rightful authority*' (Trease, 1964: 80).

Non-Englishness

In Henty we see the ideology of race at its most dominant. In one sense the uniqueness of the Anglo-Saxon, at least as far as Henty was concerned, had become the 'religion' of the Empire and the British way of doing things. Henty's feelings towards the indigenous peoples of Britain's overseas territories reflected this. He believed that no 'native', however loyal or worthy as an opponent, had in full the qualities which he saw as the God-given gifts of Englishmen. The Afghans in *For Name and Fame* (1886), for instance, were 'brave' and 'independent' but 'unruly' and 'ill-disciplined'. However:

> when **led** and **organised by English officers** there are no better soldiers in the world. . . . **Guided by British advice**, **led by British officers**, and, it may be, **paid by British gold**, Afghanistan is likely to prove an invaluable ally to us.
>
> (Henty, 1886: iv)

In each of the highlighted clauses above the focus is on process initiated by the English upon the unstated Affected, the Afghans. The processes *lead*, *organise*, *guide*, *advise*, *pay* obscure the fact of domination through displacement of terms signalling domination by terms signalling responsibility. Until the Affected have been subjected to the 'benevolent' processes initiated by the Agent they are not civilised: they are 'savages' and are unlikely to prove to be valuable allies.

Henty also evaluated different groups in hierarchical terms. Thus:

> The Sikhs and Punjaubees . . . , are **tall stately** men. . . . They had fought with extreme bravery against the English, but once conquered they became **true and faithful** subjects of the English crown. . . . The Bombay troops, upon the other hand, were drawn from races which had **long ceased to be warlike**. They possessed none of the dash and fire of the hardier troops; their organization was, and still is, **defective**; and the system of officering them was **radically bad**.
>
> (*ibid*. 328)

The Sikhs and 'Punjaubees' were subjected to the Material process of being conquered. As a result of this they went through an intensive Relational process and *became true and faithful*, thus acquiring two of the Attributes most highly valued by authors such as Henty. The description of the Bombay troops, on the other hand, represents them through a series of relational clauses in very negative terms indeed.

In the Victorian corpus there are very high frequencies for items which are, or can be, pejorative for the contemporary reader. These are: *black/s* (280 occurrences), *savage/s* (259 occurrences), *native/s* (224 occurrences), *negro/es* (76), *nigger/s* (20 occurrences). For many of today's readers it might be assumed that these items represent a cline of offensiveness. *Natives*, for example, in today's usage, is offensive in some contexts; *negro* is regarded as offensive by some; *black* can be offensive within certain contexts and both *nigger* and *savage* are particularly offensive. In the Victorian corpus the items can be substituted for each other, though interestingly of the 76 occurrences of the item *negro* 73 are from *The Three Midshipmen* and the other three are from *Peter the Whaler*, both books by W.H.G. Kingston.

One extract from *The Coral Island* exemplifies the synonymous relationship that existed between these items where *natives* was relexicalised as *savages* and *blacks* as well as being reiterated.

> the watch . . . and the look-out . . . were more than usually vigilant, as we were . . . in danger of being attacked by **natives**. . . . **Our precautions against the savages** were indeed necessary.
>
> One day we were becalmed among a group of small islands which appeared, to be uninhabited. . . . But we were mistaken in thinking there were no **natives** for scarcely had we drawn near to the shore when a band of **naked blacks** rushed out of the bush and assembled on the beach . . .
>
> (Ballantyne, 1858/1966: 121)

Before the account of this incident is concluded, the 'natives' are referred to again twice as *savages*.

Some authors did not confine themselves to the non-white races in their negative evaluation. Kingston, for example, represents the behaviour of a group of Irish Catholic emigrants during a fire on board ship thus:

> Now began the most horrible orgies imaginable. Men, women and even children, became speedily intoxicated, and entirely forgetful of their fears and awful position. They were, in fact, like the **fiercest savages** and, like them, **danced**, and **shouted** and sang, till some of them fell in fits on the deck.
>
> (Kingston, 1851/1909: 57)

The mass readership

By the end of the century more and more adolescent readers were being exposed to the genre. The appearance of magazines for juveniles ensured that youngsters of all social strata were able to avail themselves of the narratives of these writers. Wyndham Lewis (cited by Carpenter and Prichard 1984: 80) recalled the stories as being 'full of tough, hairy conquering Nordics . . . wrestling with huge apes and enormous cobras, foiling victims of Latin origin'.

However, it was not only in the fiction of magazines like *The Boys' Own Paper* (1879–1967) that stereotypes were perpetuated. Perhaps more insidiously was the attitude conveyed by some non-fiction. In *The Boys' Own Annual* for 1906 (the *Annual* is the year's collection of *The BOP*) is an article entitled 'Something about savages'. One extract is as follows:

> The great difference between man and beast is the gift of speech; and the great difference between a civilised and a **savage** man is in the use they make of it. . . . **Savages** have hardly any conversation, because they have very few ideas in their heads, and what they talk about – well . . .
>
> (*BOP*, 1906: 28)

In the same volume is another article called 'Funny faces from West Africa' which features what are called 'screamingly funny faces'. These are two caricatures of African features which are, by any standard, highly offensive. There then follows a description of 'the west coast *native*' which includes the following:

> The west-coast **native** is a constant fund of amusement, but – poor fellow – he has for many years had a very bad name as a worker. If we are to believe people who have lived with him, and who ought to know, he has generally exhibited great skill, especially when employed by Europeans, in shirking as large a portion of his fair share of work as he safely could; he has been quite content to let his wives attend to all his wants, and to do as much of the heavy work as they (and he) liked: . . .
>
> (*BOP*, 1906: 108)

We would not find such descriptions in contemporary children's reading material. Race as an institution will be approached from a different perspective. Racism is still with us but there is now a challenge to its expression in society as the setting-up in 1979 of the National Committee on Racism in Children's Books exemplifies. Furthermore, Britain, at least urban Britain, is multi-racial and the representation of race in children's fiction reflects this as the the work of authors such as Farrukh Dhondy (1944–) and his concern with Black and Asian youth illustrate.

Finally, it is worth noting that one Victorian author for young readers was not typical of the general mass of writers when it came to representing concepts of 'Englishness,' 'non-Englishness', black and white. In *Masterman Ready* Marryat chooses to use authorial voice to comment on the inevitability of the decline of empire. Much of this book is structured round long didactic passages uttered by Mr Seagrave, the father of the family, on a variety of topics. In this instance he is holding forth on colonisation and the impermanence of the hegemony of all imperial nations including England in response to a question from his son William. As he nears the end of his speech a different view from that we discussed above is given to the young reader, though the same lexical items, with the addition of *barbarians*, are employed:

> 'Recollect that when the Roman empire was at the height of its power, Great Britain was peopled by mere **barbarians** and **savages**. Now Rome has disappeared, and is only known in history, and by the relics of its former greatness, while England ranks amongst the highest of nations. How is the major portion of the continent of Africa peopled? – by **barbarians** and **savages**; and who knows what they may become some future day?'
>
> 'What! the **negroes** become a great nation?'
>
> 'That is exactly what the Romans might have said in former days: What! the **British barbarians** become a great nation? And yet they have become so.'
>
> 'But! the **negroes** father – they are **blacks**.'
>
> 'Very true; but that is no reason to the contrary. As to the darkness of the skin, the majority of the **Moors** are quite as black as the **negroes**; yet they were once a great nation, and, moreover the most enlightened nation of their time, with a great many excellent qualities – full of *honour, generosity, politeness,* and *chivalry*. They conquered and held the major part of Spain for many hundred years; introduced *arts* and *sciences* then unknown, and were as *brave* and *heroic* as they were *virtuous* and *honourable*.'
>
> (Marryat, 1841/1889: 119)

While *barbarian, black, negro* and *savage* are synonymous in this extract Marryat does, at least within the nineteenth-century context, present a less arrogant world view than some of the other writers of the genre. The italicised items in the extract are shown not to be the exclusive property and gifts of the Anglo-Europeans. For many of the other writers, and particularly those forty or fifty years on from

Marryat, this synonymy was the accepted and propagated world view labelling of the non-white races.

CONCLUSIONS

In this chapter we have been concerned with the defining characteristics of traditional juvenile literature. In terms of the representation of life as it was felt it should be conducted we noted the decidedly Christian ethos which pervades all the institutions and the fact that no one institution is mutually exclusive of any other. Lexical items were commented upon where they were seen to act as key signifiers of a moral instruction. In short, exciting events were now being presented to the young reader but there was a didacticism still present. Harvey Darton (1932/1982: 68), however, makes the point that what was new about the early adventure stories was the absence of 'any appeal to a dogmatic religious belief', but goes on to state:

> The heroes are shown as **praying**, as **trusting** in God, as **stout** Britons with a sense of **honour**, **honesty** and **duty**; and the need of those qualities is always visible and sometimes made explicit.

In *The Coral Island* Ballantyne provided a first narrator protagonist and, according to Wall (1991: 68), because of this 'Ballantyne was able to eliminate the digressions and much of the moralising which had plagued, and continued to plague, adventure stories.' Ballantyne, nevertheless, still manages to deliver the Christian message notably in the second half of the book, where much attention is given to the 'civilising' work of the Christian missionaries in the South Seas.

Piety is a characteristic of Ballantyne's heroes, their families and friends. It is even more so of Kingston's, the most popular writer of the genre. According to Avery, he 'harangues more than Ballantyne' and 'his Protestant intolerance is stronger and his sermons longer. But they are sermons on the bountifulness of the Creator and His infinite mercy rather than how one should behave' (Avery, 1965: 145).

Tom Brown's Schooldays is, not surprisingly, the most overtly didactic of the books. It represents a serious attempt to 'improve' the reader. Hughes himself said, 'My sole object in writing was to preach to boys: if ever I write again, it will be to preach to some other age. I can't see that a man has any business to write at all unless he has something he thoroughly believes and wants to preach about'

(1857/1880: xiii). There is no great strength of characterisation though the character of Tom himself is not completely unconvincing. The book is less a novel and more a documentary in which Hughes addresses his readers on what are clearly a number of hobby horses on the essence of Englishness, manliness and Christianity.

It was this genre of traditional juvenile fiction that established modern children's literature. In the nineteenth century a 'class' of writers was established. As Harvey Darton (1932/1982: 246) puts it: 'It would be tedious and unnecessary to differentiate closely, for instance, between Ballantyne and Kingston, except in the matter of dates, plots and scenes.' These authors can be seen as presenting a collection of characteristics which had 'some main unity of idea'. In terms of characterisation this means:

> the real reader makes no contact with the mind of a character except on the most superficial level. Where the story demands feelings of terror or alarm, or serious thoughts, the narratee feels or thinks them; but no attempt is ever made to explore, understand, or express how a person in such a situation might really feel. The adult narrator in fact merely reports the kind of stereotyped thought, feeling and behaviour which was marketed for the next hundred years as 'Best British Boy'.
>
> (Wall, 1991: 70)

Wall is commenting on the narrative structure of *The Coral Island* but her remarks are valid whether the traditional story is first- or third-person narrative.

The elements of the genre are all there; the conceptions of morality rooted in Christianity and Englishness. These latter two become very difficult to distinguish from imperialism by the turn of the century. The genre is defined by its institutions such as gender and friendship; the hero and his faithful male companions.

Juvenile fiction generates key lexical items in the mind: *action, suspense, challenge, adversaries, adversity, excitement.* These items can apply to other broad categories of fiction as well. We saw in chapter 1 how the traditional adventure/school stories became displaced by those from other genres, in particular the 'other strand' of fantasy, but these still contain many of the characteristics we have discussed in this chapter.

Fantasy, science fiction, history all provide frameworks for adventure. There are journeys which do not necessitate travelling to the Punjab, Africa or Antarctica; journeys can be mythical, local or, indeed, metaphorical. By the latter we mean the departure from the normal day-to-day activities of the central characters. Adventure is a term which encompasses experiences in most settings, real and imagined, but whatever the setting it usually contains danger, either actual or potential. It also involves resourcefulness and sometimes courage. As Marshall (1988: 160–1) puts it: 'The interplay of characters reveals the strengths and weaknesses of the group or the individual child, and the ending indicates the successful completion of the journey, the solving of the mystery' or the overcoming of the odds. The defining characteristics will be found, as we noted above, in other genres. In fantasy stories some will be present but also others such as notions of what is *unearthly*, *extraordinary*, *supernatural* or *magical*. There will be, as we shall see, other patterns of language occurring, other distinct transitivities and other collocations as well as language patterns which are shared.

4 Today's young reader

INTRODUCTION

The narratives which are representative of the genre of traditional juvenile fiction are, in general, best regarded as sets of characteristics with little to distinguish them one from the other. This is not to deny that with writers like Ballantyne and Kingston there was a new departure in children's literature. As well as assuming the role of instructor there was a recognisable attempt to entertain the young reader. By the early twentieth century, however, the genre was exhibiting symptoms of weariness. Overall, these narratives are alike in their uniformity, and having read one Biggles book you have read them all. The tradition of fantasy writing too was entering the doldrums as the 'First Golden Age' drew to a close. By and large the next fifty years are not noted for originality or creativity in the production of children's books. Overall, in the great majority of books published during this time there is little or no complexity of character or exploration of those emotions and feelings that are the hallmarks of the best of today's books for young readers.

In chapter 1 we saw that by the mid 1950s writers able to offer adventure and excitement with characterisation, imagination and style as opposed to presenters of stereotypes were emerging. Since the 1960s and 1970s writers already well established in the field of adult fiction were to contribute substantially to children's literature. Not least amongst them is Nina Bawden whose work has been cited in Knowles's 1989/1990 survey. Furthermore, no discussion of modern children's fiction can ignore Roald Dahl. His work has attracted a large following from childhood to adolescence as the survey demonstrates. We consider him specifically in chapter 5 from another perspective but in this chapter we wish to discuss some of the notions already explored, particularly as regards his representation of the family.

We shall also draw upon examples of the 'teen' novel, very much a phenomenon of the later twentieth century, and comment upon the representation of realism with which this genre is concerned. 'Realism', in these narratives, is a cline which ranges from the banal, on the one hand, or books which often seem 'like a sociological exploration of the inadequate' (Leeson, 1985: 122), to, on the other, those with a credibility of character and situation as well as an ability to entertain.

In discussing our examples of contemporary children's reading matter we are particularly concerned with the institution of the family. As a social unit the changes it has undergone in terms of how it is regarded in the last hundred years are profound. This is not to say that Victorian families did not experience crises and conflicts; of course they did. Challenges to the social domination of the family, however, or any other negative representation of it as an institution by the traditional authors is not, as we saw earlier, part of a world view they constructed for their readers. Characterisation is important as we consider our texts and their institutions as, unlike the majority of the traditional authors, writers like Bawden do not simply present a mixture of predictable ingredients. The range of books available today is vast. Our selection of texts exemplifies the richness and diversity of that range. It cannot represent its entirety.

CARRIE'S WAR

Nina Bawden's *Carrie's War* was published in 1973 (page references are to the 1974 edition) and is generally regarded as one of the best post-war children's books. In the book, and the later *The Peppermint Pig* (1975), Bawden represents a child's view of the world with a particular sensitivity.

The central character, equivalent of the young hero in the previous chapter, is a girl, but, unlike the traditional narratives, the story is not defined by gender. *Carrie's War*, unlike *The Coral Island* or *Tom Brown's Schooldays*, is not gender-specific in terms of implied readership. Gender is important but Bawden does not assign gender- and class-specific roles in the story as Enid Blyton's stock characters are assigned in, for example, *The Famous Five* or *The Secret Seven* series. The novel tells the story of Carrie and her brother Nick, who have been evacuated to a Welsh mining village during the Second World War. They are billeted with a shopkeeper, the bigoted and embittered Mr Evans and his brow-beaten younger sister. Mr Evans is estranged from his elder sister, Mrs Gotobed, who lives in a nearby farmhouse, Druid's Bottom, with her housekeeper Hepzibah Green, the handicapped Mr Johnny and Albert Sandwich, another evacuee. The story opens and closes in the present when the grown-up and widowed Carrie brings her own children to Druid's Bottom having believed for thirty years that she had been responsible for the destruction of the house and the deaths of its occupants.

The story evolves around the relationships that develop between Carrie and the other characters and the contrast between the bleakness of the Evans household and the warmth and security of Hepzibah's kitchen at Druid's Bottom. It is these relationships that provide the impetus for Carrie's doubts and fears and thus sustain the narrative as Carrie struggles, unsuccessfully, to heal the breach between Evans and Mrs Gotobed. The interplay of relations between Carrie and the others is not based upon a clear-cut differentiation between, for example, simplistic notions of 'good' and 'bad' normally to be found in a traditional story. Even Mr Evans is not truly bad. Rather they are based upon Carrie's perceptions of people and a world that she does not always fully comprehend. One of the most significant language patterns in the book is one of transitivity and thought presentation that Fowler (1977: 103) refers to as 'mind-style' – 'any distinctive linguistic presentation of an individual mental self'. It is a major feature in distinguishing the best of today's children's literature in general and *Carrie's War* in particular, reflecting that 'In this book we have dispensed with the drama of external situations – there are no crooks, no villains but Carrie's own guilty fears' (Kirkpatrick, 1978: 95).

As well as transitivity lexical selection is important. In *Carrie's War* significant lexical patterning complements transitivity as a conveyor of images of the world as seen by Carrie. This might mean the selection of a particular item or collocational pairing to represent her thought processes, for example, or a naming strategy when referring to one of the participants in a situation or the description of a particular set of circumstances at a particular stage of the narrative. *Said*, not surprisingly, is the most frequent lexical item but the second is the verb form *thought*, with 44 occurrences collocating with *Carrie* as node. Furthermore, when concordance lines were obtained for *thought* the pronominal *she* was the most frequent item, with 60 occurrences. Only four of these were non-referents of *Carrie*. The verb form *thought*, is a key item in the narrative as Carrie tries to make sense of the world around her and this is conveyed to the reader by what is going on in Carrie's head.

The transitivity feature of the narrative referred to above underlines the most crucial difference between this kind of modern children's fiction and the traditional stories we discussed in the previous chapter. Carrie is the Senser, in Halliday's terms, the human participant in the process. Here we are concerned with *mental* processes as opposed to *material* or *verbal* ones.

It is through this functioning of the clause that Carrie relates to the institutions represented by the people around her and the emotions they engender. If Carrie is the Senser then what she 'senses' is the Phenomenon. One of the most significant areas where these patterns occur is as Carrie meets the main characters in her new world.

Carrie as Senser

We commented elsewhere about the importance of the journey in some children's literature. In one sense there are two journeys in this narrative: first, there is the physical one, where, accompanied by her brother, she arrives in the village; second, there is the temporal and emotional one which takes thirty years to complete. Both journeys have their ultimate destination at Druid's Bottom, where Hepzibah Green is housekeeper, and are marked by *thought* clauses as Carrie meets people and has to deal with the situations and feelings that these meetings create. Note the following:

1 'Particular about what, Carrie **wondered**. But Miss Evans looked nice; a little like a red squirrel Carrie had once seen' (p. 21).
2 'But Mr Evans didn't fly into the rage she'd **expected**. He simply looked startled – as if a worm had just lifted its head and answered him back, Carrie **thought**.' (p. 28).
3 'Her voice was pitched low and soft. Her spell-binding voice, Carrie **thought**, and **looked up at** her. She was holding a candle and her eyes shone in its light and her gleaming hair fell like silk on her shoulders. A beautiful witch, Carrie **thought**' (p. 65).
4 'She **looked at** Mrs Gotobed's claw-like, ringed fingers holding her delicate cup, and **thought of** Auntie Lou's red hands that were always in water' (p. 71).
5 'Carrie **thought** she quite **liked** him. . . . He was like a bear, Carrie **thought**: a friendly, silly, strong bear' (p. 90).

In these extracts Carrie records her inner experience, the impact on her imagination which each of the above characters makes either at first acquaintance or very early on in their relationship. Carrie '*senses*', she *wonders, expects, thinks, looks up, looks at, likes* and this allows Bawden not only to present to the reader the other characters in the narrative but to give us some notion of Carrie's mental make-up at various stages. This representation of Carrie's thoughts invites the reader to see things from her point of view. In Leech and Short's (1981: 174) terms Carrie is the Reflector. There is here a 'slanting of the fictional world towards "reality" as apprehended by a particular participant, . . . in the fiction'. This heightens the reader's perception of Carrie as a person in encounters that are perfectly plausible and similar to ones which they may well have had themselves. The reader is allowed, through these processes, to identify with Carrie, to *sense* with her.

In addition Carrie's interpretation of the Phenomena metaphorically further strengthens our awareness of Carrie as a conscious being. Note in particular the animal imagery of 1, 2, 4 and 5:

    a red squirrel
    a worm
    claw-like, ringed fingers
    a friendly, silly, strong bear

This is exactly the sort of language a perceptive and sensitive child might use to record her impressions of the people who have replaced her family and thus her familiar world. 'Once more the plot concerns the precarious hold on reality of a child's imaginings' (Paton-Walsh, 1978a: 95).

None of the characters which this imagery relates to is the object of great affection on Carrie's part though all three are important in the narrative. Carrie's feelings towards Hepzibah Green, focus of her thoughts in extract 3, are, however, different and we shall return to this extract.

Hepzibah Green at home

Hepzibah Green, housekeeper to Mr Evans' estranged sister, Mrs Gotobed, becomes the surrogate mother and father figure to Carrie and her brother Nick. Their real mother appears fleetingly in the narrative and Hepzibah represents the institution of *family*. Ironically, through her story-telling, she also is the cause of Carrie's belief that she committed a terrible crime, causing the deaths of all the inhabitants of Druid's Bottom. It takes thirty years for Carrie to find out that she was not the agent of destruction she believed she was.

Under Hepzibah's roof Carrie also becomes re-acquainted with Albert Sandwich, another, slightly older, evacuee who is the friend/companion (Carrie's brother also has a companion role as well as providing the link with their 'real' family) of the narrative. It is Albert who maintains contact with Hepzibah during the thirty-year gap. It is also interesting to note at this juncture the strategies of naming Bawden employs for the people important to Carrie. *Hepzibah* Green, Albert *Sandwich*, *Mister* Johnny, Mrs *Gotobed*. In each case one element of naming provides an untypical collocation so that the unusualness of the names matches the diversity of character. They also stand in contrast to the more prosaic Evans brother and sister and the rather drab life lived in their home.

Carrie first meets Hepzibah when she and Nick go to Druid's Bottom to collect the Christmas goose. As they go through the yew wood that leads to the house they are frightened by strange noises and stumble into Hepzibah's kitchen:

A **warm**, **safe**, **lighted** place. [1] Hepzibah's kitchen was always like that, and not only that evening. [2] *Coming into it was like coming home on a bitter cold day to a bright, leaping fire.* [3] *It was like the smell of bacon when you were hungry; loving arms when you were lonely; safety when you were scared.*

(p. 46)

The kitchen is the centre of Hepzibah's universe and the symbol of the safety and security of a happy family. Note the lexical set generated by the modifiers in the nominal group which introduces the description: *warm, safe, lighted*. These key items prepare the reader for the matching relations (see Hoey, 1983: 112–15) of the successive clauses in italicised clause complexes 2 and 3:

bitter cold day	bright, leaping fire
smell of bacon	hungry
loving arms	lonely
safety	scared

This parallelism of structure allows the reader to hear the paragraph to be read in the imagination. This is another dimension of thought presentation where we are being given Carrie's and Nick's immediate experience or consciousness as they stumble through the door (see Leech and Short, 1981: 337).

A little further on Carrie becomes able to take in the scene in more detail:

> Carrie saw her, then the room. A big stone-flagged kitchen, shadowy in the corners but bright near the fire. A dresser with blue and white plates; a scrubbed, wooden table; a hanging oil lamp.
>
> (p. 46)

Note Carrie as Senser and the lexical density of the parallel nominal groups that are the Phenomena; sensing first, after Hepzibah the person, the whole, the superordinate, *the room* and then taking in its constituents:

a big stone-flagged kitchen

a dresser with blue   a scrubbed, wooden table   a hanging oil lamp
and white plates

What she perceives is to become a haven for the children and is interesting as it is a modern example of the symbolism of the kitchen in children's literature. Inglis (1981: 267) comments that 'Hepzibah's kitchen is the companion to the many beautiful kitchens of children's fiction, and a complement to the many ideal gardens.' Carpenter (1985: 161–3) draws our attention to this symbolism and the sense of security it engenders, citing Kenneth Grahame's description of Badger's kitchen from *The Wind in the Willows* amongst others. He also notes how the kitchen can be used to represent moral decay in a household as this extract from George MacDonald's *The Princess and Curdie* exemplifies:

> Everywhere was **filth** and **disorder**. **Mangy** turnspit dogs were lying about, and **grey rats** were **gnawing** at **refuse** in the sinks . . . [Curdie] longed for one glimpse of his mother's poor little kitchen, so *clean* and *bright* and *airy*.
>
> (MacDonald, 1883, cited by Carpenter, 1985: 163)

The highlighted and italicised items provide a good example of a matching contrast relation through the antonymous relationships that exist between the two sets. Curdie's mother's kitchen, like Hepzibah's, represents the ideal and we can only truly appreciate the ideal when we have experienced the opposite.

Hepzibah as family

If Hepzibah's kitchen is 'home' then Hepzibah herself is family and Carrie's first impressions of her are important. As she recovers from her fright she takes in the woman as well as the room:

she simply stood, looking down at the children and smiling. She was tall with shining hair the colour of copper. She wore a white apron, the sleeves of her dress were rolled up, showing big, fair, freckled arms, and there was flour on her hands.

(p. 46)

This description can be regarded as a process of normalisation. After the fright in the woods the safety of the kitchen re-adjusts the reader as Carrie and Nick re-adjust themselves to the security of their new surroundings The description of Hepzibah assists in this process and reinforces the warmth and safety of the kitchen. The descriptive focus (see Leech and Short, 1981: 180–5) concentrates on the physical but the reader will interpret the 'physical facts in terms of their abstract significance' (*ibid.* 181). Hepzibah is *smiling* a signal of friendship. 'She is **tall** with **shining hair** the colour of **copper**', which reinforces the security and warmth of the kitchen. 'She wore a **white apron**' and she had '**big, fair, freckled arms** and there was **flour** on her **hands**' emphasise this even further with the image of peaceful domesticity. The key lexical items here interweave; the meronyms *hair, arms, hands*; the colour modifiers *copper, white, fair, freckled*; the domestic items of *apron* and *flour*; the emphasis on size with *tall* and *big* but not size in any threatening sense.

This chapter is one of the most important in the book. It establishes the relationship between Carrie and Nick, Hepzibah, Albert and the handicapped Mr Johnny. It also features another important element in the narrative: Hepzibah's prowess as a story-teller when she recounts the history of the skull. Thus, during the next visit Carrie's imagination is at work again as the previously cited extract 3 shows. We cite it again here:

Her **voice** was pitched **low** and **soft**. Her **spell-binding voice**, Carrie thought, and **looked up** at her. She was holding a candle and her **eyes shone** in its **light** and her **gleaming hair** fell like **silk** on her shoulders. A beautiful **witch**, Carrie thought.

This physical description and the mysteriousness of Mrs Gotobed's crying which precede it, Mr Evans' unkind comments about Hepzibah after the first visit and Carrie's subsequent feelings of guilt all combine to fuel Carrie's vivid imagination.

Note how in the two *thought* clauses the Phenomena coincide with the Theme (see below), the first element in a clause and not necessarily the grammatical subject. In both clauses we have *thematic fronting* or a *marked theme* (see Halliday, 1985: 38–67). This particular fronting device allows Bawden to give special status to the two nominal groups which carry a particular significance for the reader and for Carrie.

Her spell-binding voice, . . .
A beautiful witch, . . .

Note also the collocational relationship between *spell-binding* and *witch*.

Other lexical devices include the employment of meronymy where description focuses on 'parts' of Hepzibah as illustrated below. Particularly significant are *voice* and *eyes*, which are directly related to the senses.

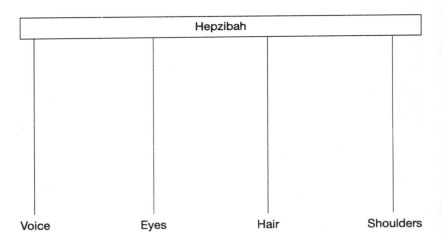

The attributes of *voice* are shown below and especially the key item, *spell-binding*.

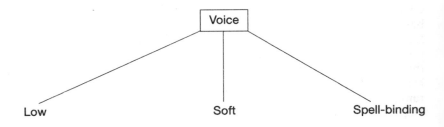

We have the imagery of *light* as illustrated below and the metaphorical use of *eyes* and *hair* as actualised participants:

She was holding a CANDLE

her eyes SHONE in its LIGHT   her GLEAMING hair
          fell like SILK

The lexical density of this extract, the fronting of marked elements, the use of meronymy and metaphor all heighten what Carrie's senses are registering, that Hepzibah is 'a beautiful witch'.

Hepzibah is not, of course, a witch, in the supernatural sense; rather, as Albert tells Carrie, she is 'a wise woman' skilled in herb lore and knowledgeable about country stories and traditions. There is, however, an element of magic in the narrative in the sense that this is in Carrie's mind. Carrie is loving and trusting but she only has a partial understanding of what is going on in terms of the relationships between Mr Evans, Mrs Gotobed and Hepzibah. This 'partial understanding' is, however, 'the mainspring of the plot' (Paton-Walsh, 1978a: 95).

Carrie is an affectionate yet lonely child and her confused feelings are well summed up in the extract below, where we note her reaction to Nick being on Hepzibah's lap during their first visit. Again we have Carrie's feelings recorded. Note the highlighted *mental* processes:

Carrie **looked at** Nick on Hepzibah's lap and **felt** jealous. Of Nick, because she would **like** to be sitting there, she wasn't too big. And of Hepzibah because she was comforting Nick in a way she **knew** she could never do.

(p. 54)

The processes direct the reader's attention to different categories of Phenomenon. Carrie *senses* or perceives both a situation, where Nick is located, and the emotion of jealousy. What Carrie wants essentially is affection and she does later in the narrative come to be comforted in the same way by Hepzibah.

It is the partial comprehension referred to above and Carrie's confusion of emotions that leads her to throw away the skull in the belief this will prevent Mr Evans from occupying Druid's Bottom. The legend of the skull, the references to the 'old religion' and Hepzibah's essential humanism are what represent the institution of *religion* in this text. There are references to the narrow non-conformist beliefs of Mr Evans but it is Hepzibah who is the essence of religion as well as family for Carrie. This is manifested in the text by statements such as Hepzibah's when she tells Mister Johnny to escort the children back through the woods. Note the italicised nominal groups where Hepzibah makes synonymous what no doubt Mr Evans would regard as antonymous by providing the inclusive *the same thing*:

> 'You'll be alright with him. No harm of the kind you're afraid of, ever comes near *the innocent*.'
> Carrie said, 'Mr. Evans says no harm can ever come to *those who trust in the Lord*.'
> 'Perhaps that's another way of saying *the same thing*,' Hepzibah said.
>
> (p. 55)

And we note at the end as Carrie leaves Druid's Bottom for the last time the highlighted significant lexical items actualising the Phenomenon. Note how *the sound* is relexicalised as *a soft gentle sigh*, *a stirring and breathing* to be finally represented as *a comforting sound*. The effect of this type of repetition is to further involve the reader with Carrie as she *hears* and *listens*, as she *senses*:

> She wasn't scared, not even when half-way up the path, dark yews all around her, and heard **the sound** she had heard the first time. **A soft, gentle sigh**; **a stirring** and **breathing**. . . . Nick was some way ahead. Carrie stood still and listened. But she wasn't afraid. It seemed **a comforting sound** now, as if the mountain had grown friendly towards her.
>
> (p. 126)

In many ways there is a sadness about the narrative. Carrie has to wait thirty years to discover that the fire she saw from the train did not destroy her friends, her 'other' family. But Bawden, as well as writing with a delicacy and complexity not found in the traditional narratives, keeps her readership in mind. Carrie, now widowed, returns with her own children, and in fact it is they who discover Hepzibah and Mister Johnny alive and still living at Druid's Bottom. James Stephens (1992: 227) sees the use of time as providing

> a model by which readers are able to extrapolate to perceive comparable functions of causality in their own lives, and causal relationships between one historical period and another. The latter conclusion is more clearly embodied by the structure of a novel such as *Carrie's War* (1973), a story framed by its narrator's return to the site of events after a period of thirty years.

In conclusion, the lexical patterns and the mental processes of transitivity we have drawn examples from illustrate clearly how Bawden epitomises the breadth and vitality of modern children's literature as opposed to the stereotypical narratives of an earlier time, examples of which are still on sale today.

ROALD DAHL: ANARCHIST

For many parents Roald Dahl's work was contrary to their view of children's literature. *Charlie and the Chocolate Factory*, which first appeared in 1964 'has been loved by children and hated by adults because it is full of fun and virtually amoral' (Carpenter, 1985: 1). The book also attracted criticism for the supposed racism in the representation of the Oompa-Loompas and the portrayal of Charlie's grandparents (see Carpenter and Prichard, 1984: 108). The representation of Charlie's grandparents is a key aspect of Dahl's work and probably why some adults have been so intensely critical of him. In other words Dahl takes a very different view of the institution of *family* and of adults in general. The submission of children to the domination of the family as a right and necessary system of control is very definitely not a part of this writer's view of the world. Ready obedience is out; anarchy is in.

Whatever the feelings of the adult population, Dahl is overwhelmingly popular with children and not least because:

> What he aims to achieve – and does – is a tone of voice which is clear, uncluttered, unobtrusive, not very demanding linguistically, and which sets up a sense of intimate, yet adult-controlled, relationship between his second self and his implied child reader.
>
> (Chambers, 1980: 256)

Dahl allies himself with the child reader against the world of adults, which is why many saw him as subversive; but he none the less exercises his own control over that reader. This can be clearly perceived in two of Dahl's works which concern themselves with the family as the main focus of representation: *Danny the Champion of the World* (1975; page references are to the 1987 edition) and *Matilda* (1988; page references are to the 1989 edition).

Danny at home

Danny the Champion of the World is not like *The Twits* (1980), which represents a grotesque husband and wife, or *George's Marvellous Medicine* (1981), about a boy with a horrible grandmother and the equally horrible revenge he takes upon her. Nor, indeed, is it involved with the power relations that characterise *Matilda* though dominance is integral to the text notably in Danny's father's view of the world as opposed to that of Mr Hazell's, the rich brewer and owner of the local estate and the pheasants Danny's father plans to poach. It does not overtly attack adults or family members in the same way as the stories cited above yet there is about the book an atmosphere of the anarchy which is so typical of Dahl. It is also a reworking of an adult text published as 'The Champion of the World' in Dahl's collection of short stories, *Kiss Kiss*, published in 1960.

The narrative centres on Danny, a motherless boy who lives in a caravan with his father whom he hero-worships. Family is highly significant, but note that it is not a typical family: it is the boy and his father alone against the world. The father represents *family* and the institution of *friendship* but he is not like the father/companion of *Masterman Ready*. This is not the key figure issuing orders and confident that his dominance will remain unquestioned; rather, as Tucker states:

> a few rogue parents still manage to make it into adventure stories as hero–companions, but only when such characters are themselves delinquent or in general set against the rest of society, as in Roald Dahl's story about a son and his poacher father, *Danny the Champion of the World*.
>
> (N. Tucker, 1989: 145)

The central characters are, therefore, male. Danny idolises his father, who has looked after him alone since his mother died when Danny was four months old. In the opening stages of the book Danny describes the caravan which is bedroom, living room and kitchen all in one, and the kitchen symbolism we discussed above is here as well:

> I really loved living in that gypsy caravan. I loved it especially in the evenings when I was tucked up in my bunk and my father was telling me stories. **The lamp was turned low**, and I could see lumps of **wood glowing red-hot** in the old stove and wonderful it was to be **lying** there **snug and warm** in my bunk in that little room. Most wonderful of all was the feeling that when I went to sleep, **my father** would still be there, **very close to me**, sitting in his chair by the fire or lying in the bunk above my own.
>
> (1975/1987: 11)

As with Hepzibah and her kitchen for Carrie, we have here for Danny the familiar symbols of *light*, *warmth*, *security*. These are represented through descriptions presented in a series of illocutionary acts as Danny speaks to us, the readers/listeners, in first-person narrative. The statements are linguistically simple presenting this idealised picture of his home and his father. The descriptive focus of these statements allows these symbols to impinge on our senses so that we know that the caravan is more than just a shabby one-room accommodation and that his father is more than a male parent for whom he has a degree of affection. This is intensified on the next page by Danny's descriptive focus concentrating on his father:

> He was actually a wildly funny person. What made him appear so serious was that he never smiled with his **mouth**. He did it all with his **eyes**. He had brilliant blue **eyes** and when he thought of something funny, his **eyes** would flash and if you looked carefully, you could actually see a tiny little golden spark dancing in the middle of each **eye**. But the **mouth** never moved.
>
> (1975/1987: 12–13).

Danny goes on to tell us that eye-smilers cannot give false smiles. If you smile with your mouth but not your eyes you are not to be trusted. The lexical item *eye* is obviously of key significance here, and we have noted the use of meronymy for positive descriptive focus in both the traditional genre and in *Carrie's War*. Both *eye* and *mouth* have a cohesive function in this extract, where they can be seen in an antonymous relationship. Note also the use of the two nominal groups with colour items *brilliant blue eyes* and *a tiny little golden spark* both of which act as positive reinforcers of the portrait Danny is presenting. They are, however, more usefully considered within the transitivity patterns of the extract where *eyes* is a key item.

The item is firstly a circumstantial element in the clause *he did it all with his eyes* referring to the means whereby the Material process took place. The next clause has *eyes* as 'possessed', they are Attributes in a possesive Relational process. Thus:

He	had	brilliant blue eyes
(Carrier/ possessor)	(Relational process/ possession)	(Attribute/ possessed)

Now *eyes* become the Agent and they *would flash* (Material process) to return in another metaphor in the final *eye* clause as part of the Phenomenon in a Mental process. Thus:

You	could see	a tiny little golden spark
(Senser)	{Mental process/perception}	dancing in the middle of each eye. {Phenomenon}

Thus the eye clauses present a succession of processes as follows: Material–Relational–Material–Mental. This pattern provides the semantic framework by which we can make sense of Danny's world both in his physical description of it and in the world of his imagination. For Danny one does not exist without the other. Danny's world centres around his father, who is *companion, comrade, friend* though interestingly these lexical items are not significant. There are only nine occurrences of *friend/s* and one of *companion* in the entire narrative. Seven of these are references to either Danny or his father. There are no occurrences of *comrade*. It is with his father, however, that the 'journey' is undertaken. The adventure that involves the capturing of the pheasants. As Danny himself says:

> That wasn't because I didn't have **good friends**. I had lots of them. Some of them were **super friends**, especially Sidney Morgan. . . . You see, the real reason I didn't want anyone else to come back and play with me was because I had such a good time being alone with **my father**.
>
> (p. 97).

Saying and telling

The picture of family represented by Dahl is not only idealised; it is, as we noted above, all male. There is only one reference to Danny's mother and that is to record the fact of her death. The relationship is probably the most characterised of all Dahl's works (Kirkpatrick, 1978: 333) and this may have something to do with its origins as an adult story. Much of this is achieved through verbal processes associated with Danny's father as Sayer.

The most common collocate of *father* is *my*. There are only 2 out of 356 occurrences of *father* where *my* is not present. and the three most common lexical items collocating with *father* are the verb forms *said* (149 occurrences), *asked* (13 occurrences), *told* (10 occurrences). *Said* is the second most frequent collocate overall of *father*. This allows, then, the pattern *my father said/asked/told* to occur 172 times in the narrative, almost exactly half the total occurrences of *father*. Thus, Danny narrates the events of the book to us not only in terms of descriptive focus of his parent but in representing him as a Sayer who can put forward statements, questions or directives. We have the following typical examples:

My father (Sayer)	told {Verbal process}	me {Recipient}	a fine story. {Verbiage}

(p. 26)

'What do you want to inspect our caravan for?' (Verbiage)	my father (Sayer)	asked. {Verbal process}

(p. 43)

'Danny did it!' {Verbiage}	my father {Sayer}	said {Verbal process}	proudly. {Circumstance}

'My son Danny is the champion of the world.'
{Verbiage}

(p. 137)

The high frequency of Verbal processes allows both direct and indirect speech and the relationship between Danny and his father is heightened for the reader through these processes of communicating. These clauses are a major contributor to the structure of the narrative and the representation of Danny's father as the focus of the boy's world. Through his statements, directives and questions, through his telling of stories, we are presented with a highly characterised relationship seen through the eyes of an adoring son.

The outside world

We have already seen how Danny wanted no other companionship but his father's. The outside world does, however, intrude. School is not a major setting for very much of the narrative as it is in *Matilda*. It does, nevertheless, allow the presentation of the vicious schoolmaster who canes Danny savagely.

On the day before the poaching expedition Danny is at school and gives the reader a portrait of the teachers. His snuffling class teacher is described thus:

Captain Lancaster, known sometimes as **Lankers, was a horrid man**. He had **fiery carrot-coloured hair** and a little **clipped carroty moustache** and a **fiery temper. Carroty-coloured hairs** also sprouted out of his nostrils and his earholes. . . . **Captain Lancaster was a violent man**, and we were all terrified of him. He used to *sit* at his desk *stroking* **his carroty moustache** *watching* us with **pale watery-blue eyes** *searching* for trouble. And as he sat there, he would make queer grunts through his nose, like some dog sniffing around a rabbit hole.

(p. 95)

The description presented to us is lexically dense though not grammatically complex. We are told firstly in a Relational process that *Captain Lancaster was a horrid man*. A second Relational process, this time of Possession, lists the following Attributes: *fiery carrot-coloured hair, a little clipped carroty moustache, a fiery temper*. The attributes are both physical and emotional and serve to characterise the schoolteacher. We illustrate this process of characterisation in figure 4.1. The presentation of these real-world phenomena are rendered particularly effective with the cohesive device of reiteration where *fiery* and *carroty* (as a colour term) are repeated. The repetition of *fiery* allows the emotional and the physical both to be included as complementary attributes of the whole as represented by the superordinate nominal group *a horrid man*.

The physical unpleasantness is ascribed agency in the next clause, where *Carroty-coloured hairs* (Agent) *sprouted* (Material process)

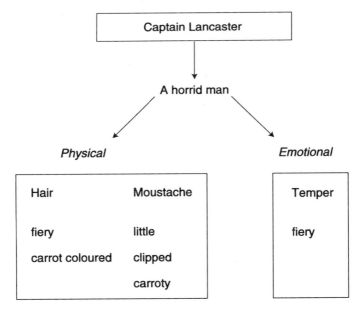

Figure 4.1   Captain Lancaster: a horrid man

out of his nostrils and his earholes (Circumstance). This clause serves to further emphasise the unpleasantness of the character and is, we maintain, illustrative of the point made by Aidan Chambers (see above) about Dahl's appeal to the young reader.

We are told a little later that Captain Lancaster is also *a violent man*, another negative attribute, and that *we all* (Carrier) *were* (Relational process) *terrified* (Attribute). If this were not enough there follows a series of clauses which characterise Captain Lancaster in a particularly sinister manner:

Captain Lancaster

A violent man
SITTING at his desk
STROKING his carroty moustache
WATCHING us (with pale watery-blue eyes)
SEARCHING for trouble

As an additional device to increase the dramatic effect Dahl introduces the animal imagery which is very much a part of his linguistic repertoire in the representation of unpleasant adult characters, as we shall see in our discussion of characterisation in *Matilda*: 'He would make **queer snuffling grunts** through his nose, like some dog sniffing round a rabbit hole.'

The main focus in the outside world is the capture of the pheasants. Danny and his father enter the woods, avoid the keepers and drug the birds. They are the property of Mr Hazell, as is most of the land round about. Where Danny and his father lived 'was a little island in the middle of the vast ocean of Mr Hazell's estate' (p. 41). The two most frequent lexical items to collocate with *Mr Victor Hazell* are *woods* and *pheasants* which are presented in possessive relational clauses.

Mr Hazell's personality and lifestyle are the antithesis of everything Danny's father believes in. In interaction he *bellows*, *screams*, *shouts and yells*. It is because Mr Hazell is Mr Hazell as much as anything else that Danny's father decides to poach the pheasants; and Danny, once he recovers from the initial shock of discovering that his father is a law-breaker, is pleased to help him.

In the social hierarchy Mr Hazell is not even an aristocrat. He is *nouveau riche*, the essence of vulgarity:

He was *a brewer of beer* and he owned *a huge brewery*. He was *rich beyond words*. . . . Mr. Victor Hazell was *a roaring snob* and he tried desperately to get in with what he believed were the right kind of people. . . . As he flashed by we would sometimes catch a glimpse of **the great glistening beery face** above the wheel, **pink as a ham**, all **soft and inflamed** from drinking too much beer.

(p. 42)

The four italicised nominal groups represent the Attributes in the four Relational processes in which they are entities. Thus, *he* (*Mr. Hazell*) is *identified* for us. There is also an evaluation here. Not only does he own a brewery but it is a *huge* brewery and the inference can be made that this is a man of wealth and power. Such an inference is confirmed by the characterising function of the Attribute *rich beyond words*. Again note the evaluation carried by the nominal group. Finally, we are told that not only is he very rich but that *Mr. Victor Hazell* (Carrier) *is* (Relational process) *a roaring snob* (Attribute). The evaluation carried in the descriptive focus has, if you like, reached a climax.

After these relational processes we are informed that he *tried* desperately *to get in with* what he believed were *the right sort of people*. To do this '**He hunted with hounds** and **gave shooting parties** and **wore fancy waistcoats**' (p. 41). Thus, we can infer that *the right sort of people* are characterised by *hunting*, *shooting* and *fancy waistcoats*. These are the people he invites to shoot his pheasants.

Lexically the focus on Hazell is two-fold. Firstly, there is a focus of progression. He is named, identified and evaluated; *Hazell/Brewer/ Rich/Snob*. Second, Mr Hazell becomes subsumed within the item *face*. In fact he becomes *the face*:

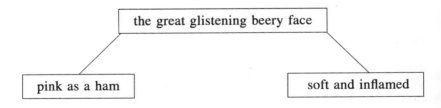

It is almost as if *the face* is ascribed agency and is also the affected participant.

We see this technique of descriptive focus employed again when Mr Hazell comes to reclaim his pheasants as they wake up from the effects of the sleeping tablets:

Behind the wheel I could see **the enormous pink beery face** of
Mr Victor Hazell staring at the pheasants. I could see **the mouth
hanging open, the eyes bulging out of his head** like toadstools
and **the skin of his face** turning from **pink to bright scarlet**.

(p. 154)

The picture is as unattractive as in the first encounter and we note that
the Senser in the Mental process of perception (*staring*) is not Mr
Hazell but his face. He is presented to the reader as:

the enormous pink beery face

the **mouth** hanging open   the **eyes** bulging out

The repetition of the colour terms adds to the dramatic effect of the
description. Overall, there is a sharp contrast with the description of
Danny's father on page 127 above.

The descriptive focus, particularly of size, shape and colour, of the
main characters is typically Dahl. He is an authorial voice which is:

a voice often heard in children's books of the kind deliberately
written for them. It is the voice of speech rather than of interior
monologue or no-holds-barred private confession. It is, in fact, the
tone of a friendly adult story-teller who knows how to entertain
children while at the same time keeping them in their place.

(Chambers, 1980: 256)

MATILDA

In this narrative the characterisation of Matilda's family acquaints the
reader with some of the most thoroughly unpleasant personalities in
children's fiction. Physical descriptions early on in the book are
particularly evaluative, carrying strong negative connotation:

Mr. Wormwood was **a small ratty-looking man** whose **front
teeth stuck out** underneath **a thin ratty moustache**. He liked to
wear jackets with **large brightly-coloured checks** and he wore
ties that were usually **yellow** or **pale green**.

(p. 23)

No positive use of meronymy here but rather significant lexical choices (note the repetition of the rat metaphor) to represent a physically unattractive male in a socially unattractive occupation, the second-hand car salesman. Such a person could only be married to:

> **a large woman** whose hair was dyed **platinum blond** except where you could see **the mousy-brown bits** growing out from the roots. She wore **heavy make-up** and she had one of those **unfortunate bulging figures** where **the flesh appears to be strapped in** all around the body **to prevent it falling out**.
>
> (p. 27)

The fact that there is a strong element of caricature serves only to heighten our perceptions of Mr and Mrs Wormwood – note the naming. Dahl, in fact, could stand accused of perpetuating stereotypes. Do his readers recognise any attributes of real-life people and if so how are they evaluated in the social hierarchy of the child's real-world experience? But Dahl is also exercising his ability to entertain children by showing how the child can retaliate by plotting revenge which humiliates her oppressors, her parents, yet leaving them unaware that Matilda is the cause of their misfortune. Philistinism – Mr Wormwood hates books and destroys them – and physical dominance cannot be defeated but life can be made more tolerable. There is a particular relish in the fact that Mr Wormwood comes to be suspicious of Matilda but is unable to articulate a reason for his suspicions.

Family is also represented negatively in the person of Miss Trunchbull the headteacher of Matilda's school. She is the aunt who brought up Miss Honey, Matilda's favourite teacher, who is the representative of the institution of friendship in the book. Miss Trunchbull is physically repulsive and a cruel woman who, it is hinted, is capable of murder.

Matilda at home

One of the most interesting linguistic features of *Matilda* is the syntactic representation of her father. We noted above the extremely high collocational relationship between *my* and *father* in *Danny the Champion of the World*. In *Matilda* the most frequent collocate to the left of *father* is the determiner *the* (63 occurrences) and to the right *said* (34 occurrences). This gives the pattern: *the father said* occurring 34 times in the text. All 63 occurrences of the structure *the father* refer to Matilda's father and the avoidance of the possessive determiner has the effect of removing any hint of affection or familial solidarity.

The pattern *the father said* permits the representation of the father as a cheat, liar and bully. This is highlighted by constant repetition of the pairing of *the father* notably in the early chapters of the book. Note the following example:

> 'I'm telling you trade secrets,' **the father said**, 'So don't you go talking about this to anyone else, You don't want me put in jug do you?'
>
> 'I won't tell a soul,' the boy said. 'Do you do this to many cars, dad?'
>
> 'Every single car that comes through my hands gets the treatment,' **the father said**. They all have their mileage cut to under ten thou before they're offered for sale. And to think I invented that all by myself,' **he added proudly**. 'It's made me a mint.'
>
> Matilda, who had been listening closely, said, 'But daddy, that's even more dishonest than the sawdust. It's disgusting. You're cheating people who trust you.'
>
> 'If you don't like it then don't eat the food in this house,' **the father said**. 'It's bought with the profits.'
>
> 'It's dirty money,' Matilda said. 'I hate it.'
>
> Two red spots appeared on **the father's cheeks**. 'Who do you think you are?' **he shouted**.

(p. 25)

From the extract we can infer *the father* is first boasting, confirmed with *he added proudly*, and second becoming irritated before becoming very angry, which is realised in the replacement of *the father said* by *he shouted*. The use of this device allows Matilda's father to be focalised and reinforces the distance that exists between father and daughter. The extract also focuses upon Matilda as the agent of disruption in her father's world. Her intervention in the discourse follows a Mental process of perception, she has been *listening closely*. The subsequent use of direct speech then causes her father's emotional state to change.

In *Danny the Champion of the World* the *my father said* structure is in sharp contrast. Danny's father's acts of communication involve declarations of affection, statements of information and questions which signify a genuine concern to be the Recipient of Danny's Verbiage. Danny's father *asks, tells, calls, whispers*. Matilda's father not only *says*, where *say* carries other connotations such as boasting, but he *shouts, yells* and *snaps*. These patterns of discourse as exemplified in the verbs listed above are reinforced by forms of address.

The narrative of the first text is, of course, in the first person. Nevertheless, *Danny* is used as a form of address 89 times out of a total of 101 occurrences and we would maintain this is a significant statistic in the structure of the narrative. In *Matilda* the father never uses his daughter's name to address her. This is in sharp contrast to Matilda's frequent use of *daddy* to address her father, a term with strong connotations of familial affection. There is a particular irony in this form of address as Matilda often uses it to criticise her father either overtly, as in the extract cited above, or to goad him when she begins to exact her revenge. The first instance of this is when she superglues his hat:

> 'What's the matter, **daddy**?' she said. 'Has your head suddenly swollen or something?'
>
> **The father *glared at*** his daughter with deep suspicion, but said nothing.
>
> He turned and *looked* again *at* Matilda who *looked back* at him with large innocent brown eyes.
>
> (p. 33)

Daddy and *the father* are significant lexical items in their conveyance to the reader of the power relations that exist between Matilda and Mr Wormwood. Note also the Mental processes of perception which generate a non-verbal exchange: *glared* (*at*), *looked* (*at*), *looked* (*back*) and which deliver a very powerful representation of the relationship between these two without a word being uttered.

Although Matilda often overtly expresses her opinions she knows that 'she was still hardly five years old and it is not easy for somebody as small as that to score points against an all-powerful grown-up' (p. 29). Her status in the family is often reinforced by the particularly unpleasant manner in which she is spoken to by both parents in the imperative, as in the examples cited below:

> 'Quite right, Harry,' **the mother said**. And to Matilda she said, 'You've got a nerve talking to your father like that. Now keep your **nasty mouth shut** so we can all watch this programme in peace.'
>
> (p. 26)
>
> 'Be quiet!' **the father snapped**. 'Just keep your **nasty mouth shut**, will you!'
>
> (p. 37)

It is only when Matilda starts school that her life takes on a new dimension. Commencing school is commencing 'the journey' of this narrative.

Matilda at school

Much of this book, unlike *Danny the Champion of the World*, is centred upon school. School represents 'the journey' in this story and the adventures attendant upon it. We mean this both figuratively, in the sense that this is the first step in a new life for Matilda, and in a literal sense. Before she can enjoy fully the new life Matilda has to overcome the vicious headteacher who would frustrate her progress up the school. School is where she meets the companion/friend of the journey in the person of Miss Honey, the companion/friend who is to become the new family, the surrogate parent. As in *Danny*, there will be one child and one parent.

The headteacher is a character of extremes both in her physical appearance and in her behaviour. She is vicious, treating the children with great cruelty. The behaviour strays into the realms of the fantastic and this is probably why it is so popular with young readers. Enough of Miss Trunchbull's behaviour, however, is rooted in the probable rather than the fantastic as to be recognisable. Dahl's savage lampooning of her is similar to his treatment of Captain Lancaster in *Danny*.

When we first meet Miss Trunchbull she is described as having about her *an aura of menace* and in the first of his animal metaphors Dahl sees her as not unlike *an enaged rhinoceros*. He also includes a military metaphor:

> When she **marched** – Miss Trunchbull never walked, she always **marched like a stormtrooper** with **long strides and arms aswinging** – when she **marched** along a corridor you could actually hear her **snorting** as she went, and if a group of children happened to be in her path, she **ploughed right on through them like a tank**, with small people **bouncing off her** to left and right.
>
> (p. 67)

The physical description of Miss Trunchbull as well as being lexically rich is also a good example of Dahl's ability to engage with his child reader directly where the narrative 'has much in common with the tone a particular kind of oral story-teller' (Wall, 1991: 18):

> She had once been a famous athlete, and even now the muscles were still clearly in evidence. You could see them in **the bull neck**, in **the big shoulders**, in **the thick arms**, in **the sinewy wrists** and in **the powerful legs**. Her face, I'm afraid, was neither a thing of

beauty nor a joy forever. She had **an obstinate chin, a cruel mouth**, and **small arrogant eyes**.

(p. 83)

In engaging with his reader Dahl leaves us in no doubt as to how he and they, it is implied, view this symbol of dominance, the head-teacher. Note the parallelism of the highlighted nominal groups. It is not difficult to conceive of this description as oral narrative with the narrator adopting suitable intonation patterns. We can represent Miss Trunchbull diagrammatically in terms of inclusive lexical relations:

Miss Trunchbull

Body	*Face*
bull neck	obstinate chin
big shoulders	cruel mouth
thick arms	small arrogant eyes
sinewy wrists	
powerful legs	

The modifiers in each pair of groups fall into three naturally occurring, but not mutually exclusive, lexical sets:

SIZE:	bull, big, small
STRENGTH:	thick, sinewy, powerful
PERSONALITY:	obstinate, cruel, arrogant

These items, with their collocating headwords, provide a vivid focalisation of this character which is centred on two animal metaphors: the stated *bull-like* and the inferred predator of *small arrogant eyes*. We noted how Dahl used the rat metaphor as a focus of distaste in the reader's introduction to Matilda's father cited above. He repeats this 69 pages later when Miss Honey goes to visit the Wormwoods: 'The door was opened by **a small ratty-looking man** with **a thin ratty moustache**' (p. 92). In a child's world power rests with parents and teachers and Dahl is helping them to get their own back for the small injustices every child experiences. For most children their reality will not be Miss Trunchbull and the Wormwoods but they will enjoy the images created by this author recognising, however slightly, something of the real world.

One final point: while the list displayed above sums up lexically the physical description of Miss Trunchbull we can infer much about her character from the metaphorical nature of the three nominal groups employed to describe her face (see the right-hand column of the list).

We see meronymy employed here for negative evaluation as we saw it used earlier for positive. The *chin, mouth, eyes* are part of the *face* which is part of *Miss Trunchbull*, who is *obstinate, cruel* and *arrogant*.

The animal imagery Dahl employs is sustained in the transitivity patterns associated with Miss Trunchbull. We list below the most frequent processes collocating with *Trunchbull* in the corpus: *said, shout, cry **bark**, look, **bellowed**, **roared**, yelled, asked, boomed, **snorted**, started, **screamed**, **snapped**, marched.* Note how the items in bold print fall into a natural set which extends the metaphor initiated by the naming device *Trunchbull* which is firmly established in the reader's mind through the effects of the descriptive focus discussed above. Thus, Miss Trunchbull as Sayer often communicates the Verbiage by *barking, bellowing, roaring, snorting, screaming* and *snapping.* The items *bellow, roar* and *snort* would not be untypical collocates of the item *bull,* and *bark* and *snap* are apposite in conjunction with the image connoted by *small arrogant eyes.* Furthermore, Miss Trunchbull is the Agent of processes 199 times and for 131 of these she is referred to as *the Trunchbull*.

Matilda and Miss Honey

In contrast to Miss Trunchbull, Miss Honey is presented to the reader in a series of matching relations when read in conjunction with the Trunchbull description above:

> She had **a lovely pale oval madonna face** with **blue eyes** and her **hair** was **light brown**. Her **body** was so **slim and fragile** . . . like a **porcelain figure**. Miss Jennifer **Honey** was **a mild and quiet person** who never raised her voice and was seldom seen to smile, but there is no doubt she possessed that rare gift for being **adored** by every small child under her care. She seemed to understand totally the bewilderment that so often overwhelms young children.

(p. 67)

We list here the physical and abstract description of Miss Honey:

	Miss Honey	
Personality	*Body*	*Face*
mild	slim	lovely
quiet	fragile	pale
adored	porcelain	oval
		madonna

In addition we are told she has **blue eyes** and **light-brown hair**, both positive attributes which further enhance the description of this character.

As Agent Miss Honey *asks*, *cries*, *looks*, *pauses*, *thinks* and *hears* as well as *says*. Miss Honey as Sayer engages in communication with her pupils but particularly with Matilda. Matilda also is a highly interactive character, with *ask* being the second most frequent lexical item (36 occurrences) to collocate with *Matilda* as node. This is important because 'a verb of speaking such as *ask* involves both a mental event and the physical act of utterance' (Leech and Short, 1981: 181). Most of these occurrences are when Matilda is talking to Miss Honey.

There are more processes attached to Miss Honey than any other character. Of the characters who appear, *Miss Honey* as a lexical item is the second most frequent (390 occurrences) after Matilda (414) occurrences. She is the only character, apart from Matilda, to be the Agent of other than Verbal processes, that is apart from Miss Trunchbull's *marching*. Thus we have Miss Honey represented as a participant in Mental processes as illustrated below:

Miss Honey	looked at	the tiny girl
{Senser}	{Mental process}	{Phenomenon}
Miss Honey	marvelled at	the child's lack of conceit
{Senser}	{Mental process}	{Phenomenon}
What a nice child she is,	Miss Honey	thought
{Phenomenon}	{Senser}	{Mental process}

These Mental processes allow the reader to see how the child becomes very much an important part of the teacher's world and her perceptions of that world. Matilda is *thought about*, *listened to*, *looked at*. She has become a focus rather than someone to be ignored or shouted at because she has intellectual gifts which threaten the dominance of the worlds of family and school as they are structured under the Wormwoods and Miss Trunchbull. The Verbal processes reinforce this. Matilda *asks* lots of questions of Miss Honey and they are *answered*. Miss Honey *asks* questions of Matilda and she also *pauses* in conversations, allowing time for more thought before she continues or for Matilda to contribute.

The *thought* clauses also contain significant lexical items. Physically Matilda is *tiny* and in terms of personality she is *nice*, she *lacks conceit*. Her vulnerability is emphasised with the item *tiny*. Although we know she is intellectually very strong we are constantly reminded by Dahl that Matilda is under threat. There are 36 occurrences of the item *girl* in the book. The three most frequent lexical collocates are *little* (7 occurrences), *tiny* (5 occurrences) and *small* (5 occurrences). They are third, fifth and sixth most frequent collocates overall. Of the 36 occurrences of *girl* 11 are references to Matilda and in each instance the headword is modified by at least one of the items in the set *tiny, small, little*. In sum, of the total 17 occurrences of the items in the set 13 are used to describe Matilda and this includes all the instances of *tiny*. The remaining 4 non-referents of Matilda all occupy a place in nominal group structure as in *a small girl/a little girl*.

The concept of size is very important in the narrative. The gross representation of Miss Trunchbull and her acts of physical violence upon the children underlines this. Matilda's father is physically small but his utterances are declamatory; he makes a lot of noise. Miss Honey, by contrast is *slim* and *fragile*. When she is a Sayer the process *said* is often presented as in 'Miss Honey said gently' or, particularly as their relationship develops, 'Miss Honey said smiling'. It is with Miss Honey that Matilda's future lies. The companion who becomes family and who represents the new school after the departure of the Wormwoods and Miss Trunchbull.

THE TEEN NOVEL

In this section we wish, briefly, to consider a dimension in literature for young readers that is very much a twentieth-century phenomenon, that is, a sub-genre written especially for the adolescent reader. We noted in chapter 1 how the 1970s saw a recognition by authors and publishers that there was a gap in the market where there were readers too old for children's stories and not yet ready for 'adult' literature, a gap ripe for exploitation. American writers were in the forefront in this new wave of 'realistic' writing and they included Judy Blume (with the first explicit description of a heterosexual encounter), Betsy Byars, Robert Cormier, S.E. Hinton and Paul Zindel.

The genre appealed to many English teachers, and writers like Zindel, for example, became set texts for some CSE examining boards. Throughout the 1970s and 1980s British publishers began to produce their own imprints for this readership and British writers began to join their American counterparts in a range of popular series. This range also reflected quality in terms ot literary merit. As well as books by writers such as Jane Gardam, Robert Leeson and Jill Paton-Walsh, to name but three, there were hundreds of titles aimed at teenage girls and a plethora of romance stories which are predictable in their structure, being written almost to a formula. Many of the books, however, tried to present 'real' issues important in the lives of teenagers. Thus, subjects previously regarded as taboo became the focus for writers. Sex, death, family tensions, social class, teenage violence and race relations were and are common themes.

The family: a new reality

The central characters of these books provide the key to the sub-genre. One of the most popular British authors is K.M. Peyton (1929–) probably best known for being creator of the Flambards series, the second volume of which earned her the Carnegie medal in 1970. Her Pennington series, however, is most representative of popular teenage fiction albeit often stereotypical in the depiction of character. The series plots the career of a teenage boy, Patrick Pennington, and *Seventeenth Summer*; (1970; page references are to the 1994 edition) the first, featured in Knowles's 1989–90 survey.

Pennington is the only son of an emotional mother and a father prone to violence. The representation of the institution of family is very different from that of traditional juvenile fiction. The following extract occurs as Pennington returns home on his father's motorbike, which he has borrowed without permission:

> His father had heard the bike, and came in from the television, his face distorted with his wild temper. His wife came with him, saying frantically, 'Leave him alone, Bill, for God's sake!'
> 'I'll leave him alone when I've finished with him – it won't take long!'
> Penn put his arms up over his face and half turned, hunching a shoulder, ducking his head. . . . Ducking neatly sideways to avoid one of his father's wilder blows, he came up sharply against the hard metal of the tin-opener fixed to the wall and nearly knocked himself out. As he went down he saw his mother pick up a frying pan and swing it like a golf club. . . . His father kicked him twice, before his mother went at him again, and Penn heard their voices, rising and falling in torrents of blame and hate while they grappled.
>
> (pp. 148–9)

And four pages further on:

> His father, having repaired to the pub for refreshment after beating up his family, learned about the theft of the motorbike from the top

of Fiddler's Creek. He went home and woke Penn up, threatening him drunkenly and loudly.

(p. 153)

The patterns of lexis and transitivity in the extracts above present a very different image from that discussed in the previous chapter. There we saw how the family was the institution presented to the young reader as the bastion of Christian values, where from *fathers/ brothers/teachers* can be learned *strength/courage/wisdom* and from *mothers/sisters/wives* can be learned *love/tenderness/purity*. For the young hero of *Seventeenth Summer* the lexical representation of mother and father is contained in sets which are potently attitudinal in their depiction of physical aggression. There are three participants in a range of processes which can be subsumed within categories we can label *defensive* and *offensive*. The mother being an agent of both defence and assault.

The father *hears*, *comes* and *attacks*. The actual physical attack is first inferred through the description of the father: '**his face distorted** with **his wild temper**'. Then we are presented with the mother's direct speech 'Leave him alone, Bill, for God's sake!' The Circumstance *frantically* in the primary projecting clause allows the writer to present to the reader the state of mind of the Sayer and thus almost convert the process of saying into one of doing, of, in this instance, defending. This gives more status to the projecting clause than had it been simply *she said*.

The third inference is the father's direct speech. There is no projecting clause. The father's words leave, however, no doubt in the reader's mind that violence is about to ensue. It does, and we have Pennington presented to us as the Agent of several processes that involve him *putting up*, *half-turning*, *hunching*, *ducking*. The Affected are parts of the boy's body: *arms*, *face*, *shoulder*, *head*.

Overall, we have a pattern of transitivity which allows the representation of the participants as follows:

1 **Father**	threatening to attack son	**sensing/doing**
2 **Mother**	attempting to defend son	**doing/saying**
3 **Father**	attacking son	**saying**
4 **Son**	defending himself	**doing**
5 **Mother**	attacking father	**doing**
6 **Father**	attacking son	**doing**
7 **Mother**	attacking father	**doing**
8 **Mother and father**	attacking each other	**saying/doing**
9 **Father**	attacking son	**doing/saying**

These patterns provide lexical sets for both the *offensive* and *defensive* superordinates, which provide a series of matching relationships when compared and contrasted with the idealised representation of the Victorian family in juvenile fiction. The items allow a descriptive focus which, although it might be in some respects stereotypical, is vivid in its depiction of the institution of family and a particular and not altogether unrealistic set of relationships that can exist within it:

Offensive	*Defensive*
distorted face	saying frantically
wild temper	put up (arms)
wilder blows	half-turn
pick up	hunching (shoulder)
swing	ducking (head)
wilder blows	avoid
kicked	ducking sideways
went at	
voices (rising/falling)	
torrents	
blame	
hate	
grapple	
beat up	
woke up	
threatening	
loudly	
drunkenly	

The items come from all word classes and we see that there are far more associated with attack than there are with defence. Furthermore, all the attack items collocate with adult participants and in trying to avoid his father's assault Pennington knocks himself out.

Thus, in this representation of the family there is violence and drunkenness and there are parents whose interaction often involves 'torrents of blame and hate'. Yet there is also presented a moral code. Pennington's father lies to the police on his behalf, causing the boy to ponder albeit somewhat ironically, 'Thank God, he thought, for a father you can trust' (p. 150).

Reality and violence

The violence of the description above reflects succinctly the 'reality' of this sub-genre of fiction for young readers. The violence does not always have to be physical: it may be verbal. Again there is a stark contrast with the world of the nineteenth century where violence was distanced, either being committed by 'savages' who were themselves violent and were thus being justly punished or between schoolboys indulging in the 'English way of doing things'. Violence in the family was taboo and the type of exchange recorded below would not feature easily in the works of Ballantyne or Kingston. This is an exchange between a father (Maurice) and son (Nick) where the mother has left home. Broken homes are often a definitive feature of the family in the teen novel:

> 'I'm not having this staying-in-bed business,' said Maurice. He stepped forward and snatched the bedclothes off. Naked, Nick grabbed at his coverings and yelled, 'Fuck off!'
>
> (Prince, 1986: 109)

The depiction of this relationship is bleak and the father, a drunk, is eventually killed off. One of the features, of course, of the discourse of realism is contained in the above extract and that is the use of language previously regarded as taboo. In this particular instance it serves to emphasise just how stark is the relationship between father and son.

Violence is not just verbal, nor is it the prerogative of family members. In Robert Cormier's (1925–) *The Chocolate War* (1974; page references are to the 1992 edition) we have a narrative in which domination through brute force or, more accurately, the powerlessness of the hero is the central focus. In this novel virtue is not its own reward, for good does not triumph over evil. Indeed, for some critics the book epitomises what has been called a 'didactic negativity' (see Abrahamson, 1983: 319–23).

The Chocolate War is a tale of hopelessness. It concerns Jerry Renault, the hero, a pupil at a private, though by no means exclusive, Catholic high school. The acting head, Brother Leon, plans to raise funds by having the boys sell 20,000 boxes of chocolates. At first Jerry is a figure of admiration for his peers as he refuses to participate. Brother Leon, however, obtains the support of the school secret society, the Vigils, led by Archie Costello. Thus, we have an alliance between the legal authorities and a group of young gangsters; a powerful force in terms of domination. Jerry ceases to be a hero, becoming 'an outcast ripe for destruction' (Carpenter and Prichard, 1984: 116).

The book opens and concludes with violence. In the first chapter Jerry is trying for a place on the school football team and is being subjected to intense physical aggression to test him. Following the football practice:

> [1] He managed to make it back to the school. [2] By the time he had sprawled himself on the floor of the lavatory, his head hanging over the lip of the toilet bowl and the smell of disinfectant stinging his eyeballs, the nausea had passed and the bleep of pain had faded. [3] Sweat moved like small moist bugs on his forehead. [4] And then without warning, he vomited.
>
> (Cormier, 1974: 12)

The extract charts a progression of loss of control which exemplifies well the theme of powerlessness, and thus hopelessness, in this book. Time is very important in the narration of this progression. It is almost like watching a series of slow-motion sequences which are contained within the numbered clause complexes. In sentence 1 *managed to make it* shows that agency is still in the control of the grammatical subject, the hero of the story, but only just. He is weak and the implication is that it has taken Jerry some considerable time to get back to the school. Clause complex 2 reinforces Cormier's message of control slipping by the thematization of *by the time*. This clause complex then proceeds to locate Jerry specifically within the school and in so doing removes his control for his own actions even more. If we return to our cinematic analogy we can visualise him in sequence (a) half-staggering half-crawling back to the school. In sequence (b) we see him *sprawling* (Material process) *himself* (Affected) slowly it is inferred on the floor of the *lavatory* (Circumstance).

In the clause cited above, the Circumstance provides us with the precise location of the hero. The humiliation of his position is further emphasised by the descriptive focus of all that is entailed by the process of *sprawling*. Not only is he on the floor of the lavatory but we are told he is *sprawled* with *his head hanging over the lip of the toilet bowl and the smell of disinfectant stinging his eyeballs*. Control has left him and even though the nausea and pain have subsided (3) summarises the powerlessness, the loss of control, which presents Jerry as a victim early in the book but which is a strong indicator that to be a victim is to be his fate. The animal imagery of sentence 3 combines with the transitivity pattern to powerfully present the reader with this picture of victim:

Sweat	moved	like small moist bugs
{Agent}	{Material process}	{Circumstance}
on his forehead		
{Circumstance}		

And finally, the seemingly long drawn-out sequence of Jerry's helplessness is suddenly compounded with the last clause: slow-motion ceases. Time again features in Theme position and the focus in the clause is not only temporal but violent: *then, without warning* (and Jerry becomes Agent again but hardly of a process that he controls), *he vomited*.

Two hundred and sixty-five pages further on the narrative reaches the final episode of savagery. There is no preferred outcome here, corruption and brutality have won. Our final glimpse of Jerry is through the eyes of a friend who sees him collapse, having been horribly beaten:

[1] Goober watched helplessly as Jerry finally sank to the stage, bloody opened mouth, sucking for air, eyes unfocused, flesh swollen. [2] His body was poised for a moment like some wounded animal and then he collapsed like a hunk of meat cut loose from a butcher's hook.
   [3] And then the lights went out.

(p. 277)

If we return to our film metaphor Goober is symbolic of the cinema audience. As Senser he:

watched	Jerry	helplessly
{Mental process}	{Phenomenon}	{Circumstance}

In the Phenomenon we have the complete victory of the power system as represented in the alliance between the school authorities and the adolescent gangsters, the Vigils. The fact that Goober *watched helplessly* implies that he *felt* also hopeless and powerless and the intensity of the ensuing physical descriptive focus reinforces this.

Goober as audience, then, sees another slow-motion sequence. We can imagine the camera panning towards the stage as:

Jerry	finally	sank
{Agent}	{Circumstance}	{Material process}
to the floor		
{Circumstance}		

In the school lavatory extract above Jerry was also on the floor but this time *finally* is a powerful circumstantial signal. The message is that Jerry is finished, he has been defeated and not just physically. It is, however, the lexically dense physical description of clause complexes 1 and 2 and the dramatic suddeness of the final clause that allows us to infer this. Note how Cormier reduces Jerry to his constituent parts in the following nominal groups from clause complex 1:

bloody opened *mouth*
eyes unfocused
flesh swollen

Note also the landed fish imagery of *sucking for air*, which reinforces the notion of helplessness.

In clause complex 2 'the camera' has held on Jerry: *His body was poised* for a moment. The *mouth*, *eyes* and *flesh* are now *his body* which is the Identifier in a Relational process. The collocational relationship between *poised* and *for a moment* is very powerful in terms of our image of slow motion sequencing. The audience have a final close shot of this defeated boy before *he collapsed*. He is now well and truly down. *Poised*, he was *like some wounded animal*; down, he becomes like *a hunk of meat cut loose from a butcher's hook*. Finally, the sudden and dramatic closure (like the *he vomited* above) to Jerry's active involvement in the narrative: *And then the lights went out.*

There is no happiness in this book. Just before he collapses Jerry sees himself as having been reduced to the level of the young thugs of the Vigils. He has become 'another animal, another beast another violent person in a violent world, inflicting damage, not disturbing the universe but damaging it' (p. 276). For Fred Inglis, Cormier is dealing in the 'sentimentalities of disenchantment'. He comments after Jerry's final, brutal beating:

Hero–victim and reader are left with the pain, and the clichés of concussion. The crude lesson is threefold: that all institutions systematize violence; that violence upholds power without reason; that individuals cannot hope to change these facts.

(Inglis, 1981: 278)

Reality and sex

Of all the previously taboo subjects in children's fiction it was sex that became the central concern of much of the early writing for teenagers in the 1970s. It is still an important area for the producers of books dealing with the mid-teen or 'young adult' readership. Imprints for this readership such as Point, Teens and Tracks will usually have sexual relationships as part of the social and emotional realities that the author purports to be concerned with. The focus on these relationships will vary. In some sex is important but part of the dilemma of attaining adulthood rather than providing the whole concentration of the narrative. In *The Chocolate War*, for example, Cormier appears to present sex as part of the overall bleak scene occupied by his characters. Attaining adulthood for Cormier is a process of becoming part of a trapped and hopeless community unless, like Brother Leon, you have attained a particular and brutal power. Cormier's adults are, by and large, a rather pathetic lot. Even Brother Jacques, who epitomises decency, cannot combat the forces ranged against him.

Sexual references in *The Chocolate War* have a depressing if not sordid resonance. Early in the narrative, as he is struggling back to the school after the football practice, as cited above, he thinks, briefly, of his dead mother. The thought is fleeting:

[1] He thought of his mother and how drugged she was at the end, not recognizing anyone, neither Jerry nor his father. [2] The exhilaration of the moment vanished and he sought it in vain, like ecstasy's memory an instant after jacking off and encountering only shame and guilt.

[3] Nausea began to spread through his stomach warm and oozy and evil.

(Cormier, 1974/1992: 11–12)

In clause complex 1 we have Jerry as Senser of a Mental process. The Phenomenon concerns his mother's dying and focuses on her physical and mental powerlessness being subject to the domination of both medication and disease. The fronting of *the exhilaration of the moment*, referring to his reminiscence of his mother, in clause complex 2 is highly significant as it is relexicalised as *ecstasy's memory*, which projects the reader forward to the masturbation metaphor and would appear to place both Mental processes on an equal footing. Lexis plays an important role here in representing the young hero's mental confusion. *Exhilaration* and *ecstasy*, on the one hand, *shame* and *guilt*, on the other. His mental state is matched in the final clause complex by the physical. *Nausea* assumes the role of an animate Agent and *spreads* (Material process) *through his stomach* (Affected). The lexical set *warm, oozy, evil* provides a further metaphor to highlight the descriptive focus of Jerry's wretchedness and lead the reader into the lavatory scene described earlier.

Other references to sex do nothing to dispel the starkness of this novel. In one a rather physically unattractive boy called Tubs is desperately trying to sell the chocolates so as to be able to buy a bracelet for Rita, a girl who, when she walks beside him, has 'her breast brushing his arm, setting him on fire'. 'Him – Tubs Casper, forty pounds overweight which his father never let him forget. Him – with this beautiful girl's breast pushed against him'. The girl is 'beautiful in **a ripe wild way, faded blue jeans hugging her hips, those beautiful breasts bouncing under her jersey**'. As far as Tubs is concerned he loves Rita and the bracelet is all important because 'Rita loved him – tomorrow she'd probably let him get **under her sweater**' (pp. 104–5).

Rita, the implication is, is exploiting Tubs and there is something stereotypical in the language used to convey this relationship. There is a concentration on *brushing against, rubbing against, pushing against* either by the girl herself or her breast, which is ascribed agency. The stereotype is continued in the description of her body and the agency ascribed to the jeans and again to her breasts. While Cormier certainly captures the frustration of male adolescence there is, none the less, a reductiveness in his references to sex in general and to females in particular. In a sense sex is another power system which can only oppress and exploit because it is corrupt.

Not all 'teen novels' represent budding sexual relations in such a comfortless manner. K.M. Peyton's Pennington, referred to above in *Seventeenth Summer*, despite his dismal home life and a bullying schoolmaster, develops a relationship with a girl which is not viewed as part of a repressive social order. In *It's My Life* (1980) Robert Leeson presents a sensitive and sympathetic portayal of a teenage girl who believes she is pregnant. The girl, whose mother has left the family, has every reason to feel part of a world as bleak as that of Cormier and, at times, it is. Nevertheless the book concludes on a hopeful rather than a negative key. It is Judy Blume (1938–), however, who provided the 'pioneering' work in the depiction of teenage sexual discovery.

Sex and Judy Blume

Judy Blume has written a number of works of fiction which concern themselves with 'realism' and the types of problems which can face adolescents: the onset of puberty, physical handicap, divorcing parents, obesity and sexual relationships. *Forever* (1975; pages references are to the 1986 edition) set out to explore, for a teenage readership, the latter area. Although it was not written for adults it was first published as an adult title 'presumably because of the semi-explicit but decidely soft-core sex scenes' (Abrahamson, 1983: 319).

Blume's heroines are almost always, unlike Leeson's, from prosperous middle-class backgrounds. *Forever* charts the love affair between two adolescents, Katherine and Michael, who have just graduated from high school, and the nature of their sexual progression. It is a book still decidely popular amongst girl readers. Out of 60 second-year women undergraduate students interviewed in 1991–2 57 said that they had read the book between the ages of thirteen and fifteen and over 40 said that they had read it without their parents' knowledge. While this is only a small sample it does indicate a continuing popularity throughout the last twenty years.

While Blume's sex scenes are described in detail it is of interest to note that words formerly taboo in children's literature are used sparingly. A manual search yielded only 3 occurrences of *fuck*, 1 of *screw* and 8 occurrences of *laid*. It is not so much the use of taboo language that marks Blume's style as a writer but her use of language as she addresses her implied reader. As Wall (1991: 248) puts it in commenting on this aspect of narrative technique in adolescent fiction: 'The most common stance is . . . where the child voice directly addresses a child audience in something approaching a child's idiom' or, to put it another way, a 'simulated peer relationship' (Kirkpatrick, 1978: 888). The technique, therefore, adopted by Blume is that of first-person narrative which is, no doubt, because it is assumed this will sustain the realism and make it readable. John Stephens (1992: 252) makes the point that a very restricted discourse in terms of lexis, register and syntax is then produced. Indeed, commenting upon another of Blume's works, *Are You There God? It's Me, Margaret* (1970), he emphasises the point by saying:

Sentence structures here are simple and rather repetitive, and with little attempt to construct sentences without an overt, pronominal narratorial presence (as 'I', 'we', 'me' or 'my'). This sets the norm for a text which tells all, uses no focalizing strategies, and swamps the readers subjectivity, leaving nothing for it to do.

Certainly, *Forever* is complex neither in character nor situation, but neither is the progression towards full sexual relationships sensationalised although the opening sentence, 'Sybil Davison has a genius I.Q. and has been laid by at least six different guys' (Blume, 1986: 5) might lead one to think otherwise. The narrative, however, concerns two well-adjusted protagonists in Katherine and Michael. Much of the book reads so factually as to be clinical in style, and from the point of view of entertaining narrative it is actually rather boring – a point made by a number of our undergraduate informants. Katherine does all the sensible things: she reads the pamphlets on birth control, abortion and venereal disease sent to her by her grandmother; she discusses issues with her mother; and she visits a birth control clinic. What is apparent is that from the beginning Katherine is represented as a character who, when she loses her virginity, wants ' *it to be special*' in contrast to her friend Erica: '*"You're a romantic," Erica said, "You always have been. I'm a realist. . . . We look at sex differently. . . . I see it as a physical thing and you see it as a way of expressing love"*' (p. 26). The two lexical sets below provide a neat summary of the competing value systems inherent in the adolescent world according to Blume:

Erica	*Katherine*
Physical	Romantic
Realist	Expressing love

These value systems provide Blume with a framework for instructing her reader, which she does throughout.

Blume's main contribution to the genre is that books like *Forever* play an informative role. She seems to want to provide something more entertaining than a standard pamphlet on birth control or sexual intercourse. Katherine, for example, compares for her addressee her actual experience of male genitalia with what she has read about in books. She informs us: 'Ralph [Michael's penis] felt like ordinary skin' (p. 60). There are around 23 occurrences of the lexical item *Ralph* in the book and while this is not a high degree of frequency the item is highly significant as it marks the progression of the narrative and thus Katherine's developing sexual experience. Eventually she takes the initiative in their physical relationship and is represented as being able to direct it for her own pleasure as well as for Michael's. The emphasis of the novel is supposed to be on real experience rather than actual abstract description. The entertainment value of the book is restricted and information from our student respondents cited above would indicate curiosity as the motive for reading. The fact, of course, that the book is informative gives it an ideological orientation of social responsibility. Great literature *Forever* is not, but at least, as Patricia Craig (1978: 137) informs us, 'Judy Blume is out to repudiate the false connotations of for ever: as an absolute concept it is meaningless.'

CONCLUSIONS

In this chapter we have considered a sample of the great variety of texts available to young readers in the latter part of the twentieth century. In Nina Bawden we have a writer who exemplifies what many commentators have called the 'Second Golden Age' of writing for children (see chapter 1). In *Carrie's War*

> There is a portrait of a whole community of people, their oddities and their feuds, seen through the bemused and only half understanding eyes of childhood.
>
> (Paton-Walsh, 1978a: 95)

We saw how important was the representation of Carrie as Senser in her attempts to comprehend this community. How Mental processes were central in the reader's identification with and understanding of Carrie's psychological make-up. We have now what we called 'credibility of character' integral to this stream of children's literature. Through Carrie's eyes we are made aware of real people rather than sets of uniform characteristics. We share with Carrie, through her impressions of the world about her, 'the reality of what most threatens our children – that they will lose those they most love, uncomprehendingly destroy what they most cherish' (Inglis, 1981: 269).

In Roald Dahl we have, arguably, the most popular children's writer of the last thirty years. All of Dahl's narratives contain fantastic events in the central character's struggle against the odds. The elements of fantasy are present in both *Danny, the Champion of the World* and *Matilda*. Both these narratives, however, are concerned with the reality of domination. In Danny and his father's case it is the domination of greed as personified by Mr Hazell. But there is also the ideology of the idealised family and companion. Danny's father represents both. We noted lexical patterns playing an important role in this representation, notably in the opposition portrayed to the reader in the description of Danny's father as opposed to that of Mr Hazell or the violent schoolmaster Captain Lancaster. The characterisation is exaggerated but none the less it has a reality recognisable to the young reader mainly because Dahl 'speaks directly and overtly to his narratees' (Wall, 1991: 272).

In *Matilda* the element of fantasy is more focal than in *Danny*. Nevertheless, the particularly unpleasant family represents a recognisable reality. The domination of insensitive and, verbally at least, very aggressive parents presents a stark contrast to the idealised relationship that is Danny's and his father's. The physical domination of the gross over the physically weak is represented to us in the character of Miss Trunchbull. Even though highly caricatured, reality is there. Matilda does win through against her family and the bullying headteacher to meet her ideal friend and surrogate family, Miss Honey.

It is, perhaps, Dahl's powerful descriptive focus in his representation of the unpleasantness of the domination of adulthood that has caused him to be greeted with suspicion by many parents. For Inglis (1981: 236)

> Dahl has a vigorous feel for the raucous crude vengefulness of children: he catches and endorses this nicely. But . . . is stuck forever in the second and third stages – the legalistic, retributive stages – of Piaget's and Kohlberg's moral development.

Finally, we considered what is a new departure in the history of children's literature, the teen or young adult novel. At their best they attempt to represent the turbulent and complex emotions of adolescence in a realistic and compassionate manner. Often, in so doing they are concerned with adolescents in conflict with parents and the adult establishment. Sometimes this can mean violence being represented as a part of family life.

We noted that sometimes hopelessness is a dominant theme. This was particularly so in Cormier's *The Chocolate War*, where the narrative concludes with violence and corruption having conquered. Sex, formally taboo, is, of course, important in these narratives and not always as reductively portrayed as it is by Cormier. Judy Blume's *Forever* combines an instructional, almost moralistic voice – the girl who sleeps around, becomes pregnant and does not know who the father is – with its theme of first love.

The teen novel varies considerably. If it chooses it can be competitive with serious adult fiction in its seriousness of purpose and in effectiveness of techniques. It can also, as Bator (1983: 303) points out, be considered purely in terms of 'its extraliterary values' as a situation type written to a formula rather than a creative and sensitive presentation of issues in a manner that has both substance and technique. An awareness of linguistic description can greatly assist in differentiating.

5 The fairytale

THE FAIRYTALE AS GENRE

Fairytales are standardly considered a sub-genre of the folktale, itself a sub-genre of folklore, 'traditional verbal materials and social rituals that have been handed down solely, or at least primarily, by word of mouth and by example rather than in written form' (Abrams, 1957/1971: 63). The literary fairytale is perceived as based on, or at least as sharing certain features of the traditional fairytale, but since motifs and plots from every type of folktale may surface in the works of writers of all types of literature for children, it will be useful to establish some criteria for the identification of fairytales as such. Folklorists have a similar concern, and we base our effort at definition on the folktale typology of Katharine Mary Briggs (1898–1980). However, since we are dealing with the fairytale as a sub-genre of literature for children, rather than as a sub-genre of the folktale, we shall have to move on from Briggs' definition towards a definition which allows us, as hers does not, to distinguish the fairytale from the sub-genre of children's literature which arguably resembles it most closely, namely children's fantasy fiction.

Briggs (1970) distinguishes, first, between folk legends, once believed true, and folk narratives which have always been conceived as fiction, 'told for edification, delight or amusement' (1970: 1). Second, within the genre of folk narrative, Briggs perceives five groupings: (i) fables and exempla, 'those animal stories after the manner of Aesop that point a moral or satirize human frailties'; (ii) jocular tales, 'a great body of drolls, noodle stories, bawdy tales, and so on, that are handed about for entertainment'; (iii) novelle, 'narratives in which there is no explicitly supernatural element'; (iv) nursery tales like 'Henny-Penny', 'obviously invented for small children and of a type to be appreciated by the very young'; and

(v) fairytales, 'narratives containing or hinging upon supernatural happenings' (1970: 2). While the use in this definition of the term 'supernatural' allows for inclusion in the genre of the numerous literary fairytales which contain clear theistic motifs, its disjunctive (or) form does not allow us to distinguish fairytales from fantasy fiction, in which the supernatural may also play a part. Yet there are differences between the fairytale and fantasy fiction which affect the use of language in them, and in order to retain the distinction between the two genres here, we shall define fairytales as 'narratives predicated upon magic'. The fairytale *assumes* magic in the same way that the realistic novel assumes its absence. Fantasy fiction may incorporate a magical element, but when it does, the magical element, far from being assumed, is fantastic relative to the realistic aspects of the work.

Fairytale and fantasy

The term 'fairy' derives from Old French *faerie*, meaning 'enchantment' or 'magic'. It is in this sense that Spenser used the term in *The Faerie Queene* (1590) (Ayto, 1990: 217), and it also appears to be in this sense that Briggs uses the term 'supernatural' in her definition: she contrasts the 'small creature' sense of 'fairy' with the 'state of enchantment' sense, which is the sense pertinent to fairytales (whether or not they include fairies among their characters), and she discusses the magical element in fairytales. We prefer 'magic' to 'enchantment' because while 'enchantment' carries a strong sense of agency – of the presence of an enchanter responsible for the enchantment – 'magic' lends itself more easily to being used in an agent-free sense. If a world is enchanted, something or someone must have enchanted it, whereas if a world is magic, then that is simply what it is: no-one need have made it so. And it is exactly the hallmark of the fairytale that no causal statement about the magic which permeates it is required. A prince may become a toad through the agency of a witch; but no explanation is provided, and none is expected, for the existence of the witch herself, because we are dealing with a magical world in which witches are commonplace.

When, as in the case of several of the tales we discuss below, the supernatural takes a divine form, the deity operates within a magical world, not outside it. The divine serves as an explanation within the narrative as a whole, but not as an explanation of it. For example, a Christ-like figure moves Oscar Wilde's Selfish Giant, but is not responsible for his giant-ness. That the giant is a giant is a function of the genre, rather than of any agent within the tale itself. As Zipes (1979: xi) puts it, fairytale magic 'is not ethereal hocus pocus but the *real* symbolic potential of the tales to designate ways for creating . . . concrete utopias in the here and now'. To remain in the here and now while creating what Zipes somewhat misleadingly refers to as a 'utopia' requires an act of 'seeing as', and in the fairytale, the world of the here and now is seen as magical. An action of seeing x as y is a metaphorical action, and the fairytale world can be considered a metaphor for the world of the here and now.

In spite of its potential for creating utopias, the fairytale differs from utopian stories proper in so far as it typically lacks the fully fledged Utopia's explicit exposition of social structures and arrangements (see, for example, Moore, 1516; Morris, 1890). It is not necessary to explain the social structure in great detail in fairytales, because, as it is our own, it is familiar and available for metaphorical representation in the fairytale.

Furthermore, utopian fiction is less likely than either fantasy fiction or fairytales to make use of a magical component, except, possibly, to explain the protagonists' arrival in the Utopia.

FAIRYTALE NARRATIVE

The magical nature of the fairytale world is reflected in the characteristic realisations in the genre of three major aspects of narrative, namely spatiotemporal staging, characterisation and progression.

Spatiotemporal staging

In order to retain for the fairytale an anchorage in the reality of one universe and one stream of time while also allowing this universe and this stream of time its magic character, writers of fairytales typically employ one of three means of staging:

1 Absence of spatiotemporal staging: 'Curdie was the son of Peter the miner' (MacDonald, 1883); 'Sophie couldn't sleep' (Dahl, 1982: 9).
2 Inexplicitness of spatiotemporal staging: 'There was once a little princess' (MacDonald, 1872); 'High above the city, on a tall column, stood the statue of the Happy Prince' (Wilde, 1888a).
3 Explicit distancing of the spatiotemporal stage of the story from the place and time of writing/reading: 'Once upon a time, so long ago that I have quite forgotten the date' (MacDonald, 1864); 'More

than a thousand years ago, in a country quite on the other side of the world' (De Morgan, 1877).

Character and plot: Propp's morphological approach

The interaction of characters and plot in fairytales has been examined from a functionalist/structuralist point of view by Vladimir Propp (1895–1970).

According to Propp, different examples of the fairytale genre exhibit sufficient regularity of structure to enable us to speak of a morphology, or 'study of form' of fairytales, just as we might study the structure of an organism (1928/1968: xxvi). He classifies fairytale characters and events according to the underlying roles and functions they perform in the tales, rather than according to their surface descriptions. This enables him to frame the varied details of the plots in the tales he examines within thirty-one functions, not all of which need be realised in every tale, but which always follow each other in the same order (*ibid.* 64, 22). The varied characters can similarly be reduced to seven character roles (functions), each of which has a particular sphere of action: the villain, the donor (provider of magical agent), the helper, the princess (sought-for person) and her father, the dispatcher (who sends the hero on the search), the hero and the false hero (*ibid.* 79–80).

Each of the thirty-one plot functions is 'an act of a character, defined from the point of view of its significance for the course of the action' (1968: 21). After an initial situation is outlined, each tale concerns the fulfilment of a lack, for example of another human being, of a magical object, of a wonderful object, or of means of subsistence (1928/1968: 35).

No doubt the kinds of regularity of plot structure and of character and action type which Propp isolates (and which his method, argu-ably, exaggerates – see Rimmon-Kenan, 1983: 21–2) play some part in many people's impression of fairytales as 'universal, ageless, and eternal' (Zipes, 1983: 6). It would also be foolish to deny the psychological reality – that is, the perception in people's minds as units or entities – of those types of plot, character and action on which it is obvious that writers of literary fairytales draw extensively and explicitly in their own creations. The perception of these entities had clearly influenced typologies drawn up by scholars earlier than Propp, but Propp attempts to clarify and justify earlier scholars' intuitive definitions of fairytales by showing not only that the tales are similar, but also what the underlying basis for our perception of their similarity might be: different events and characters can realise identical functions; similar events and characters can realise different functions; and the functions are in either case identifiable in terms of their contribution to the plot. As he points out:

> If the hero jumps to the princess's window on horseback, we do not have the function of jumping on horseback (such a definition would be accurate only if we disregard the advance of the narrative as a whole) but the function of performing a difficult task as part of courtship. Likewise, if an eagle takes the hero to the country of the princess, we do not have the function of flying on a bird but one of transfer to the place where the object of search is located.
>
> (1976/Liberman, 1984: 74)

Propp highlights the underlying constants which we recognise when we perceive the tales as similar; but in addition to this, he explains that the reason we are able to isolate *these* as the respects in which different occurrences are similar is that we perceive them as functioning as units of plot composition. The question of where this perception comes from is not raised.

There is an excellent explanation and critique of Propp's method in Liberman's Introduction to Propp (1984), together with references to other critics. From our point of view, a major difficulty with his approach is that the search for similarity between the texts below the surface level of language obscures both those differences in and similarities between linguistic choices which interest us. Propp deals with character functions, but not with character selection and description; his plot develops through the functions of actions, but he neglects the importance of the selection of a particular action and the manner in which it is described. As Zipes (1983: 5–6) points out, when form becomes meaning (or comes to replace meaning), 'the historicity of the individual creator (or creators) and society disappears'.

Characterisation

As mentioned in the discussion of staging above, fairytale writers may facilitate our perception of our own world as magical by refraining from explicit spatiotemporal staging, or by providing an impression of temporal and spatial distance between reader (and writer) and story.

In the case of characterisation, acceptance of the equation 'our world = magic world' is encouraged by keeping characters 'flat'. The 'flat' character, which, in its purest form, is 'constructed round a single idea or quality' (Forster, 1927: ch. 4: I), is unlikely to encourage readers to identify particularly closely with it, but is, at the same time, drawn in sufficiently precise outline for readers to understand its thoughts and actions.

Reader identification with a character typically requires not only that the reader temporarily adopts aspects of the psychology of the character, but also that the reader imposes aspects of his/her own psychology on the character. In the fairytale, such interaction would disrupt the identity relation between our world and the magic world, since the fairytale character has to accept as commonplace a great many phenomena which the reader would find astonishing.

Psychological interaction between character and reader is promoted in texts which encourage readers to make inferences about character intentions, feelings, motives and psychological traits which are not explicitly mentioned, but which are suggested by the behaviour, speech and thought of the characters. To discourage such inferencing on the part of fairytale readers, writers tend to tell readers exactly what they need to know about the characters' mental life (and possibly a little more for the sake of entertaining them), but to refrain from hints and insinuations: 'And the king said to himself, "All the queens of my acquaintance have children . . . and my queen has not one. I feel ill used"' (MacDonald, 1864); '"My own garden is my own garden", said the Giant; "any one can understand that, and I will allow nobody to play in it but myself." . . . He was a very selfish Giant' (Wilde, 1888b). Descriptions like these provide sufficient information for readers to be able to understand why characters act as they do without having to live along with them. It allows for understanding without identification.

Descriptions of characters' physique tend to be equally clear-cut: the focus is typically on one or a few salient characteristics, as in the following example from MacDonald (1872): 'Her face was fair and pretty, with eyes like two bits of bright sky, each with a star dissolved in the blue.' Such descriptions provide instant, clear impressions of the characters as either attractive or unattractive physically, so that readers do not have to dwell on the characters' physique any more than on their minds.

Character selection in the fairytale has a similar effect of balancing detachment with recognition. The list of typical fairytale characters is well known: Kings, Queens, Princesses, Princes, Dragons, Witches, Fairies (who may be Godmothers), Dwarfs, Giants, Beasts (who may be enchanted) and so on, and in many tales we find interaction between these extraordinary characters and relatively normal children and their parents, who marvel no more at the extraordinary creatures than we, as readers, do. But it is not only through familiarity with the conventions of the fairytale genre that readers are able to perceive the socially elevated or otherwise extraordinary characters as normal. As Rörich (1986: 7) points out, in traditional fairytales, royal characters bear little resemblance to actual royalty, about whose lifestyle the tale-teller and his/her audience knew very little; rather, the royal characters resemble the rich peasant, a character better known to teller and audience. In literary fairytales, too, the fantastic characters are brought down to earth by being made to behave like and share the emotions of ordinary people, or by explicit statements of normalisation: 'Of course you know that dragons were once as common as motor-omnibuses are now, and almost as dangerous' (Nesbit, *c.* 1900). Some writers, furthermore, make it explicit that social elevation is metaphorical for nobility on dimentions other than that of social scale: 'every little girl is a princess' (MacDonald, 1872; magazine version; 1990: 343).

The tension between this normality and the extraordinary status that is claimed for the characters is just the tension required to retain reader interest and recognition while preventing identification. In addition, there are obvious advantages in terms of plot in having extraordinary characters with extraordinary powers: some characters can exercise magic, others achieve power through wealth and social position, and writers can give a royal personage 'every beautiful thing' (MacDonald, 1872, magazine version; 1990: 344) they please.

Narrative progression

Lüthi (1975/1984: 41) remarks that narration in the European fairytale tends to be linear: 'The teller of fairytales narrates primarily incrementally rather than by using subordination', and there is little or no use of retrospection or flashback (*ibid.* 56). Like the strategies observed for staging and characterisation, linearity in narration ensures that the story is easy to follow. The events of which the plot is composed are told in the sequence that mirrors their natural order of occurrence (*ordo naturalis*) so that even if readers may on occasion wonder at what happens and at how it happens, they will, at least, not need to dwell on the question of sequentiality.

FAIRYTALE LANGUAGE

The magical nature of the fairytale world, and the effect of this on staging, characterisation and narrative structure, have a number of consequences for the language of the fairytale.

Because the magical is commonplace in the fairytale, the language of the fairytale is fairly matter of fact, and devoid of long explanatory passages. The flatness of characters inhibits prolonged passages of indirect thought or speech, and because of the reluctance to concentrate on character psychology, the language of characterisation is predominantly physical, even when a mental state is, in fact, at issue: 'The wrinkles of contempt crossed the wrinkles of peevishness' (MacDonald, 1864, Lurie, 1993: 62).

Both character normalisation and character description in terms of a few salient properties frequently take a comparative form, and fairytales abound with similes in which the relevant aspect of a character is compared to a well-known, very often physical, phenomenon, so that the similes serve to link the magical world to the observable, everyday world, and to reinforce the impression of clarity of characterisation. This clarity is further enhanced through the selection of the most general descriptive adjective from sets sharing a basic meaning. For example, *red* is preferred to *vermilion* or *crimson*. In the case of gradable adjectives (terms for scalar concepts like temperature and general physical appearance: hot – warm – cool – cold; beautiful – good-looking – ugly) the terms selected are often at the ends of the scales in question. No doubt these phenomena play a part in creating the impression that 'fairytales love oppositions' (Rörich, 1986: 8).

All of this means that the language of fairytales is relatively simple and that the stories are generally easy to follow, even though the stories told in them are fantastic. For this reason, partly, the genre appealed to those writers of the nineteenth century who wished at once to instruct, entertain and develop the imaginations of the children of the Industrial Revolution.

LANGUAGE AND CONTROL IN NINETEENTH-CENTURY LITERARY FAIRYTALES

In this section, reference will be made to the following fairytales by George MacDonald: 'The Light Princess', first published as an interpolated story in the novel *Adela Cathcart* (1864; page references to Lurie, 1993); 'Little Daylight', first published in *Dealings with Fairies*

(1867a; page references to Mark, 1993); *The Princess and the Goblin* (first published as a serial in *Good Works for the Young* between November 1870 and June 1871; book version 1872; page references to the 1990 Oxford World Classics paperback edition); *The Princess and Curdie*, first published as a serial in *Good Things: A Picturesque Magazine for Boys and Girls* between January and June 1877; book version 1883; page references to the 1990 Oxford World Classics paperback edition).

By Oscar Wilde: from *The Happy Prince and Other Stories*, 'The Happy Prince' (1888a) and 'The Selfish Giant' (1888b); from *The House of Pomegranates*, 'The Young King' (1891a); and 'The Star Child' (1891b). All page references to *Oscar Wilde: Complete Shorter Fiction* (1980).

By Edith Nesbit: 'The Island of the Nine Whirlpools', first published in *The Strand* (1899; page references to Mark, 1993); 'The Book of Beasts', first published in *The Book of Dragons* (1900; page references to Lurie, 1993); 'The Last of the Dragons', probably written in 1900, but first published in *Five of Us – and Madeleine* (1925; page references to Zipes, 1987).

George Macdonald (1824–1905)

George MacDonald was born in Huntley in Aberdeenshire of a Calvinist farming family. According to the Calvinists faith, only the elect will be saved, but the young MacDonald became convinced that it was possible for everyone, whether faithful, 'heathen', animal or even devil, to attain salvation through a wilful pursuit of good, because every creature contains the divine essence. Such a view was subversive, not only of Calvinism, but of the creeds of other 'established' churches, none of which was able to accept MacDonald as a minister for long. He turned, instead, to creative writing as a vehicle for the expression of his vision and for criticism of a society misguided, as he saw it, by materialism and the teaching of the established churches.

MacDonald was one of the first British writers to use the literary fairytale successfully in the furtherance of his subversive ends, often through parodies of the themes of traditional tales (Zipes, 1983: 175–6). In his early stories, he plays deliberately, entertainingly and purposefully with the theme of the wicked fairy who, because she has not been invited to the christening of the princess, casts an evil spell:

'Of course somebody was forgotten' (Lurie, 1993: 62).
'Of course all the known fairies were invited to the christening' (Mark, 1993: 103).

'Of course the old hag was there without being asked' (Mark, 1993: 104).

However, the traditional tales also offer MacDonald an alternative history on which to base a rationalisation and eternalisaton of his own message. In 'Little Daylight', historisation is spelt out: 'In all history we find that fairies give their remarkable gifts to prince or princess . . . always at the christening' (Mark, 1993: 103), and the eternalisation and rationalisation strategies are equally obviously at play:

> Now wicked fairies will not be bound by the laws which the good fairies obey, and this always seems to give the bad the advantage over the good. . . . But it is all of no consequence, for what they do never succeeds; nay, in the end it brings about the very thing they are trying to prevent. So you see that somehow, for all their cleverness, wicked fairies are dreadfully stupid, for, although from the beginning of the world they have really helped instead of thwarting the good fairies, not one of them is a bit the wiser for it.
>
> (Mark, 1993: 115)

Here, 'so you see' is a clear marker of rationalisation, and 'from the beginning of the world' of eternalisation. What is being eternalised is the triumph of good over wickedness, and what is being rationalised is the vanity of any attempt at gain through evil means. In addition, since we have already been told that 'the power of the fairies they have by nature; whereas a witch gets her power by wickedness' (Mark, 1993: 103), goodness is linked to obedience to natural laws, and wickedness to rebellion against them, as well as to stupidity.

Rebellion against natural laws can take the form of a desire to master these laws and make them work, not naturally, but according to human design. MacDonald's 'philosophers' seek to achieve this goal through the method of empirical science, the method which had led to the industrialisation which MacDonald deplores in the fairytales – not in and for itself, but because it proceeds according to the wrong principles. This is most clearly evident in *The Princess and Curdie*, where we meet a member of the clergy preaching the principle 'that every One should take care of that One' (1883/1990: 315) and using sophistic reasoning to convince his audience that this will lead to the good of all.

MacDonald's first children's story, 'The Light Princess', begins with the birth of a princess to a king and queen who have waited a long time for this desirable event, and assumes, as we have seen, the theme of the forgotten fairy, Makemnoit, who turns up uninvited at the christening of the infant. Makemnoit adds something to the water with which the princess is to be christened, thereby depriving her of gravity. She is able to do this because she is

> a philosopher, and knew all the *ins* and *outs* of the laws of gravitation as well as the *ins* and *outs* of her boot-lace. And being a witch as well, she could abrogate those laws in a moment; or at least so clog their wheels and rust their bearings, that they would not work at all.
>
> (Lurie, 1993: 63)

By linking the laws of gravitation with boot-laces, MacDonald suggests that philosophers denigrate the laws of nature by seeking to master them, and by the mechanical metaphors he suggests that philosophers consider natural laws as mechanical as machinery made by humans. In *The Princess and Curdie*, the very minds of thinkers of the materialist persuasion are likened to machines. The preacher we met above is a 'sermon-pump' (1883/1990: 315), and the clergy in general is 'always glad to seize on any passing event to give interest to the dull and monotonic grind of their intellectual machines' (*ibid.* 314).

For the moment, Makemnoit's design appears to have succeeded. The princess has lost, not just gravity of body, but also gravity of mind. She is as light of mind as she is of body, and MacDonald makes great play of the multiple meanings of 'light'. The king and queen quarrel about the merits of being 'light-hearted', 'light-headed', 'light-handed', 'light-fingered', 'light-footed', 'light-bodied', 'light-minded' and 'light-haired' – at which point MacDonald's love of ambiguity and his awareness of the power of language are evidenced in the king's uncertainty about 'whether the queen meant light-*haired* or light-*heired*; for why might she not aspirate her vowels when she was ex-aspirated herself?' (Lurie, 1993: 67).

The lightness of the princess's mind is reflected in numerous references to her tendency to laugh. As soon as Makemnoit's spell takes effect, 'a shudder went through' everyone present at the christening except the baby, who immediately begins to laugh. She is to continue to laugh immoderately and indiscriminately throughout much of the story, and, as the narrator remarks on several occasions, her laughter is unnatural. It lacks 'a certain tone, depending on the possibility of sorrow – *morbidezza*, perhaps. She never smiled' (Lurie, 1993: 70).

However, in MacDonald's universe, nothing unnatural can last.

Nature is divine, and therefore eternal, and the eternal is non-negatable. Therefore, the unnatural contains the seed of its own destruction, and as the princess grows older, her mirth becomes a hindrance to her. As a baby, she laughs and crows naturally enough, as babies do, although she also laughs 'amazingly' (Lurie, 1993: 63). Even poetic references to 'her peals of tiny laughter' are accompanied with reference to the surprise of those who observe her, and the sweet simile of the princess as 'a baby-laughter-cloud in the air' is followed immediately with the more sinister expression 'exploding continuously' (p. 64). As the story progresses and the princess grows older, the sound of her laughter is repeatedly described in unappealing terms: the princess is heard 'screeching with laughter' (pp. 66, 76); she laughs 'hugely' and 'immoderately' in 'outbursts' (p. 69), and is likened to 'a musical box' (p. 70). Her laughing takes the form of a 'violent fit' which 'checked her' (p. 71), and it begins to sound like 'screaming' (pp. 77, 78). Later, when the prince who eventually saves her speaks to her in lovelorn terms 'about being in heaven, the princess laughed at him dreadfully' (p. 83).

In contrast, the deity's laugh, as described in *The Princess and Curdie* (1883/1990: 217), 'was . . . sweeter than running brook and silver bell; sweeter than joy itself, for the heart of the laugh was love'. The Light Princess lacks the ability to relate to either heaven or love: 'perhaps the best thing for the princess would have been to fall in love. But how a princess who had no gravity could fall into anything is a difficulty – perhaps *the* difficulty' (Lurie, 1993: 74).

It is, however, through hearing the princess scream, as he thinks, that the prince who will be her salvation is drawn to her, and the princess's innate divinity causes her to recognise, subconsciously, her own lack. She comes to love the lake below the palace 'more than father and mother', because when in the lake 'she recovered the natural right of which she had been so wickedly deprived – namely gravity' (Lurie, 1993: 74). In fact, the lake restores to her not only physical gravity, but the ability, first to wish to be like other people so that she could more easily get into the water (p. 75); second to become angry, when the prince, having mistaken her laughter for screaming, pulls her out of the water (p. 78); and third to grieve for herself, when the lake begins to dry up (p. 85) through the agency of Makemnoit, who begrudges the princess the pleasure she finds in the water. However, the princess still lacks the ability to grieve for another human being, and it is this ability which is required to repair the princess's humanity. She find it by contemplating the prince's love for her. The price is prepared to sacrifice himself, to save the princess from dying of grief, by plugging the hole in the lake, an action which would cause him to drown as the lake filled up again. The princess pulls the drowning prince into her boat, rows him ashore and takes him to her room where 'just as the sun rose, the prince opened his eyes' (p. 96). Then the princess bursts into tears and regains her gravity, and all is resolved in the most harmonious way with the marriage of the prince and princess who 'lived and were happy; and had crowns of gold and clothes of cloth, and shoes of leather, and children of boys and girls, not one of whom was ever known, on the most critical occasion, to lose the smallest atom of his or her due proportion of gravity' (p. 98).

The theme of due proportion and the play on the meanings of 'light' are taken up again in 'Little Daylight'. Daylight, like the Light Princess, is the first baby to appear at the palace. A palace, declares MacDonald, 'ought to be open to the sun and wind', with which the princess herself is equally closely associated. She is 'a beautiful baby, with such bright eyes that she might have come from the sun, only by and by she showed such lively ways that she might equally well have come out of the wind' (Mark, 1993: 102). However, Daylight's innate association with the sun is broken by a spell which is cast as a pun on the princess's name. On being told that the princess's name 'is little Daylight', the wicked fairy cries: 'And little daylight it shall be. . . . I bestow upon her the gift of sleeping all day long' (p. 104). Another fairy, however, has yet to bestow her gift, and seeks to temper the spell by decreeing that Daylight shall then, at least, be awake all night. But the wicked fairy had been interrupted and claims the right, therefore, to continue her spell: 'If she wakes all night she shall wax and wane with its mistress the moon' (p. 104–5). Fortunately, there is still one fairy left, and she adds: 'Until . . . a prince comes who shall kiss her without knowing it.'

The effect on Daylight of the spell is described using a simile which introduces explicit social criticism into the story:

> When the moon was at the full, she was in glorious spirits, and as beautiful as it is possible for a child of her age to be. But as the moon waned, she faded, until at last she was wan and withered like the poorest, sickliest child you might come upon in the streets of a great city in the arms of a homeless mother.
>
> (Mark, 1993: 105)

However, the old fairy's curse cannot reach Daylight's heart: 'she was Daylight still, only a little in the wrong place' (p. 105), and her appearance remains linked to day:

As she grew older she had grown more and more beautiful, with the sunniest hair and the loveliest eyes of heavenly blue, brilliant and profound as the sky of a June day.

(Mark, 1993: 106)

As the moon wanes, her skin and posture come to resemble those of a woman of eighty. But as her hair and eyes do not change, her appearance is as 'unnatural' as the laughter and condition of the Light Princess, and therefore as unlikely to last.

Daylight delights in the moon, whose movements she emulates in a circular dance she performs in a forest glade when the moon is full. But as the moon wanes, she retreats further and further into the wood, and she is as aware of her predicament as the Light Princess. When Daylight meets her prince, she asks him about the sun, which she has never seen 'Because I can't wake' (Mark, 1993: 113). She cannot wake, neither to see the day, nor from her enchantment. Having explained this to the prince, 'she hid her face in her hands' (p. 113). The prince observes Daylight's moon-dance for many nights. Finally, one dawn, he finds her in her waning state, and, with deep compassion for the weeping old creature before him, whom, of course, he does not recognise as the beautiful princess, '"Mother, mother!" he said – "Poor mother!" and kissed her on the withered lips.' The spell is broken, and Daylight is revealed to him and daylight to her: 'The first gleam of morning was caught on her face: that face was bright as the never-ageing Dawn, and her eyes were lovely as the sky of darkest blue.'

In these two fairytales, MacDonald begins to build his fairytale world of forests, lakes and mountains, with sun, wind and rain, and to place his creatures in it. The royal family is located in a palace 'high and brave', and, as we have seen, 'open to the sun and the wind'. However, 'no house of any pretension to be called a palace is in the least worthy of the name, except it has a wood near it'. The wood is the habitat of good and bad fairies alike, though wicked fairies are located further away from the palace than good fairies. The wicked 'swamp fairy' (Mark, 1993: 115) in 'Little Daylight', lives 'in a mud house, in a swampy part of the forest' (p. 103). The good fairy who gives the prince food and shelter lives in 'the palace wood' in 'the strangest little house', also described as a 'cottage' (pp. 108, 110, 112, 114, 116).

The two spheres of palace and forest interrelate. The laws of nature are used by both kinds of fairy, in their separate ways, to influence palace events; palatial characters seek out the forest and its inhabitants in times of need. The palace imposes a degree of order on the forest, but MacDonald's concern is, again, for due proportion. Consider his description of the setting for Daylight's father's palace:

[1] And there was a very grand wood indeed beside the palace of the king who was going to be Daylight's father; . . . [2] Near the house it was kept very trim and nice, and it was free of brushwood for a long way in; but by degrees it got wild, and it grew wilder, and wilder, until some said wild beasts did what they liked in it. [3] The king and his courtiers often hunted, however, and [4] this kept the wild beasts far away from the palace.

(Mark, 1993: 102; numbers added)

Section 2 of this passage is ambiguous in two respects. First, it is ambiguous between gradual descriptive movement through space, and narration of gradual temporal alteration: are we moving further and further away from the palace, or are we moving through a time during which the wood grows wilder and wilder? The fact that the wild beasts are kept away from the palace (section 4) does not prevent them getting wilder or doing as they please in the parts which the hunting parties do not reach.

Second, it is not clear whether the pronoun 'it', refers in section 2 to the entire 'grand wood' of section 1. Because section 2 introduces a part of the wood near the house, it is possible that 'it' refers to this part, and this interpretation supports the notion of temporal alteration. Of course, the story indicates that, at the time of telling, the part near the house is 'trim and nice', and the customary sequentiality of narration in fairytales (see p. 162 above) draws attention away from the possibility that this passage might be predictive. It is, however, strongly predictive of the *The Princess and the Goblin* where the Goblins are sufficiently close to the princess and the miners to threaten them, and of *The Princess and Curdie* in which bad government allows greed to run wild and destroy a civilisation.

There are a number of suggestions that if wildness is kept too far from the palace, it goes underground, and may be ignored and forgotten, and that it is this which causes it to develop into wickedness. Makemnoit was the king's sister, who had displeased their father, who had therefore forgotten her in his will, so that 'it was no wonder that her brother forgot her in writing his invitations' (Lurie, 1993: 62). The swamp-fairy is unknown to all but the other fairies, and 'the king and queen never thought of inviting an old witch' (Mark, 1993: 103). The goblins in *The Princess and the*

Goblin are reputed once to have been humans displeased with their rulers, and to have retreated underground.

Clearly the scale of distance from the high palace on which characters are placed assists in MacDonald's metaphor-making, since his projected contemporary audience would have been well versed in the Christian metaphor according to which heaven is situated high above hell, with the earth in between, on a vertical scale. However, MacDonald's characters are also ordered according to their degree of 'nobility', and this scale need not match their physical nearness to the royals. In Victorian society, nobility of birth was becoming undervalued in comparison with purely financial status, and MacDonald can appear to be concerned to return to a pre-industrialised social order. However, his main concern is to establish nobility as a moral, rather than a social, concept.

By birth, everyone is noble: 'every little girl is a princess' as he puts it in the magazine version of *The Princess and Curdie* (McGillis, 1990: 343, note 5), and many instances 'have been known in the world's history' of boys like Curdie who 'was not a miner only, but a prince as well' (1872/1990: 138). Nevertheless, nobility must be nourished by individuals or their guardians because everyone has the freedom to turn ignobel through willing forgetfulness of their nobility and its divine source. MacDonald does his share of nourishing by explaining how true princesses and princes should behave (LD = 'Little Daylight'; *PG = The Princess and the Goblin*; *PC = The Princess and Curdie*; numbers refer to pages in the works listed at the head of this section):

LD	113	like a true gentleman-prince, he obeyed
PG	9	she was as brave as could be expected of a princess of her age
		like a true princess, she resolved on going wisely to work to find her way back
PG	12	she did as she was told (two mentions)
PG	18	a real princess cannot tell a lie
PG	19	is never rude
PG	33	must *not* break her word
PG	54	never forgets her debts until they are paid
PG	60	Some little girls would have been afraid . . . but Irene was a princess
PG	137	loves all her brothers and sisters best
PG	138	If a true princess has done wrong, she is always uneasy until she has had an opportunity of throwing the

wrongness away from her by saying 'I did it; and I wish
I had not; and I am sorry for having done it.'

PC   117   we must accept righteous sacrifices as well as make them
the road to the next duty is the only straight one

PC   213   It is greed and laziness and selfishness, not hunger or
weariness or cold, that take the dignity out of a man, and
make him look mean

So nobility resides in obedience, bravery, resolve, wise work, truthfulness, politeness, honesty, family affection, the ability to repent, and to accept and make sacrifices, righteousness, the will to do one's duty and in regard for others. This clearly suggests a Victorian value system. However, MacDonald interprets and presents it in terms of his own egalitarian theism.

Everyone, indeed everything, natural is inherently noble, in the sense of coming 'from the place where all lovely things were born before they began to grow in this world' (1883/1990: 194). Therefore, dictinctions between people in terms of nobility cannot be made according to the norms generally accepted in society, whether agrarian or industrialised. Nobles, in the social sense, can be wicked: 'in a neighbouring kingdom, in consequence of the wickedness of the nobles, an insurrection took place upon the death of the old king' (Mark, 1993: 107), and so can kings, for that matter, if they are greedy and pay no attention to their people (see Chapter XXXV of *The Princess and Curdie*).

MacDonald's nobility knows no snobbery: Daylight's prince finds his breakfast 'nothing the worse for being served in the kitchen' (Mark, 1993: 110). It is nourished through contact with nature: the prince awakes in the fairy's cottage 'amazed to find how well and strong he felt' (p. 108), and he considers the bread and milk she feeds him 'the most delicious food he had ever tasted, wondering that they did not have it for dinner at the palace sometimes' (p. 108). Nobility, furthermore, honours its elders and its family: the good fairy appears to the prince in the guise of 'a very tidy motherly old woman' (p. 108) whom he addresses as 'mother', 'for that was the kind way in which any young man in his country would address a woman who was much older than himself'; she in turn addresses him as 'son' (p. 114). In *The Princess and the Goblin*, Curdie feels his duty to and love of his family deeply, and the king commends him for it (1872/1990: 164–5): 'He was a right good king, and he knew that the love of a boy who would not leave his father and mother to be made a great man, was worth ten thousand offers to die for his sake, and would prove so when the right time came' (1883/1990: 176).

The observance of duty is characteristic of nobility at every level. In *The Princess and Curdie*, MacDonald explains that 'a real king' is 'one who ruled for the good of his people, and not to please himself' (1883/1990: 175–6). In the case of the highest authority of all, this dual characteristic, ruler/benefactor, is given physical expression in the deity's dress, which is that of a ruler, on the one hand, and her actions, which are those of a servant, on the other: 'she made them all sit down, and with her own hands placed at the table seats for Derba and the page. Then in ruby crown and royal purple she served them all' (p. 339).

The identification of power to govern with willingness to serve clearly goes some way towards enabling MacDonald to allow one of his innately noble creatures to rule other, equally innately noble, creatures. It does not, however, explain the *need* for the one to govern the others, or the need to have any hierarchy at all. For this purpose, MacDonald uses (i) the notion of free will, and (ii) an evolutionary theory of reincarnation.

The deity explains to Curdie that 'all men, if they do not take care, go down the hill to the animals' country' (1883/1990: 219), and that 'it is always what they *do*, whether in their minds or their bodies, that makes men go down to be less than men, that is, beasts' (p. 220). Curdie is convinced that the terrible creature, 'Lina is a woman, and that she was naughty, but is now growing good' (p. 278), although 'Doubtless she *had been* a goblin's creature' (p. 234). Everyone in MacDonald's stories begins each life in a state fitted to their rank on the moral scale. The deity explains to Peter 'you have got to thank me that you are so poor. . . . Hadst thou been rich, my Peter, thou wouldst not have been so good as some rich men I know' (p. 208). However, once in the world, they can choose good or evil ways, and are open to good or bad influences. Therefore, agents of socialisation are particularly important, and MacDonald is at pains to stress the need for socialisation to take place through good, natural agents, and to criticise any that are unnatural.

The primary natural agent of socialisation, according to MacDonald, is the family. Its importance is suggested by the use of the modal auxiliary verb *ought*, in 'The Light Princess', where the king 'ought not to have forgotten' the wicked fairy because she was his 'own sister' (Lurie, 1993: 62). Good family relationships are characterised by love and affection. It is the king and queen's 'tenderness for their . . . offspring' which saves the Light Princess from death by metaphysical cure (p. 74), and, as we have seen above, a true princess 'loves all her brothers and sisters best' (1872/1990: 136). This remark, however, refers to 'the miner's children' the princess meets 'on the mountain' (*ibid.*), *so MacDonald's noble family is wider than the nuclear. It is, in fact, universal, a family of human and beast, grounded in the divine guardian of all nature whom we meet in The Princess and the Goblin* and *The Princess and Curdie*. There, we also come to understand that a well-turned nuclear family is a microcosm of the universal family and that the child becomes socialised into both as it grows up with its mother and father.

MacDonald's faith in the family is reflected in many aspects of his stories, but particularly interestingly in his expressions of disapproval of the Victorian middle-class custom of leaving the care of children to nurses. In 'Little Daylight', this disapproval is made explicit: the king and queen love the princess 'far too much to give her up to nurses, especially at night, as most kings and queens do – and are sorry for it afterwards' (Mark, 1993: 104). MacDonald's nurses are, on the whole, fearful and dishonest *because* they are not the natural carers of their charges, but employees. They are afraid of losing their jobs, and this fear interferes with their ability to do the job properly. They become petrified, ineffectual creatures, from whom MacDonald's princesses have a habit of escaping at every given opportunity. They cannot understand children (the nurse in *The Princess and the Goblin* misinterprets the princess's statement that her grandmother is prettier than the nurse to mean that the princess thinks that the nurse is ugly), and cannot understand the truth of what children say (the same nurse is unable to believe in the princess's story about her grandmother). If they love their charges, they love them jealously ('Bother your grandmother!') and are open to manipulation through both flattery and threats. Their innocent charges often teach them, and are their superiors in wisdom.

In 'The Light Princess', there is one passage in which the nurse is seen in a positive light: 'the princess and her old nurse were left with the prince. But the old nurse was a wise woman, and knew what to do' (Lurie, 1993: 96). There are four mentions of *nurse* in a neutral context: 'the nurse began to float the baby up and down'; 'the nurse's experience' (p. 63); 'the nurse returned' (p. 65); and 'answered the nurse' (p. 97). Against this, there are three examples of the nurse in fear, in one of which this fear is directed at the employer: 'the nurse gave a start and a smothered cry'; 'the nurse in terror flew to the bell' (p. 63); and 'Oh! don't frighten me, your Majesty!' exclaimed the nurse, clasping her hands, (p. 65). There are two instances of uncontrolled behaviour on the part of the nurse: 'the nurse rushed about the palace screaming "My baby! my baby!"'; and 'her old nurse uttered a yell of delight, and ran to her screaming' (p. 97).

In 'Little Daylight', we find, apart from the statement that the king and queen loved the princess 'far too much to give her up to nurses . . . as most kings and queens do – and are sorry for it afterwards' (Mark, 1993: 104), that 'the lady at the head of the nursery department was anything but comfortable in the prospect before her' (p. 105).

It is, however, in *The Princess and the Goblin* that MacDonald's antipathy towards nurses stands out most clearly, even though he makes no explicit statements of disapproval in that story. The terms *nurse*, *nursey* or *Lootie* (the princess's petname for the nurse) are used approximately (the works discussed in this chapter have been analysed manually, so some inaccuracy can be expected) 185 times in the story. Occurrences of immediate repetition, such as 'Lootie, Lootie', are counted only once.

Of these, 20 occurrences are framed in a context which appears to show the nurse in a positive light. Of these, one might be considered a positive evaluation by the narrator, given his views on repentance: 'the nurse was ashamed of herself' (p. 19). Two indications of positive qualities in the nurse are filtered through the princess: 'The princess and her nurse were the best of friends' (p. 21); and 'that was her pet-name for her nurse' (p. 21). In addition to these, there are ten instances where the nurse is shown to give comfort and assistance to the princess, Irene; for instance, '"Lootie! Lootie!" cried the princess. "Take me home"' (p. 29). On seven occasions, the nurse seems to show genuine love and concern for her charge; for example, 'Lootie was very glad to please the princess' (p. 24).

There are, however, ten mentions in which the nurse herself is an object of concern; for example, 'sprung to Lootie's rescue' (p. 149).

Of the 57 mentions which are not evaluatively framed, 11 are simply neutral mentions, like 'among the rest came the nurse' (p. 140), or cases of conventional address like 'Good night, Lootie' (p. 34). Seven have frames where Irene is asking the nurse questions like 'What more is my name, Lootie?' (p. 30), and two have the nurse being asked to do something: 'ask the nurse to' (p. 21); 'requested Lootie to' (p. 150). Four frames cast the nurse as the asker of questions, but only one has her being answered: 'Only when the nurse spoke to her, she answered her' (p. 19). There are seven instances of *the nurse/Lootie* in collocation with *said*, and one each with *exclaimed* and *returned*. The nurse is directly mentioned as the object of discussion on five occasions, for instance 'Is it naughty of Lootie then?' (p. 62), and on three as a possession: 'her nurse'; 'your nurse'. On six occasions, Irene is telling the nurse to look or see or otherwise directing her behaviour: 'Nursie! Lootie! I can't run any more. Do let us walk' (p. 26). In five instances, Irene contradicts the nurse: 'No, no, Lootie. I won't be called names' (p. 31), and four times she explains something to her, for example: 'And you know it was, Lootie' (p. 30).

There are 27 occurrences of the nodes *nurse* or *Lootie* in what might be termed 'mildly or ironically negative' frames. These include, for instance: 'Now the nurse, as she said herself afterwards, could not be every moment in the room' (p. 22)'; 'Lootie was longer in returning than she had intended' (p. 75); and 'How the nurse came to sleep through it, was a mystery' (106).

There are six links between the nurse and lack of knowledge, as in 'Nursie doesn't know' (p. 14), and ten links with lack of understanding, as in 'The nurse was not lady enough to understand' (p. 33). Her inability to believe is expressed on six occasions, for example: '"I can't believe you," said the nurse' (p. 19). The nurse's inability to believe gives rise to three occasions on which she speaks sarcastically, as in: '"Oh I dare say!" remarked the nurse' (p. 17). On one occasion, she is indecisive: '"What *am* I to do?" said the nurse' (p. 26), and on five, she is angry: 'the nurse, now thoroughly vexed' (p. 18). She cries in association with five mentions such as 'the nurse came into the room, sobbing' (p. 87), and is jealous once: 'Bother your grandmother!' (p. 19). Seven mentions demonstrate her snobbery, as in '"Who are you?" asked the nurse, offended at the freedom with which he spoke to them' (p. 28), and four mentions show that she is rude: 'said the nurse rudely' (p. 27). The nurse and fear are directly associated on 19 occasions, including 'Lootie was almost silly with terror' (150). Seven times she is seen to be at the mercy of her employer, for instance, 'If his majesty, Irene's papa, were to hear of it, Lootie would certainly be dismissed' (p. 25). On five occasions, she is out of control, as in 'the senseless Lootie' (p. 149), and once she is escaped from: 'contrived to give Lootie the slip' (p. 151).

So, against 20 positively framed mentions, and 57 which might be considered neutral, we have ten where Lootie is an object of concern, 27 which are mildly or ironically negative, and 71 which are certainly negatively framed. In addition, there are hints that the nurse could be a danger to the princess: 'She kept foolishly whispering to the servants, however – sometimes that the princess was not right in her mind, sometimes that she was too good to live' (1872/1990: 137).

Lootie's is given two 'wise insights', though each is mixed with delusion, rather like the wisdom of witches. On the first occasion, the nurse tells Irene that it must have been Irene's long-dead mother who gave Irene the ring which she has in fact received from her grandmother the night before (1872/1990: 88). The king later tells Irene 'It was your queen-mama's once' (p. 89). On the second occasion, the nurse recognises the sound of mining under the house. She expresses her belief: 'Sometimes they sound . . . like the noises you hear in the mountains from those horrid miners underneath' (p. 142). The assembly take the nurse to mean by 'those horrid miners' the real miners. On that interpretation, she is wrong, since the sounds are made by the goblins trying to break into the house. In so far as the goblins are 'horrid miners', her utterance is true, but the actual miners in this story are not, as Lootie thinks, horrid – on the contrary, they are the king's servants, and are instrumental in saving the princess from the goblins' wicked designs.

In addition to nurses, MacDonald disapproves, in *The Princess and Curdie*, of 'evil teachers' who, unknown to the king, 'had crept into the schools' (1883/1990: 290), and of the established churches. We have already discussed his use of mechanistic metaphors for the minds of the clergy in *The Princess and Curdie*, but there is also a hint that the clergy is somewhat ineffectual and prone to act mechanically, without due contemplation, when the archbishop who presides over the christening of Little Daylight addresses the wicked fairy as 'my good woman' (Mark, 1993: 104).

There are a number of differences between MacDonald's two almost novel-length fairytales and the shorter stories. The two novels, are, first of all, explicitly linked in so far as the main characters are the same in both, and in so far as the first chapter of the second novel ends with a summary of the action of the first which, it is said, took place 'about a year before this story began' (1883/1990: 176). This temporal development is mirrored in the increased clarity in the second novel of scenes and themes introduced in the first. However, the major difference between the short stories and the novels is that, in the latter, the divine is personified in the figure of the young-and-old great-great-grandmother. Along with this personification goes a general tendency towards externalisation of forces. Individual characters in the novels do not carry the effects of explicit magic spells within them; nevertheless, they are prevented by other characters from relating naturally to the world around them. Princess Irene is prevented by the threat posed by the goblins 'from seeing the real sky with stars in it', and this impediment contrasts as much with the link between her and the night sky which the description of her establishes: 'with eyes like two bits of night sky, each with a star dissolved in the blue' (1872/1990: 5), as Daylight's spellbound behaviour contrasts with her name. Furthermore, the urban society we meet in *The Princess and Curdie* is under the 'spell' of greed and corruption, and this has physical consequences: the king is ill and weak.

There are, however, also very clear links between the early stories and the novels in landscaping and social organisation, although the greater length of the novels permits a widening of the society presented to include a number of social groups whose interrelations and activities forge the link between the magic world and Victorian society strongly. In particular, the countryside is contrasted with an urban society, the city Gwyntystorm, where the king has his court. The link between novels and reality is also strengthened by the naming of characters with apparently ordinary, everyday names. These do not display their meanings as clearly as descriptions like 'The Light Princess' or as pseudo-names like 'Daylight'. Nevertheless, the origins of some, and the well-known connotations of others contribute to the metaphor.

The name of princess Irene derives from the Greek word for 'peace' (McGillis, 1990: 344), and is also an anagram of *reine*, the French word for 'queen' (Willis, 1985: 24). The princess shares this name with her eternal young-and-old great-great-grandmother to whom she is directly linked in a number of ways in the story. Irene is the descendant of the queen of peace and becomes a queen of peace herself in *The Princess and Curdie*.

Curdie is the name of her husband-to-be. This is 'a pastoral name of MacDonald's invention. Here, as elsewhere in the book and throughout his writing, MacDonald is aware of the symbolic nature of naming' (McGillis, 1990: 349), and the symbolism of the coming together of the namesake and descendant of the queen of peace with Curdie Peterson, whose father is Peter Peterson, is clear.

The palace where Irene's father lives 'was built upon one of the mountains, and was very grand and beautiful' (1872/1990: 5). Irene, however, lives in 'a large house, half castle, half farmhouse, on the side of another mountain, about half-way between its base and its peak' (p. 5). In the garden around this house, MacDonald locates his preferred proportion of civilisation and wilderness:

> The garden was a very lovely place. Being upon a mountain side there were parts in it where the rocks came through in great

masses, and all immediately about them remained quite wild. Tufts of heather grew upon them, and other hardy mountain plants and flowers, while near them would be lovely roses and lillies, and all pleasant garden flowers. This mingling of the wild mountain with the civilized garden was very quaint, and it was impossible for any number of gardeners to make such a garden look formal and stiff.
(1872/1990: 57)

Rocky wildness is elevated; it is 'upon the mountain side', and it cannot be tamed by Victorian attention to stiff formality. It is quite unlike the low, swampy parts of the forest where Makemnoit resides, unknown, ignored and destructive. It is, furthermore, related to Curdie, the son of Peter, namesake of the Bible's apostle of the rock, whose 'poor little house' is built against 'a huge rock' (p. 156). The princess is saved by Curdie, to whom she relates freely and naturally, without stiffness or formality, from their first meeting, and whom she later marries. Furthermore, the string by which Irene is connected to her grandmother is spun on what the grandmother calls 'the rock' (p. 63), referring to the distaff of her spinning wheel.

Curdie is a miner. The miners are an important social class in this story, because it is only through their work that 'the hollow places underneath' (1872/1990: 5) the mountains are known. The miners' 'business was to bring to light hidden things', and these things, in the physical shape of silver, stem from the heart of the earth, which is 'a great wallowing mass . . . of glowing hot melted metals and stones . . . a huge power of buried sunlight' (1883/1990: 173) – hence the sanctity of rocks. But the passage also explains MacDonald's extensive use of terms for gold, silver, sun and moon in descriptions of morally elevated characters, and the relationships between these terms. MacDonald declares that 'the earth flew off from the sun', that the sun is the 'grandfather' of the mountains, and that the moon is 'their little old cold aunt' (p. 174).

The miners, we learn, 'were a mingled company – some good, some not so good, some rather bad – none of them so bad or so good as they might have been . . . they knew very little about the upper world' (1883/1990: 179), in particular, about the princess's grandmother, and are contrasted with men 'of the upper world where the wind blew' (p. 180). However, their potential is great, because 'those who work well in the depths more easily understand the heights, for indeed in their true nature they are one and the same' (p. 184).

Curdie is in touch both with the high, in the form of the princess, her father and her grandmother, and with the low, in the form of the

goblins of whom he has no fear. He is therefore able to combat the
goblins, and he also has the potential to come to know and understand
the princess's divine grandmother, a potential denied to the nurse:
'Curdie is much farther on than Lootie' (1872/1990: 123), explains
the grandmother to Irene. Again, his moral elevation makes him a
prince. He regrets an incident when he behaved badly to the princess,
so 'there is some ground for supposing that Curdie was not a miner
only, but a prince as well' (p. 138). His position relative to the divine
(and to Irene) is also exemplified in his habitat. He lives with his
mother and father 'on the high hillside', and there are a number of
parallelisms between descriptions of Curdie's family life and Irene's
relationship with her grandmother, which reinforce Curdie's position.
These include the explicit authorial statement: 'I doubt if the princess
was very much happier even in the arms of her huge-great-grandmother than Peter and Curdie were in the arms of Mrs Peterson' (p.
66). Mrs Peterson 'was such a nice good mother' and she 'made and
kept a little haven in that poor cottage on the hillside – for her
husband and son to go home to out of the low and rather dreary
earth in which they worked' (p. 67). Irene, similarly, describes her
grandmother's room as 'Oh, what a lovely haven to reach from the
darkness and fear through which she had come!' (p. 78), and the room
is situated high above the nursery which Irene often finds dreary.
Furthermore, Mrs Petersen teaches Curdie to find his way through the
mines, and therefore back to her again, by using a ball of string; Irene
is guided in a similar manner by her grandmother. If Curdie's thread
becomes tangled, Mrs Peterson untangles it, explaining her skill to
Curdie: 'I follow the thread . . . just as you do in the mine' (p. 68),
and just as the princess does in Chapters XX and XI. Curdie has 'a
huge ball of fine string' (p. 67); Irene has 'a shimmering ball . . .
about the size of a pigeon's egg' containing 'more . . . than you think'
(p. 82) of thread 'too fine for you to see. You can only feel it' (p. 84).
In Chapter XXVIII, this string leads first Irene and then Curdie to
Curdie's mother who, Irene declares, 'has been so kind to me – just
like my own grandmother!'. Also like the grandmother, Curdie's
mother spins. When Curdie seeks out the grandmother:

> As he hesitated, he heard the noise of a spinning-wheel. He knew it
> at once, because his mother's spinning-wheel had been his govern-
> ess long ago, and still taught him things. It was the spinning-wheel
> which first taught him to make verses, and to sing, and to think
> whether all was right within him.
>
> (1883/1990: 186)

Through such parallelisms of description and theme we come to understand the nuclear family as a microcosm of the universal family of divine creation.

The goblins who threaten Irene and the miners live in the 'subterranean caverns' (1872/1990: 6) below the mountains. They only come out at night, and have established an anti-society (Halliday, 1978: ch. 9) with 'a king and a government of their own, whose chief business, beyond their own simple affairs, was to devise trouble for their neighbours' (1872/1990: 7). These were once ordinary people, but have retreated underground because they felt unjustly treated by the then king. Here they plan their insurrection, a theme which calls to mind the rebellion of the peasants against the nobles in 'Little Daylight'. While 'the goblins themselves were not so far removed from the human' (1872/1990: 6) in appearance, their animals, which are referred to as their 'creatures', are so 'sub-natural' that humans fail to find names for them. MacDonald describes them as 'grotesque', 'misshapen', 'hideous', 'ludicrous', and their sounds as

> as uncouth and varied as their forms . . . neither grunts nor squeaks nor roars nor howls nor barks nor yells nor screams nor croaks nor hisses nor mews nor shrieks, but only . . . something like all of them mingled in one horrible dissonance.
>
> (1872/1990: 71)

After this breathless series of negated descriptive terms, and an explanation that the creatures have developed over the centuries from normal animals, the reader is startled by the information that 'what increased the gruesomeness tenfold, was that, from constant domestic, or indeed rather family association with the goblins, their countenances had grown in grotesque resemblance to the human' (p. 72). The shock-effect of this statement is increased by the witholding of the term 'human' until the very end of the sentence. We have been lulled into accepting these creatures as so far differentiated from us that they are unnameable and almost indescribably horrible, and the term 'human' is quite unexpected, in virtue of which it becomes the more effective. It is like the kind of shock the deity describes to Curdie in *The Princess and Curdie*:

> Many a lady, so delicate and nice that she can bear nothing coarser than the finest linen to touch her body, if she had a mirror that could show her the animal she is growing to, as it lies within the

fair skin and the fine linen and the silk and the jewels, would receive a shock that might possibly wake her up.

(1883/1990: 222)

Looking back at the assertion that the goblins themselves are human-like, we find, in fact, that this is doubtful praise:

> The goblins themselves were not so far removed from the humans as [heresay] would imply. And as they grew misshapen in body, they had grown in knowledge and cleverness, and now were able to do things no mortal could see the possibility of. But as they grew in cunning they grew in mischief.

(1872/1990: 6)

The link between the two first sentences here with 'And' strongly suggests that humans, in fact, have grown so much in the type of knowledge and cleverness which the passage equates with cunning and mischief, that they can do things which ought to be unimaginable to human, that is, things that are inhuman.

Irene is cared for by a nurse in her country-people house–castle, and her first action in the story is to revive from the stupor of boredom on a rainy day, as her nurse leaves the room:

> The next moment after you see her sitting there, her nurse goes out of the room.
>
> Even that is a change, and the princess tumbles off her chair, and runs out of the door, not the same door the nurse went out of, but one which opened at the foot of a curious old stair of worm-eaten oak.

(1872; 1990: 8–9)

At the top of this stair, she finds her own kin in the shape of a character initially introduced as 'a very old lady who sat spinning'. In the 135-word paragraph that follows, the term 'old' appears five times and 'older' once. This old lady, however, is also 'beautiful', her skin is 'smooth and white', and her hair is long and loose. The structure of the paragraph mirrors the contradictoriness of the lady's appearance. After the clear statement of the previous paragraph that what the princess saw was 'a very old lady', MacDonald introduces this paragraph with a modal adverb: 'Perhaps you will wonder how the princess could tell that the old lady was an old lady, when I inform you that not only was she beautiful, but her skin was smooth and white.' After the hair has been mentioned, there is another assertion, 'That is not much like an old lady', but this is immediately followed by a tag question held onto the statement with a dash: '– is it?' There follows an exclamation and a contrastive linker: 'Ah! but it was white almost as snow.' In fact, the uncertainty is resolved for Irene when she observes the lady's eyes which 'looked so wise that you could not have helped seeing she must be old' (pp. 11–12). The emphasis on age continues to predominate in the linguistic picture of the grandmother, although it is regularly mingled with youthful features. On page 12, four mentions of 'the old lady' and one of her 'sweet, but old and rather shaky voice' are followed by a reference to her hands as 'so smooth and nice!' On the following page, Irene

> wondered to see how straight and tall she was, for, although she was so old, she didn't stoop a bit. She was dressed in black velvet with thick white heavy-looking lace about it; and on the black dress, her hair shone like silver.

> (1872/1990: 14)

This is followed by two further narrator references to 'the old lady', who then introduces herself to Irene: ' "I'm your great-great-grand-mother." ' Irene replies, ' "You must be a queen too, if you are my great big grandmother"', as MacDonald continues, through a play with the small girl's inability to comprehend the exact relationship between herself and the old lady, to reinforce the mingling of qualities in the latter. This mingling continues throughout both books. In the first, in addition to the mentions quoted so far, she is referred to or addressed as 'grandmother' 110 times; as 'lady' 84 times; as 'great-great-grandmother' four times; and as 'mother', 'queen', 'Irene', 'great-great-great-great-grandmother', 'huge-great-grandmother' and 'granny' (by a doubting Curdie) once each. She is described as 'old' 42 times; as 'great' seven times; as 'big' twice; as 'huge' three times; as 'beautiful' six times; and as 'dear', 'diligent' and 'sweet' once each.

When we come to the second novel, the initial reference is to 'one particular personage', but we immediately learn that 'That personage was the great-great-grandmother of the princess's (1883/1990: 178). After that, she is referred to or addressed as 'princess' 50 times; as 'ma'am' 35 times; as 'lady' 24 times; as 'grandmother' 11 times; as 'great-great-grandmother nine times; as 'woman' seven times; as 'the maid' and 'Queen Irene' twice each; and as 'creature', 'thing', 'marvel', 'countrywoman', 'the Lady of the Silver Moon', 'the mother of all the light that dwells in the stones of the earth', and 'old Mother Wotherwop' once each. She is described as 'old' 37 times; as 'grand' three times; as 'young' and 'great' three times each; as 'withered', 'filmy' and 'beautiful' twice each; and as 'small', 'huge', 'little', 'thin', 'tall', 'strong', 'lovely' and 'wonderful' once each.

In addition, on page 184 we find the chapter heading 'The mistress of the silver moon', and pages 206–12 constitute a chapter entitled 'What *is* in a name?', in which the lady is also referred to as 'the Mother of Light', 'she who had gone from them', 'she who with her absence darkened their air' and 'the Lady of the Light'.

Finally, there are three descriptive passages which deserve special attention. In the first book, the lady appears:

> dressed in the loveliest pale-blue velvet, over which her hair, no longer white, but of a rich golden colour, streamed like a cataract, here falling in dull gathered heaps, there rushing away in smooth shining falls. And ever as she looked, the hair seemed pouring down from her head, and vanishing in a golden mist ere it reached the floor. It flowed from under the edge of a circle of shining silver, set with alternated pearls and opals. On her dress was no ornament whatever, neither was there a ring on her hand, or a necklace or carcanet about her neck. But her slippers gleamed with the light of the milky way, for they were covered with seed-pearls and opals in one mass. Her face was that of a woman of three-and-twenty.
>
> (1872/1990: 79)

In the second book, she appears to Curdie as:

> a lady, 'beautiful exceedingly', dressed in something pale green, like velvet, over which her hair fell in cataracts of a rich golden colour. It looked as if it were pouring down from her head, and, like the water of the Dust-brook, vanishing in a golden vapour ere it reached the floor. It came flowing out from under the edge of a coronet of gold, set with alternated pearls and emeralds. In front of the crown was a great emerald which looked somehow as if out of it had come the light they had followed. There was no ornament else about her, except on her slippers, which were one mass of gleaming emeralds, of various shades of green, all mingling love-lily like the waving of grass in the wind and sun. She looked about five-and-twenty years old.
>
> (1883/1990: 203–4)

It is obvious that MacDonald had a keen eye on the passage quoted above in composing the present one. We encounter again 'velvet', though green rather than blue; hair 'of a rich golden colour'; 'cataract'; 'pouring'; 'vanishing in a golden – ere it reached the floor'; 'flow'; 'set with alternated pearls and –'; 'no ornament'; and 'slippers'. Finally, on page 217, the lady appears to him,

> fairer than when he saw her last, a little younger still, and dressed not in green and emeralds, but in pale blue, with a coronet of silver set with pearls, and slippers covered with opals, that gleamed every colour of the rainbow.

Here, the picture from page 203 has been altered to match that of page 79 of the earlier novel as her age is reduced, the green is replaced by blue, and the emeralds by opals. Only 'the milky way' of the first picture has been replaced by 'the rainbow'. There can hardly be any doubt in the mind of any reader that this lady is the universal, eternal, elemental young-and-old princess who is the light in our darkness.

Her femaleness serves a number of purposes: it links her to the good fairies of traditional fairytales; it links her to the other, little princess served, sought and revered by Curdie, also in fairytale fashion, but in addition so that human love can be seen as a reflection of divine love; it links her to the Virgin Mary; it subverts, for the moment of the fairytale, the established churches' emphasis on the maleness of God, although MacDonald elsewhere refers to God as the Father of Light (see MacGillis, 1990: 358, note 206) – or it redresses the balance.

In this divine, eternal mother, Irene finds herself: 'If I hadn't found the beautiful lady, I should never have found myself' (1872: 18). In Curdie, too, she finds her kin in so far as he is her natural counterpart: her complementary opposite, not only in sex and colouring, but also within the framework of MacDonald's dual-gendered, royally divine universe. Curdie 'was a very nice-looking boy, with eyes as dark as the mines in which he worked, and as sparkling as the crystals in their rocks' (1872/1990: 28).

The miners mine silver. This and other shining metals are constantly related to the royal characters. For example, Irene's father, the king, has 'a long dark beard, streaked with silvery lines', and 'as Irene sat on the saddle . . . it mingled with the golden hair which her mother had given her, and the two together were like a cloud with streaks of sun woven through it' (1872/1990: 55). Most importantly, however, silver relates to the moon and to the grandmother whose moon it is. In the centre of one of the rooms in which she appears hung the most glorious lamp that human eyes ever saw – the Silver Moon itself . . . with a heart of light so wondrous potent that it rendered the mass translucent, and altogether radiant.

(1883/1990: 217–8)

This lamp and relations of it are referred to regularly throughout both books. It is part of the essence of the grandmother, whose hair is repeatedly linked with silver, and who uses a 'silvery voice' (1872/1990: 78).

As the story of *The Princess and the Goblin* progresses it becomes clear that the goblins wish to steal Irene to be the bride of their own king's son, or, failing that, they intend to flood the mines from which the kingdom gets its wealth. Curdie saves the princess and the mines, though not before Irene, with the aid of her grandmother's guiding thread, has released Curdie from imprisonment by the goblins. The king promises Curdie that he shall marry the princess when they are both old enough, and rides away to his palace with Irene. In *The Princess and Curdie*, the king is being poisoned by his evil, self-seeking courtiers, who want to take over the kingdom. Here MacDonald explains the role of kings, the possible consequences of good government and the process of social perversion. The king,

was a real king – that is one who ruled for the good of his people, and not to please himself, and he wanted the silver not to buy rich things for himself, but to help him govern the country, and pay the armies that defended it from certain troublesome neighbours, and the judges whom he set to portion out righteousness amongst the people, that so they might learn it themselves, and come to do without judges at all. Nothing that could be got from the heart of the earth could have been put to better purposes than the silver the king's miners got for him. There were people in the country who, when it came into their hands, degraded it by locking it up in a chest, and then it grew diseased and was called *mammon*, and bred all sorts of quarrels, but when first it left the king's hands it never made any but friends, and the air of the world kept it clean.

(1883/1990: 175–6)

By the time Curdie reaches Gwyntystorm, 'lying and selfishness and inhospitality and dishonesty' are everywhere (1883/1990: 275), but Curdie, Irene and the grandmother heal the king and win a great battle against the wicked.

To guide Curdie on his way to Gwyntystorm, the grandmother gives Curdie two guides beside herself. One is an ability to feel the good or evil in a person by touching their hands. The second is the monstrous Lina. Lina has remarkable eyes which have a similar ability to light up the darkness as the grandmother's moon-lamp. They are 'green eyes with a yellow light in them' (1883/1990: 236); 'her two green eyes flaming yellow as sunflowers and seeming to light up the dungeon . . . two faint spots of light cast from her eyes upon the ground' (p. 255); and, with a highly significant choice of verb, the unusual 'lamping', Curdie 'had no light but the lamping of Lina's eyes' (p. 256). Nor is the divine spark, which is physically manifest in Lina's eyes, confined to her. On his journey, Curdie meets again the goblins' creatures from *The Princess and the Goblin*, though now, apparently, on the way towards redemption. Lina calls them to her to help in the coming struggle, and appears

> followed by forty-nine of the most grotesquely ugly, the most extravagantly abnormal animals imagination can conceive. To describe them were a hopeless task.
>
> (1883/1990: 237)

Nevertheless, the narrator succeeds, and Curdie names the creatures with descriptive, fairytale names; for example:

> the serpent with the long body, the four short legs behind, and the little wings before. . . . 'That's all very well for you, Mr Leg-serpent!' thought Curdie.
>
> (1883/1990: 302)

Clearly, the creatures are no longer so out of proportion with the divine universe that description and naming of them is impossible. They are now also prepared to 'obey at once' (p. 307). They help Curdie clean out the king's house of its wicked inhabitants and other dirt, they provide wholesome food for the king's company, and they play an important role in restoring order to the city.

Zipes (1983) entitles the chapter in which he deals with MacDonald and Wilde 'Inverting and subverting the world with hope', but he finds some difficulty in reconciling the ending of *The Princess and Curdie* with this heading:

> Irene and Curdie were married. The old king died, and they were king and queen. As long as they lived Gwyntystorm was a better city, and good people grew in it. But they had no children, and when they died the people chose a king. And the new king went mining and mining in the rock under the city, and grew more and more eager after the gold, and paid less and less heed to his people.

Rapidly they sunk to their old wickedness. . . . And so greedy was the king after gold, that . . . he caused the miners to reduce the pillars which Peter and they that followed him had left standing to bear the city. . . .

One day at noon, when life was at its highest, the whole city fell with a roaring crash. The cries of men and women went up with its dust and then there was a great silence.

Where the mighty rock once towered, crowded with homes and crowned with a palace, now rushes and raves a stone-obstructed rapid of the river. All around spreads a wilderness of wild deer, and the very name of Gwyntystorm has ceased from the lips of men.

(1883/1990: 341–2)

John Rowe Townsend (1965 [1990]: 76–7) finds this conclusion disturbing and 'savagely pessimistic', and believes that it expresses MacDonald's condemnation of 'the state of civilization in his own day'. According to Zipes, it embodies a warning, but may also be evidence of MacDonald's 'sober optimism: humanity must raise itself from a beastly state to form the utopian society and must constantly exercise creative and moral powers to pursue the ideal society. Otherwise, there will be a return to barbarism' (1983: 110). According to McGillis (1990: xvii–xviii), however, this interpretation, and, by implication, Townsend's, too, ignores MacDonald's deeply held religious faith:

the end of *The Princess and Curdie* is more than a warning; it is MacDonald's most uncompromising vision of what he calls in *Lilith* (1895) 'the endless ending'. . . . MacDonald . . . has the Christian's belief . . . in a time no longer when all dualities are reconciled. The wilderness of wild deer and the raving river of the book's final paragraph are, in the age of Darwin, a sign of renewal, of new beginnings. Creation begins anew in an unpeopled world. The possibility of hope fills this as yet untainted wild. MacDonald's imagination is apocalyptic; the conclusion of *The Princess and Curdie* is what MacDonald calls in his sermon, 'The Consuming Fire', a 'partial' revelation. In a universe of infinite meaning, created by an infinite God, all revelations must be partial, encouragements to keep us on the look-out for further revelations [see *Unspoken Sermons: First Series* (Alexander Strahan, 1865), 35].

Of course, McGillis's interpretation draws upon sources other than the story itself. Within the story, it is not the entire world that is destroyed, only Gwyntystorm, which, we know, has neighbours. Besides, there are 'men' left, from whose lips the town's name has ceased – though in the telling of the story it has obviously been revived. In these respects, the story itself supports MacGillis's optimistic interpretation; but the strongest support for it within the fairytales themselves comes from the contrast between, on the one hand, the remaining 'wildness of wild deer' and the rushing and raving of the 'rapid of the river' of this actual ending, and, on the other hand, the image presented in 'The Light Princess' of the unmaking of a world:

> It was fearful to think of the mud that would soon lie there baking and festering, full of lovely creatures dying, and ugly creatures coming to life, like the unmaking of a world.
>
> (1864; Lurie, 1993: 85)

Here the princess is imagining what will happen as a result of the swamp fairy Makemnoit's evil action. The deity's action has quite different results, and her image remains in the rushing river whose movement mirrors the impressions of her hair in the long descriptive passages quoted above.

Oscar Wilde

Oscar Fingall O'Flahertie Wilde (1854–1900) was born in Dublin, Ireland, but spent most of his adult life based in England. While studying at Oxford, he met John Ruskin and Walter Pater, whose views he synthesised in his own concept of social aesthetics, blended later in his life with a strong influence from the American Transcendentalist Ralph Waldo Emerson (1803–82) (Murray, 1990: xi–xii).

Wilde's first collection of fairytales, *The Happy Prince and Other Stories*, was published in 1888 and the second, *The House of Pomegranates*, in 1891, the same year which saw the appearance of his essay 'The Soul of Man under Socialism' in *The Fortnightly Review* (February 1891; quoted here as 1891c; all page references to the World's Classic Edition, Oxford University Press, 1990). This essay contributed to current debate in the periodical journals on 'Individualism, Socialism, Anarchism, poverty, philanthropy, and the limitations of freedom' (Murray, 1990: xi). It is also, according to Zipes (1983: 114–15), a key to understanding the fairytales.

In it, Wilde expresses his belief that human society will inevitably evolve towards socialism, and that socialism will lead to Individualism (1891c/1990: 2). According to Individualism, 'the proper aim of human life is not a self-denying altruism but rather a perfecting of the self' (Murray, 1990: xi) which is achieved by opposing 'conformity, consistency, imitation, philanthropy, charity, property, and the mob' (*ibid.* xii–xiii). The perfecting of the self, however, is not by any means to be confused with selfishness, which is the pushing away of the other, exemplified in the fairytales by 'the very lofty wall' (1888a/1979: 95) around the garden of the Happy Prince, and the 'high wall' (1888b/1979: 110) the Selfish Giant builds around his garden. These walls are built to protect from others what lies within them, that is, belongings, as expressed in the Giant's truism: 'My own garden is my own garden' (p. 110). But 'the true perfection of man lies, not in what man has, but in what man is' (1891c/1990: 7), and about what man is, or rather, will be, Wilde is thoroughly enthusiastic:

It will be a marvellous thing – the true personality of man – when we see it. It will grow naturally and simply, flower-like, or as a tree grows. It will not be at discord. It will never argue or dispute. It will not prove things. It will know everything. And yet it will not busy itself about knowledge. It will have wisdom. Its value will not be measured by material things. It will have nothing. And yet it will have everything, and whatever one takes from it, it will still have, so rich will it be. It will not be always meddling with others, or asking them to be like itself. It will love them because they will be different. And yet while it will not meddle with others it will help all, as a beautiful thing helps us, by being what it is. The personality of man will be very wonderful. It will be as wonderful as the personality of a child.

(1891c/1990: 9)

According to Murray (1979: 9), Wilde saw his fairytales as attempts 'to mirror modern life in a form remote from reality – to deal with modern problems in a mode that is ideal and not imitative' (Murray, 1979: 9). The problems in question include, among others, the relationship between poverty and privilege, outward form and inner worth, and between freedom and servitude. These problems, however, all arise from the same source, namely the institution of private property, for it is this which leads to the confusion of having with being. Attempts to use private property to alleviate poverty are immoral, since poverty arises in the first place from the institution of private property, and charity merely prolongs suffering by obscuring its ugliness. The only proper solution to poverty is 'to try to reconstruct society on such a basis that poverty will be impossible' (1891c/1990: 1–2). This solution is never proffered in the fairytales, and in this absence resides their most scathing criticism of the Victorian social order. Wilde's reformed characters may be rewarded, but their rewards take the form of ultimate retreat: 'In my garden of Paradise this little bird shall sing for evermore, and in my city of gold the Happy Prince shall praise me' (1888a/1979: 103); 'You let me play once in your garden, to-day you shall come with me to my garden, which is Paradise' (1888b/1979: 114).

Outcomes of this kind do nothing to solve fundamental social problems, and they suggest that in a social order such as the Victorian, even God is powerless, because by its very nature the system perpetuates the evils which may be temporarily alleviated through good deeds.

In view of Wilde's opinion of the institution of private property, it is unsurprising that his use of terms for those things that people consider precious is rather different from MacDonald's.

As we saw, MacDonald – who considers it right and proper that the miners should work to provide riches for a king to control and administer fairly for the good of all – constantly associates his deity and its universe with precious stones and metals, partly by decking out the deity's physical shape in them while explaining that apart from this she wore no ornaments, and partly through his similes. In the four Wilde stories analysed here, in contrast, precious stones and metals are presented, on all but thirteen occasions of mention, as either: ornaments (thirty-eight contexts); currency (thirty-one contexts); replacements for living creatures and parts of them (twelve contexts); contrasting with natural phenomena (five contexts); objects of worship (five contexts); associated with trade (five contexts); associated with death (four contexts); associated with frost (three contexts); and as replacements for other jewels (HP = 'The Happy Prince'; SG = 'The Selfish Giant'; YK = 'The Young King'; ST = 'The Star Child)':

Ornaments

HP	95	a large red ruby glowed on his sword-hilt
HP	96	a golden bedroom
HP	98	the great ruby from the Prince's sword
HP	100	amber beads
HP	103	The ruby has fallen out of his sword
YK	172	steps of bright porphyry
YK	173	bracelets of jade
YK	173, 180	robe of tissued gold
YK	173	ruby-studded crown

YK	173	sceptre with its rows and rings of pearls
YK	174	inlaid with agate and lapis-lazuli
YK	174	panels of powdered and mosaiced gold
YK	174	cup of dark-veined onyx
YK	174	tall reeds of fluted ivory bare up the velvet canopy
YK	174	the pallid silver of the fretted ceiling
YK	174	a flat bowl of amethyst
YK	176	great earrings of silver dragged down the thick lobes of his ears
YK	179	rubies for a king's crown
YK	181	bright porphyry staircase
YK	181	gates of bronze
YK	183	crown of gold
YK	183	sceptre of pearl
YK	183	marvellous vessels of gold
ST	238	a thing of gold
ST	238, 243	cloak of golden tissue
ST	240	the curious cloak of gold
ST	240, 242	a chain of amber
ST	242	a cloak of gold tissue
ST	242, 243	the amber chain
ST	246, 250	inlaid with gilt flowers
ST	246	a ring of graved jaspar
ST	246, 247	steps of brass

Currency

HP	97	He . . . is asking for oranges. His mother has nothing to give him. . . . Will you not bring her the ruby . . .
HP	98	laid the great ruby on the table
HP	99	Shall I take him another ruby
HP	100	Alas! I have no ruby now
HP	100	he found the beautiful sapphire
HP	101	slipped the jewel into the palm of her hand
HP	102	Leaf after leaf of the fine gold he brought to the poor
ST	238	a crock of gold
ST	238	the gold
ST	239	pieces of gold
ST	247	three pieces of gold. One is of white gold, and another is of yellow gold, and the gold of the third one is red

ST	247 (two mentions); 248 (three mentions): the piece of white gold
ST	247	the white gold
ST	247–8	a piece of white gold
ST	248 (two mentions); 249 (six mentions): piece of yellow gold
ST	249 (three mentions); 250 (two mentions): piece of red gold

Replacement

For skin

HP	95	He was gilded all over with thin leaves of fine gold
HP	102	I am covered with fine gold
HP	102	Leaf after leaf of the fine gold the Swallow picked off

For eyes

HP	95	for eyes he had two bright sapphires
HP	100	My eyes . . . are made of rare sapphires

For creature

HP	97	What, is he not solid gold
HP	98	the white marble angels were sculptured
HP	103	he is golden no longer
YK	172	lions of gilt bronze
YK	173	the marble brow of an antique statue
YK	173	a silver image of Endymion
YK	174	A laughing Narcissus in green bronze

Contrast with natural phenomena

YK	183	lilies that were whiter than pearls
YK	183	roses that were redder than rubies
YK	183–4	Whiter than fine pearls were the lilies, and their stems were of bright silver.
YK	184	Redder than male rubies were the roses, and their leaves were of beaten gold.
ST	239	no gold was in it, nor silver . . . but only a little child

Object of worship

HP	101	worships a large crystal
YK	172	the cry of pleasure that broke from his lips when he saw the . . . rich jewels
YK	177	he took the pearl, and . . . pressed it to his forehead and bowed.
YK	183, 184	jewelled shrine

| YK | 184 | the crystal of the many-rayed monstrance |

Association with trade

HP	98	weighing out money in copper scales
YK	173	merchants . . . to traffic for amber
YK	173	. . . to look for that curious green turquoise
YK	173	buy . . . moonstone and bracelets of jade
YK	176	ivory scales

Association with death

HP	98	The King is there himself in his painted coffin. . . . Round his neck is a chain of pale green jade, and his hands are like withered leaves
YK	173	turquoise which is found only in the tombs of kings
YK	177	a pearl in his right hand; a beautiful pearl; the pearl that he brought with him was fairer than all the pearls of Ormuz. . . . But his face was strangely pale, and as he fell upon the deck the blood gushed from his ears and nostrils. He quivered a little, and then he was still.
YK	180	There is Blood in the heart of the ruby, and Death in the heart of the pearl

Association with frost

SG	111	The frost painted all the trees silver
HP	102	the streets looked as if they were made of silver
HP	102	long icicles like crystal daggers

Replacement for other jewels

| HP | 100 | I will bring you back two beautiful jewels in place of those you have given away |

Exceptions

HP	99	eyes like green beryls
HP	100	The ruby shall be redder than a rose, and the sapphire shall be as blue as the great sea
HP	101	gold fish
HP	102	the living always think that gold can make them happy
HP	103	city of gold [God's]
SG	110	delicate blossoms of pink and pearl
SG	113	Its branches were all golden, and silver fruit hung down from them
YK	173	a Greek gem carved with the figure of Adonis

YK	174	the whole world was to be searched for jewels
YK	176	He was black as ebony
YK	180	a mirror of silver
ST	238	the Earth seemed to them like a flower of silver, and the moon like a flower of gold.
ST	240	he was white and delicate as sawn ivory

As is clear from the above listing, precious metals and stones figure most prominently in 'The Young King'. Thirty-nine of the contexts cited, and four of the exceptions, are drawn from that story. 'The Star Child' provides thirty-seven contexts and two exceptions; 'The Happy Prince' provides twenty-five contexts and one exception; and 'The Selfish Giant' provides just one context and two exceptions. The stories cover the following number of pages, respectively: YK: 13.5, ST: 16.25, HP: 9, SG: 9. This means that the average numbers of contexts for jewels and precious metals per page in each story are as follows:

	Non-exceptions	*Exceptions*	*Undifferentiated*
YK	2.9	0.3	3
ST	2.3	0.1	2.4
HP	2.9	0.1	3
SG	0.2	0.4	0.6

In other words, there are proportionally most mentions in 'The Young King' and 'The Happy Prince', with 'The Star Child' some way behind, and 'The Selfish Giant' a definite fourth. This, of course, is related to what the stories are about: three deal with royal personages while the fourth deals with a giant, his garden and a group of children. It is, however, interesting to observe that where the terms *pearl*, *silver* and *golden* occur in 'The Selfish Giant', the usage supports the connectivity between the stories which is clearly observable in the theme of personal development shared by them all.

The Young King is just about to become a king when we meet him, and the story traces his growth from one fascinated by the finery of kingship to one who rejects it because of its human cost and who understands and teaches his subjects that kingship is a moral or spiritual state. He is the only one of our main characters who is allowed to stay alive at the end of the story, and his is the only story in which a divine nature effectively replaces ornamentation and is recognised as superior to the trappings of luxury:

the sunbeams wove round him a tissued robe that was fairer than the robe that had been fashioned for his pleasure. The dead staff blossomed, and bare lilies that were whiter than pearls. The dry thorn blossomed, and bare roses that were redder than rubies . . . and the Bishop's face grew pale, and his hands trembled. 'A greater than I hath crowned thee,' he cried, and he knelt before him.

(1891a/1979: 184)

The Happy Prince is already a prince (although a dead one) when we encounter him. He persuades a swallow to distribute his finery among the poor of the city whose suffering he can see from his pedestal. This causes the Swallow's death as his deepening compassion for the Prince prevents him from flying away from the deepening winter. The story centres on the personal development of the Swallow, the Prince having already come to realise how isolated he had been from reality within the walled palace where he lived.

The Star Child is found in the forest on a winter's evening, wrapped in the golden cloak and wearing the amber chain which figure in the listing above, and he spends part of the story among the peasants who find him. The numerous references to pieces of gold in the listing derive from scenes during which he is acquiring the virtues he needs to be accepted as a king. His learning process, however, takes such a toll on him that 'after the space of three years he died. And he who came after him ruled evilly' (1891b/1979: 252).

'The Selfish Giant' contains neither royal persons nor their trappings, and *pearl*, *golden* and *silver* are used here only as colour terms. *Pearl* occurs in association with spring. In the Giant's garden 'were twelve peach-trees that in the spring-time broke out into delicate blossoms of pink and pearl' (1888b/1979: 110). *Golden* and *Silver*, however, are associated with winter. Silver is first encountered during the winter created in the Giant's garden by his selfishness: 'Only in the garden of the Selfish Giant it was still winter. . . . The frost painted all the trees silver' (p. 111). Towards the end of the story, *golden* and *silver* appear within the spring created during a natural winter by the appearance of the redeemer of the reformed Giant, who is about to die:

One winter morning he looked out of his window as he was dressing. . . . Suddenly he rubbed his eyes in wonder. . . . It certainly was a marvellous sight. In the farthest corner of the garden was a tree quite covered with lovely white blossoms. Its branches were all golden, and silver fruit hung down from them, and underneath it stood the little boy he had loved. . . .

And the child smiled on the Giant, and said to him, 'You let me play once in your garden, to-day you shall come with me to my garden, which is Paradise.'

And when the children ran in that afternoon, they found the Giant lying dead under the tree, all covered with white blossoms.

(1888b/1979: 114)

As these summaries suggest, there is both thematic and metaphorical continuity between the two sets of stories, those which concern royalty and the one that does not. There is thematic continuity in so far as each story traces the development of a character, and there is metaphoric continuity in so far as images of winter, with their associated terminology, appear in all the stories except for the 'The Young King', the one story in which the possibility of a happy ending is not precluded, in so far as we leave him alive and admired by his subjects (though it is also possible to read the ending as another withdrawal from society: 'no man dared look upon his face, for it was like the face of an angel' (1891a/1979: 184)). 'The Young King' is the most literal of the four stories in its presentation of social and personal immorality, and it is to this that the winter imagery is linked in the other three stories.

In 'The Happy Prince', the winter metaphor complements explicit statements of social criticism, and the increasing cold which eventually kills the Swallow contrasts sharply with the Swallow's improved spiritual state. The Swallow is a promising character from the start, because he is a non-conformist: he stays behind when his fellows fly to Egypt. However, there is a hint that his non-conformity is motivated by his rather high opinion of himself. He stays behind to be with a Reed who 'made him a low bow. So he flew round and round her' (1888a/1979: 96). Here, 'So' strongly suggests that the reason for the Swallow's courtship is the Reed's low bow, and there are several other indications that the Swallow is self-centred. He likes to feel distinguished and important: 'I come from a family famous for its agility, but still it was a mark of disrespect' (p. 98); 'the sparrows . . . said to each other "What a distinguished stranger!" so he enjoyed himself very much' (p. 99); 'I am waited for in Egypt' (pp. 97, 99). Furthermore, he is not yet ready to allow others to non-conform with himself 'I love travelling, and my wife, consequently, should love travelling also' (p. 96).

His progress is tracked through a change from being 'in love' to loving, from ego-centrality to altruism, and from concentration on outer form to concentration on inner state.

Prior to the Swallow's point of entry into the story, we learn, 'he was in love with the most beautiful Reed' to whom 'he had been so attracted by her slender waist that he had stopped to talk to her' (1888a/1979: 95), that is, he was attracted by her physical qualities. At this stage, he treats love as an action one can decide to engage in or not: '"Shall I love you?" said the swallow' (p. 95). He leaves the Reed because she will not come away with him, and alights at the feet of the statue of the Prince to spend the night in the 'golden bedroom' he provides. He feels a drop of what he takes to be rain and remarks: 'The climate in the north of Europe is really dreadful' (p. 96). However, the drop is really a tear from the sapphire eye of the Prince, who is weeping, we subsequently discover, at the misery of his city. So this misery is linked to climate through the Swallow's remark. With the Swallow's first good deed comes the first explicit mention of 'cold': 'It is curious . . . but I feel quite warm now, although it is so cold' (p. 98). Obviously this cold is external to the Swallow, who feels warm '"because you have done a good action", said the Prince'. Indeed, on the following morning the Swallow is seen by the Professor of Ornithology, who remarks, 'A swallow in winter.' The Swallow's second good deed, too, is associated with cold; it is directed at a poor poet who is 'too cold to write any more' (p. 99). The Swallow is reluctant to pick out the Prince's eye to give to the poet, and 'he began to weep'. However, the Prince persuades him, and asks him, subsequently, to stay just one more night. The Swallow replies: 'It is winter . . . and the chill snow will soon be here' (p. 100), adding *snow* and *chill* to the winter image. Yet he agrees to stay: 'but I cannot pluck out your eye. You would be quite blind then.' Still, the Prince prevails, and when the Swallow returns the third time he declares: 'You are blind now . . . so I will stay with you always', and insists 'I will stay with you always', in spite of the Prince's protestation that the Swallow must now go to Egypt. Still, the Swallow's education is not complete; the Prince has yet to explain to him:

> you tell me of marvellous things, but more marvellous than any-thing is the suffering of men and women. There is no Mystery so great as Misery. Fly over my city, little Swallow, and tell me what you see there.
>
> (1888a/1979: 101)

Eventually, the Prince is quite stripped of finery which the Swallow has distributed among the poor in the city. But 'Then the snow came, and after the snow came the frost. The streets looked as if they were made of silver . . . the poor little Swallow grew colder and colder, but he would not leave the Prince, he loved him too well' (p. 102). Then the swallow dies, and the Prince's leaden heart breaks. The narrator remarks: 'It certainly was a dreadfully hard frost' (p. 103).

The Frost recurs, along with the Snow, the North Wind and the Hail, in the garden of the Selfish Giant, when he has built the wall around it to keep the children out:

> Then the Spring came. . . . Only in the garden of the Selfish Giant it was still winter. . . . The only people who were pleased were the Snow and the Frost. . . . The Snow covered up the grass with his great white cloak, and the Frost painted all the trees silver. Then they invited the North Wind to stay with them. . . . 'This is a delightful spot,' he said, 'we must ask the Hail on a visit.' So the Hail came. . . . He was dressed in grey, and his breath was like ice.
>
> (1888b/1979: 111)

The Giant fails to comprehend the reason why winter stays in his garden, until one day the children make a hole in the wall and creep into the garden again. Then 'the Hail stopped dancing over his head, and the North Wind ceased roaring' (pp. 111–12). This gives the Giant the opportunity to act with mercy and to feel pity for one child:

> It was a lovely scene, only in one corner it was still winter. It was the farthest corner of the garden, and in it was standing a little boy. He was so small that he could not reach up to the branches of the tree, and he was wandering all round it, crying bitterly. The poor tree was still quite covered with frost and snow, and the North Wind was blowing and roaring above it. 'Climb up! little boy,' said the Tree, and it bent its branches down as low as it could; but the boy was too tiny.
>
> And the Giant's heart melted as he looked out. 'How selfish I have been!' he said; 'now I know why the Spring would not come here. I will put that poor little boy on the top of the tree, and then I will knock down the wall, and my garden shall be the children's play-ground for ever and ever.'
>
> (1888b/1979: 112)

Here, in the metaphor of the melting heart, Wilde clearly links the frost outside with the frost in the Giant's heart, and this image is strengthened in 'The Star Child', which begins:

> Once upon a time two poor Woodcutters were making their way home through a great pine-forest. It was winter, and a night of bitter cold. The snow lay thick upon the ground, and upon the branches of the trees; the frost kept snapping the little twigs.

Although this seems a realistic description, the animals' discussion of the weather soon puts paid to the impression of realism:

> So cold was it that even the animals and the birds did not know what to make of it.
> 'Ugh!' snarled the Wolf . . . 'this is perfectly monstrous weather. Why doesn't the Government look to it?'

The discussion culminates in the Woodpecker remarking 'it is terribly cold', and the narrator's agreement 'Terribly cold it certainly was' (1891b/1979: 237).

The Woodcutters continue on their realistically described way over 'caked snow', in and out of 'a deep drift', slipping 'on the hard smooth ice', and getting temporarily lost, which terrifies them, 'for they knew that the Snow is cruel to those who sleep in her arms'. It is in their relief at seeing the lights of their village that 'the Earth seemed to them like a flower of silver, and the moon like a flower of gold'. However, immediately after their relief they remember their poverty, and reason that 'seeing that life is for the rich, and not for such as we are' it would have been 'better that we had died of cold in the forest' (p. 238). Here they, like the Wolf, liken the cold conditions to affairs of state. At this point, they find the Star Child instead of the gold they had expected to lie where a star seems to fall in the forest. One argues that the child should be left to die

> But his companion answered him: 'Nay, but it were an evil thing to leave a child to perish here in the snow, and though I am as poor as thou art, and have many mouths to feed, and but little in the pot, yet will I bring it home with me, and my wife shall have care of it.'
> So very tenderly he took up the child, and wrapped the cloak around it to shield it from the harsh cold.
>
> (1891b/1979: 239)

When the Woodcutter returns home, the child is initially greeted with a coldness no less harsh than that expressed previously by his companion. This has grown from his wife's appreciation of how unjust and uncaringly wintry her society is; but the good Woodcutter works in his wife a conversion like that which the small child worked in the Giant:

'Our children lack bread, and shall we feed the child of another? Who is there who careth for us? And who will give us food?'

'Nay, but God careth for the sparrows even, and feedeth them,' he answered.

'Do not the sparrows die of hunger in the winter?' she asked. 'And is it not winter now?' And the man answered nothing, but stirred not from the threshold.

And a bitter wind from the forest came in through the open door, and made her tremble, and she shivered, and said to him: 'Wilt thou not close the door? There cometh a bitter wind into the house, and I am cold.'

'Into a house where a heart is hard cometh there not always a bitter wind?' he asked. And the woman answered him nothing, but crept closer to the fire.

And after a time she turned round and looked at him, and her eyes were full of tears. And he came in swiftly, and placed the child in her arms, and she kissed it.

(1891b/1979: 240)

From then on the story concerns the beautiful Star Child's development. He starts out proud, wicked and cruel to all the living creatures around him and his narcissism culminates in his rejection of his mother, who comes to him in the form of a beggar. This makes him so ugly that everyone except the Woodcutter's little daughter rejects him. He realises his sin and sets out to find his mother, but it is not until he has been prepared to sacrifice his life to save that of a leper that he becomes beautiful again. He finds his mother, the leper reveals himself to him as his father, 'and lo! they were a King and a Queen' (p. 251).

This is the only one of Wilde's fairytales in which the family motif plays a major role. No doubt this is partly because Wilde's main protagonists tend to be male, and males in fairytales tend to travel out from the family or be away from it for the major part of the story. They do, however, tend to end up in the family again, through marriage, and this is not the pattern in Wilde's stories. In fact, the clear difference in emphasis on the family motif in Wilde and MacDonald is connected with their different treatment of riches, and springs from their very different understanding of the ideal society.

The overriding theme in each of MacDonald's stories is inheritance. Characters inherit their physical appearance from nature – sun, wind, stars, gold, silver, crystals and so on – and they obey natural laws. In the two long fairytales, these laws spring from a source presented as the princess's great-great-grandmother, whose relationship with humankind is that of a servant–ruler. Her person is constantly associated with riches, silver in particular, and this metal is linked to her lamp of whose light every living creature inherits a portion. The metal itself also springs from her initially, but is inherited, administered and apportioned by the king for the benefit of his people, so the king, too, is both servant and ruler. This mingling in one person of authority and servitude does not disturb the person's place in a hierarchy; it justifies the hierarchy through eternalisation, naturalisation and rationalisation. The king's position is passed from parent to child (the exception spells the end of Gwyntystorm). The great-great-grandmother's kinship with the royal family is mirrored in earthly family relationships within the stories, in particular those which obtain within Curdie's family. The family is the seat of love, and this love is also found at the heart of the deity's laugh, which sounds like silver. But we also know that MacDonald considered every little girl a princess by nature, and every father, consequently, a king. So the naturally authoritarian-and-serving institution of the family is the natural centre for the good use and administration of a just portion of those riches which humanity inherits from nature. In the fairytales, MacDonald presents his social critique through processes of restoration of his ideal, natural social order.

Wilde's main concern in the fairytales is to show how things are, that it is the institution of private property which is responsible, and that while it remains, all good acts are ultimately fruitless, no matter whose they are and even if they are divine. Loving one's parents is simply one good sentiment among others, all equally ineffectual in procuring any lasting, general improvement in society. Wilde's fairytales do not present his vision of the ideal society, but, as we have seen, the vision in 'The Soul of Man under Socialism' is one of a community of equal, although varied, individuals existing in mutual love and respect. It is unlikely that the family would have any major political part to play in a property-free community of equals.

Edith Nesbit

Edith Nesbit (1858–1924) was born in London of middle-class parents. She is, according to Julia Briggs (1987: xi), 'the first modern writer for children', and although she falls into Zipes' category of basically conformist writers, in so far as her characters in the final analysis integrate into the established social order, her use of the genre is non-conventional. She is among the first fairytale writers to approach the genre from what might be called a feminist perspective, in so far as some of her female protagonists struggle against males who are demonstrably unjust and unreasonable. In addition, her fairytales are more precisely related to her present time than those of MacDonald and Wilde, and in this respect she foreshadows Dahl (see chapter 5 below).

Nesbit's career as a fairytale writer began with a commission she received in 1899 to write a sequence of modern fairytales for *The Strand*, entitled 'Seven Dragons', and later published as *The Book of Dragons* (1900) (J. Briggs, 1987: 218–19). The first story for *The Strand* was 'The Book of Beasts' (March 1899). In this story, Lionel is called upon to go and be king because his great-great-great-great-great-grandfather has died. He first hears of his impending coronation when his nurse says to him, 'Master Lionel, dear, they've come to fetch you to go and be King' (1900/1993: 203). As the referents for 'they' are at this stage unknown, the use of the pronoun sets the adult referents apart from Lionel's child-world, and this differentiation is reinforced through a contrast between their sphere of formality and Lionel's natural, childish behaviour.

The referents for 'they' are introduced into the story in the drawing-room to which Lionel 'bolted off without waiting for his clean handkerchief' as 'two very grave-looking gentlemen in red robes with fur, and gold coronets with velvet sticking up out of the middle like the cream in the very expensive jam tarts' (p. 203). The simile achieves two effects: first, it relates the gentlemen's apparel to something familiar to Nesbit's projected audience; second, it ridicules the gentlemen's apparel by reducing it to the level of expensive jam tarts. Lionel's reaction to the gentlemen's attempts at being scrupulously precise in referring to his paternal ancestor is equally effective. After two mentions by the grave gentlemen, Lionel refers to 'my great-great-however-much-it-is-grandfather', and is subsequently careful not to let them get beyond 'your great-great-', or 'Your great-' (pp. 205, 206) before interrupting them. In fact, the gentlemen's formal behaviour turns out to be a mere outward covering which can hide true intent, as we see in the following example, which contrasts low bows and politeness of tone and expression with the propositional content of the question asked:

when Lionel came in they bowed very low, and were beginning to ask Lionel most politely what on earth he was coming bothering for now.

(1900/1993: 205)

Similarly, in 'The Island of the Nine Whirlpools', where 'the dragon and the griffin were sitting primly on each side of' the Princess (1899/1993: 275), their prim demeanour obscures the fact that they are keeping the Princess prisoner.

As we might expect, the death of Lionel's male forebear is not a recent event. However, Lionel's subjects have, with typical Victorian thrift and loyalty to royalty, been saving

so much a week, you know, according to people's means – sixpence a week from those who have first-rate pocket-money, down to a halfpenny a week from those who haven't so much. You know it's the rule that the crown must be paid for by the people.

(1900/1993: 205)

Nesbit was a founder member of the Fabian Society (established 1884), and the example just quoted is a good illustration of her skill at introducing socialist propaganda in her children's stories (Ruck, 1935: 145–7, quoted in J. Briggs, 1987: xvi). By making the loyal subjects into children having to spend their pocket-money to pay for the crown, the message is no doubt easier for a child to relate to. She continues to voice her critique of people's attitude to the institution of monarchy in terms specially suited to her audience:

though the Prime Minister and the Chancellor and the Nurse might have the very poorest opinion of Lionel's private judgement, and might even slap him and send him to bed, the minute he got on his throne and set his crown on his head, he became infallible – which means that everything he said was right, and that he couldn't possibly make a mistake.

(1900/1993: 208)

However, there is not universal agreement about Nesbit's degree of commitment to the socialist cause. According to Julia Briggs (1987: xii), 'she remained a committed, if distinctly eccentric, socialist all her life', whereas Zipes (1987: 351) claims that Nesbit's commitment to socialism was 'superficial'. The fairytales give an impression of ambivalence or, to put it in more positive terms, moderation of attitude. Lionel remains king, and we meet, in his lifetime, his own 'great-great-great-great-grandchildren'. As king, he restores order, and releases beauty into the initially stiff and formal sphere of the palace, by learning to control and justly administer the magic held in check there since the death of the previous king.

About the previous king, too, Nesbit is temperate in her critique. He sold all the jewels in his crown, hence the need to purchase a new one. However, he sold the jewels to buy books and he had the crown itself 'tinned over, for fear of vanity' (1900/1993: 205). In Nesbit's writing, knowledge is, on the whole, a good thing, and books are the repositories of learning. On seeing the books in his library, Lionel exclaims: 'I shall read them all. I love to read. I am so glad I learned to read' (p. 205). The grave gentlemen, now revealed as the Chancellor and the Prime Minister, advise Lionel not to read any of the books, and explain that the old king had been 'too clever by half', and that he 'was *called* a wizard' (p. 206), although by now we may suspect that this modification is another surface gloss of polite deference to the old king, and that the latter really *was* a wizard. Lionel, in contrast, is not clever enough, and needs to learn how to be a responsible king. He releases from one of the forbidden books beautiful creatures, but also a dangerous dragon. In his defeat of the dragon, Lionel is aided by personal experience of the adverse effect of the dragon, but also by the beautiful creatures released from the book, who give him, on the one hand, determination and, on the other, practical help:

> At last came a Saturday when the Dragon actually walked into the Royal nursery and carried off the King's own pet Rocking-Horse. Then the King cried for six days, and on the seventh he was so tired that he had to stop. Then he heard the Blue Bird singing among the roses and saw the Butterfly fluttering among the lilies, and he said:
> 'Nurse, wipe my face, please. I am not going to cry any more.'
> Nurse washed his face, and told him not to be a silly little King. 'Crying,' said she, 'never did anyone any good yet.'
> 'I don't know,' said the little King. 'I seem to see better, and to hear better now that I've cried for a week.'
> (1900/1993: 211)

After this, Lionel manages to force the Dragon back into the book and to release everyone it has carried away, including a football team, whereas 'the Blue Bird and the Butterfly sing and flutter among the lilies and roses of the Palace garden to this very day' (p. 214).

The theme of beneficial crying recurs in Nesbit's feminist fairytale,

'The Island of the Nine Whirlpools', where, again, effective action follows when the three female characters 'had all cried as much as was good for them', and when the queen 'cried for a day and a night' (1899/1993: 275).

The characters in 'The Island of the Nine Whirlpools' are adult, but Nesbit was conscious of the parallels between the positions in society of children and women. According to Briggs, part of Nesbit's continuing appeal to children is that their social position remains effectively unaltered:

> Something within her clearly responded and coresponded to the position of the child in her society: second-rate citizens, then as now, they practised a quiet subversiveness, an irony at the expense of the absurd world of adults, which appealed strongly to her. She experienced all the child's primitive desires to control the world around her, yet she was conscious, as the children in her books are, of being a subject in a world where the rules are laid down by full-grown men – and where women, like children, are relegated to marginal positions and occupations.
>
> (J. Briggs, 1987: 399)

The female protagonists in 'The Island of the Nine Whirlpools' also share with Lionel a propensity for kissing: Lionel 'kissed Nurse' (1900/1993: 204); 'kissed the Prime Minister' (p. 207); and tells Nurse, 'kiss me in case I never come back' (p. 211). The Queen in 'The Island of the Nine Whirlpools' 'kissed [the witch] half a hundred times' (1899/1993: 273), and the witch subsequently helps her 'for the sake of the twice twenty-five kisses you gave me' (p. 275). The Queen, the Witch and the Princess 'kissed each other again and again' just before parting, and then the Princess waits for 'the day when her mother would come out of the stone and kiss her again' (p. 276). 'She kissed Nigel' (p. 282), who, it is true, also kisses her: 'He shut a little kiss in each hand before he let them go' (p. 278) and 'Nigel took his Princess in his arms and kissed her' (p. 280). However, Nigel is a young man to whom the narrator repeatedly refers as a boy: 'a certain sailor-boy'; 'the boy'; 'as good a boy as you'd find in a month of Sundays' (p. 276); 'the boy'. The Princess, 'pretending to be very grown up' calls him 'a silly boy' (p. 278) and tells him to 'be a good boy' (p. 279); he is elsewhere referred to by his name or as 'he'. This boy is, in any case, on the side of the women against the enchanter–King who has spellbound the Princess, his own daughter, as a punishment for insubordination.

Female/childish honest shows of affection, and the cathartic power of crying are contrasted in both stories with male attention to form, and the predominant male emotion of anger. Lionel's Prime Minister 'gave the King a good shaking, and said: "You're a naughty, disobedient little King," and was very angry indeed' (1900/1993: 207). In contrast, the Nurse tempers her non-physical scolding, 'You are a naughty little King', with the explanation, 'and nobody will love you' (p. 208). In 'The Island of the Nine Whirlpools', apart from being 'the Queen's husband', the King is 'an enchanter' (1899/1993: 271); 'would be very much annoyed' (p. 272); 'tore his black hair with fury' (p. 273); 'grew more and more clever at magic and more and more disagreeable at home'; appears 'looking as black as thunder'; 'was not a King with pretty home manners'; 'said . . . angrily'; 'could not utter a word for several minutes. He was too angry'; and 'was going to be disagreeable' (p. 274). The King's fury at discovering that his child is a girl lasts and grows for eighteen years, at which point he imprisons her on an island surrounded by nine whirlpools. She is further guarded by a dragon, who resembles the king in being 'hot-tempered' (p. 282).

Finally, 'the wicked King died' (1899/1993: 276), though his spell remains effective until the natural forces of love and knowledge conquer the magic of rage. The witch-turned-happy-old-woman reveals that 'Those whirlpools were made by the enchanter–King's dropping nine drops of blood into the sea. And his blood was so wicked that the sea has been trying ever since to get rid of it'. Nigel gradually recovers 'the wicked King's blood' in the form of rubies, which, it turns out, can be used for ploughing. 'So the wicked King did some good after all' (p. 283).

The enchanter–King's nasty temper contrasts with his wife and daughter's love and compassion, emotions shared by the female enchanter, the witch. The Queen pays the witch for her child with love, and the witch returns her love and helps her defeat the King's spell. In administering her own spell, the witch is de-witched:

> In doing this for you I lose all my witch's powers, and when I say the spell that changes you to stone, I shall change with you, and if ever we come out of the stone, I shall be a witch no more, but only a happy old woman.
>
> (1899/1993: 276)

The only time the Queen is associated with anger, she speaks 'crossly, for she was frightened' (p. 274) about what her husband might do to punish their daughter for defending her mother against the King.

However, although this tale is a clear expression of Nesbit's objection to male tyranny, the fact remains that it takes a wedding to a good boy to bring the tale to a happy close. This is also true of 'The Last of the Dragons', in which love again conquers anger, as Nesbit has a princess socialise a growling dragon by addressing it with a term of endearment. It is well known that Nesbit's feminism was as moderate as her socialism, at least following her marriage in 1880 to Hubert Bland. She was not in favour of the women's vote, or of economic and political equality, which, according to Bland, was unnatural, and likely to undermine family life (1900/1987: xviii). She takes care to differentiate between the sexes, reserving a separate paragraph for the remark concerning Lionel that

> He was a little sorry at first that he had not put on his best clothes, but he soon forgot to think about that. If he had been a girl he would likely have bothered about it the whole time.
>
> (1900/1993: 204)

Where a princess is allowed to engage in male pursuits, and to acquire characteristics which many writers might consider typically male, the princess must only excel in comparison with other *princesses*, and it must still be stated that she is nice and pretty:

> . . . said the Princess and went off to her fencing lessons, with which she took great pains. She took great pains with all her lessons – for she could not give up the idea of fighting the dragon. She took such pains that she became the strongest and boldest and most skilful and most sensible princess in Europe. She had always been the prettiest and nicest.
>
> (Zipes, 1987: 354)

Nor can Nesbit bear to dismiss the actions of a *pater familias* altogether, even when he is her wicked enchanter–King, who, when he takes his daughter to the Lone Tower: 'gave her a dowry, and settled a handsome income on her' (1899/1993: 275). The story ends with the narrator explaining that during the long years of waiting, the Princess 'lived on her income: and that is a thing which a great many people would like to be able to do' (p. 283).

'The Last of the Dragons' was published posthumously in *Five of us – and Madeleine* (1925), though Zipes (1987: 351–2) believes that it was probably written about 1900 along with her other dragon tales, even though here 'she did not portray the dragon as sinister'. In fact, there is nothing sinister in this tale at all; in particular, the portrait of the King is quite different from that in 'The Island of the Nine

Whirlpools', even though both tales are distinctly feminist. This king is at once conformist – 'It's always done my dear' (p. 353) – and ready to relax with his daughter in the garden. It is also the King himself who in the final sentence of the story completes the normalisation process of the dragon – by turning it into 'the first aeroplane' (p. 358) – which the narrator began in the first sentence: 'Of course you know that dragons were once as common as motor-omnibuses are now, and almost as dangerous' (p. 353).

This is perhaps the most 'realistic' of Nesbit's fairytales, and it is the fairytale tradition which is held responsible for the process of 'real-isation' of the genre:

> as every well-brought-up prince was expected to kill a dragon . . . the dragons grew fewer and fewer till it was often quite hard for a princess to find a dragon to be rescued from.
>
> (Zipes, 1987: 353)

The story concerns the 'last real live dragon', who resided in Cornwall 'a very long time ago, before what you call English History began' (p. 353). Yet its preferred food is petrol, the story's prince owns a motor-car and the dragon ends up as an aeroplane.

The three writers whose fairytales we have discussed in this section have different convictions. MacDonald writes from a theist position and desires a society organised along conventional, though divinely inspired, lines. Wilde writes from an Individualist position, is anarchic relative to the society of his day, but believes that human nature will evolve towards a state of perfection, which will guarantee joyous social harmony and mutual love and respect. Nesbit writes from the position of the mildly oppressed child/woman and seeks a catharsis of a basically desirable social order through a re-evaluation and readjustment in it of masculine and feminine virtues: more love and compassion; less anger and attention to form for form's sake.

The major difference between these writers and those of their twentieth-century colleagues to be dicussed in the following section and in chapter 6 below is that the grand solutions proffered by the former have no counterparts in the work of the latter.

LANGUAGE AND CONTROL IN TWENTIETH-CENTURY LITERARY FAIRYTALES

The second half of the twentieth century has not been a period of grand solutions, but, rather, of a number of avoidance strategies aimed at preventing universal annihilation. By the end of the

1960s, certainly, if not before, it had come to seem highly unlikely that either international co-operation, a good deal of which had followed in the wake of the 1939–45 war, or any form of national government would bring about the ends that Wilde foresaw for socialism. At the same time, aided by the media revolution, awareness had been raised about the possibility of planetary destruction in the wake of overpopulation, overconsumption and pollution, or as a result of the kind of war which would be the natural successor to that of 1939–45. As Zipes (1991: xxvii) remarks, the terrors which concern writers of literary fairytales after World War II include 'the demented and perverse forms of civilization that had in part caused atrocities and threatened to bring the world to the brink of catastrophe'.

The only twentieth-century writer of literary fairytales who figures as a favourite of Knowles' respondents is Roald Dahl (we discuss C.S. Lewis in chapter 6 on fantasy fiction), and discussion in this section is confined to the following works by Dahl: *James and the Giant Peach* (first published in the United States in 1961; published in Great Britain by Allen & Unwin in 1967; page references to the Puffin reprint, 1990) and *The BFG* (first published by Jonathan Cape 1982; page references to the Puffin edition, 1984).

In chapter 4, we discussed aspects of Dahl's mode of dealing with adult–child relationships, particularly within families and in school. In the fairytales, Dahl casts his net wider, as the BFG's remark, 'Grown-up human beans is not famous for their kindness' (1982/ 1984: 116), among many others, demonstrates. The fairytales are clearly both subversive and didactic; as Sophie is aware, the 'extraordinary giant' author of *The BFG* 'was disturbing her ideas. He seemed to be leading her towards mysteries that were beyond her understanding' (p. 102).

Apart from *The Gremlins*, which was published as a Disney picture-book in 1943, all of Dahl's fairytale-like children's books were written after World War II, and some, including *The BFG*, show clear signs of what Treglown calls Dahl's 'humanitarian revulsion against war' (1994: 65). This revulsion is matched by a clear intention to promote compassion for and knowledge about other species.

James and the Giant Peach was the first of Dahl's children's books to attain widespread popularity. Within a year of its publication, it had sold 6,500 hardback copies; by 1971 the sales figure for the United States alone was 266,435; and by 1975, British sales figures were 115,000 paperback and 45,000 hardback copies (Treglown, 1994: 137, 177, 186). The book contains a number of pleasing plays on words in which what are normally figures of speech are made to function literally. For example, chapter 12 ends with the Grasshopper asking, 'So would you be kind enough, Miss Spider, to make the beds?' (1961/1990: 42). Chapter 13 begins with a description of a bed which the spider has literally created. When the peach begins to move, the giant ladybird asks James 'would you like me to take you under my wing', immediately turning the figure literal by adding 'so that you won't fall over when we start rolling?' (p. 47). This type of play on the figurative/literal is fully matched in Dahl's manipulation of fairytale conventions which blurs the boundary between fiction and reality.

The book appears to begin as realism, outlining the 'happy life' of James, who lived 'peacefully with his mother and father in a beautiful house beside the sea', with 'plenty of children for him to play with'. His, claims the narrator, was 'the perfect life for a small boy'. It is not a lifestyle granted to the majority of Dahl's characters; nor does James remain thus blissful for more than a paragraph of story-space, covering the first four years of his life.

With the demise of James' parents in the second paragraph – 'Both of them suddenly got eaten up . . . by an enormous angry rhinoceros which had escaped from the London Zoo' (1961/1990: 7) – and James' removal to 'a queer ramshackle house on the top of a high hill in the south of England' (p. 8), where he is to live with his horrible Aunts Sponge and Spiker, the story moves into the fairy realm. As perceived from this realm, however, the realism in which James had lived before takes on fairytale characteristics. From the garden of his aunts' house:

> he could see a tiny grey dot far away on the horizon, which was the house that he used to live in with his beloved mother and father. And just beyond that, he could see the ocean itself – a long thin streak of blackish-blue, like a line of ink, beneath the rim of the sky.
>
> (1961/1990: 8)

As time goes on, and James becomes 'sadder and sadder, and more and more lonely',

> he used to spend hours every day standing at the bottom of the garden, gazing wistfully at the lovely but forbidden world of woods and fields and ocean that was spread out below him like a magic carpet.
>
> (1961/1990: 10)

By placing this reality, fairytale-like, in the distance and by using the ink-line and magic-carpet similes, the narrator suggests that it is not, in fact, reality at all, but a wishful interpretation which cannot be sustained any more than the happy ending can be transferred to real life.

Through the agency of a magician whose magic green living seeds James spills on the ground, a tree in his aunts' garden sprouts a giant peach inside which James travels to America together with seven giant insects. Here, 'every one of them became rich and successful in the new country':

> The Centipede was made Vice-President-in-Charge-of-sales of a high-class firm of boot and shoe manufacturers.
>
> The Earthworm, with his lovely pink skin, was employed by a company that made women's face creams to speak commercials on television.
>
> The Silkworm and Miss Spider . . . set up a factory together and made ropes for tightrope walkers.
>
> The Glow-worm became the light inside the statue of Liberty, and thus saved a grateful City from having to pay a huge electricity bill every year.
>
> The Old-Green-Grasshopper became a member of the New York Symphony Orchestra, where his playing was greatly admired.
>
> The Ladybird, who had been haunted all her life by the fear that her house was on fire and all her children gone, married the Head of the Fire Department and lived happily ever after.
>
> (1961/1990: 133–5)

Everyone finds their proper place, and proper places, as we see, can include most spheres of modern life. However, America is not actually 'the new country' any longer, and the characters who thus happily find their right place in life are so firmly fantastic that we cannot easily transfer their fulfilment to reality.

James himself takes up residence inside the peach stone in Central Park, where he holds open house for the 'hundreds and hundreds of children' who come 'from far and near' to play with him. When James lived with his aunts, the narrator reminds us, he 'had been the saddest and loneliest little boy that you could find'; but now he 'had all the friends and playmates in the world'.

> And because so many of them were always begging him to tell and tell again the story of his adventures on the peach, he thought it would be nice if one day he sat down and wrote it as a book.

So he did.

And *that* is what you have just finished reading.

(1961/1990: 135–6)

So the fiction is presented as James', and in it he turns himself from 'a small boy' to a sad and lonely little boy, and finally into 'a famous person' who is a writer. His plenty of friends become none at all for the three years he spends living with his aunts, and then 'all the friends and playmates in the world'. His home turns from 'a beautiful house' to 'a queer, ramshackle house' and finally to a peach stone. His 'gentle parents' are replaced by the nasty aunts. But at the end of the story, there are no adult guardian figures. There is only James, the writer for children – a benevolent figure, albeit a fictional one, but a child-figure liberated from adult control.

Adult control has a tendency, in Dahl's fairytales, to be linked with inhibition and abuse. Aunt Sponge and Aunt Spiker contrast sharply with James' lost 'gentle', 'beloved' parents of the fiction of his early life. The aunts 'were both really horrible people. They were selfish and lazy and cruel, and right from the beginning they started beating poor James for almost no reason at all' (1961/1990: 8). Clearly, the two contrasting pictures of adults presented here correspond fairly well to the ambivalent feelings children often have towards their parents or guardians: total adoration when the adults are being what the child perceives as reasonable, and total, if only momentary, hatred on the other, when the adults restrict the child. In Dahl's fairytales, however, either type of parenting is restrictive, and so is either type of child reaction. The natural development from child to adult of the mouse-boy in *The Witches* is arrested as much by his love for his grandmother as by the witches' spell. James' love for his parents would have been as restrictive as the terror he experiences while living with the aunts.

The restriction of the aunts' regime is made explicit in Dahl's use of the terminology of imprisonment, punishment and force:

His room was as bare as a prison cell.

Terrible punishments were promised him, such as being locked up in the cellar with the rats for a week.

(1961/1990: 8)

James was forced to stay locked in his bedroom, peeping through the bars of his window.

(1961/1990: 30)

As well as physical abuse, James is subjected to verbal abuse by the aunts who 'always referred to him as "you disgusting little beast" or "you filthy nuisance" or "you miserable creature"' (p. 8).

This regime makes James fearful. His only way of countering his aunts' abuse is to run, hide and cry, or to look at them 'with large frightened eyes' (1961/1990: 14); when he encounters the magician, 'James was too frightened to move' (p. 15); he is afraid of the dark: 'He stared straight ahead with large frightened eyes, hardly daring to breathe' (p. 32); and when he enters the peach and encounters the giant insects, 'his face [was] white with horror'; 'he started to stand up, but his knees were shaking so much he had to sit down again' (p. 35); and his 'large frightened eyes travelled slowly round the room' (p. 36). Of course, he has good reason to be frightened on each of these occasions, but his fear here is in marked contrast to his resourcefulness in the face of equally terrifying occasions during his escape, when he is never frightened into pure inactivity and withdrawal.

In fact, James' release from fear begins with his first encounter with beauty, magic and wonder, closely intertwined. The magician shows James

> a mass of tiny green things. . . . They were extraordinary beautiful, and there was a strange brightness about them, a sort of luminous quality that made them glow and sparkle in the most wonderful way.
>
> (1961/1990: 16)

After James has had this experience, there is no reference to fear on his part, in spite of the frightening image presented in the immediately following description of the magician's animal-like crouching and subsequent sudden mad behaviour when he explains how the beautiful things have been created:

> He was crouching a little now and pushing his face still closer and closer to James. . . . Then suddenly he jumped back and began waving his stick madly in the air. 'Crocodile tongues!' he cried. 'One thousand long slimy crocodile tongues boiled up in the scull of a dead witch for twenty days and nights with the eyeballs of a lizard! Add the fingers of a young monkey, the gizzard of a pig, the beak of a green parrot, the juice of a porcupine, and three spoonfuls of sugar. Stew for another week, and then let the moon do the rest!'
>
> (1961/1990: 16–17)

When James first sees the giant peach his reaction to its beauty contrasts sharply with his aunts' reaction to it as a meal and a business venture. They begin 'shouting all sorts of silly things in their excitement', including 'Hallelujah!', 'What a peach', 'Magnifico!', 'Splendifico!' and 'And what a meal!' In contrast to these remarks which the punctuation signals as exclamations and which are accompanied by the reporting verbs 'shouted' and 'cried out', the 'spellbound' James murmurs quietly to himself, 'Oh, isn't it beautiful. It's the most beautiful thing I've ever seen' (p. 26). On the following page, this sentiment is confirmed by the narrator: 'The skin of the peach was very beautiful.' However, James' murmured remark is greeted by his Aunt Spiker snapping 'Shut up you little twerp! . . . It's none of your business!' To the aunts, it is all business. They agree not to eat the peach because 'There's a pile of money to be made out of this' (p. 28) and they sell tickets for people to come and see the peach.

James' encounter with the magician has awakened in him a sense of magic which takes the form of premonitions:

> *Something is about to happen*, he told himself. *Something peculiar is about to happen any moment*. He . . . could feel it in his bones that something was going to happen soon. He could feel it in the air around him . . . [*sic*] in the sudden stillness that had fallen upon the garden . . . [*sic*]
>
> (1961/1990: 23)

This sense of magic liberates James from his petrification in the dark garden. It is triggered by the sight of the magic peach:

> And what a dazzling sight it was! The moonlight was shining and glinting on its great curving sides, turning them to crystal and silver. It looked like a tremendous silver ball lying there in the grass, silent, mysterious, and wonderful.
>
> And then all at once, little shivers of excitement started running over the skin on James's back.
>
> *Something else*, he told himself, *something stranger than ever this time, is about to happen to me again soon*. He was sure of it. He could feel it coming.
>
> He looked around him, wondering what on earth it was going to be. The garden lay soft and silver in the moonlight. The grass was wet with dew and a million dewdrops were sparkling and twinkling like diamonds around his feet. And now suddenly, the whole place, the whole garden seemed to be *alive* with magic.
>
> (1961/1990: 32–3)

James, in contrast to his aunts' hunter-like reaction to the peach as to a dead animal, approaches the peach as if it were a living animal. He 'put out a hand and touched it gently with the tip of one finger. It felt soft and warm and slightly furry, like the skin of a baby mouse. He moved a step closer and rubbed his cheek lightly against the soft skin' (p. 34).

It is this talent for wonderment and gentleness, along with a desire to learn, which Dahl's adult controllers of children restrict. While James lived with his aunts, he 'had never even *wondered* how a grasshopper made his sounds' (1961/1990: 84). But when he enters the peach, he begins a journey of discovery of wonders, helped by his travelling companions from whom he receives fun, friendship, kindness, trust and lessons in natural history and in the need to come to understand the world:

> 'My dear young fellow,' the Old-Green-Grasshopper said gently, 'there are a whole lot of things in this world of ours that you haven't started wondering about yet.'
>
> (1961/1990: 84–5)

James, along with the reader, learns about the nature of the creatures he encounters inside the peach. We learn, for instance, that centipedes have not 100, but only forty-two legs, and that they have jaws as sharp as razors; that glow-worms are not worms but female fireflies without wings; that there are two kinds of grasshopper, and that they make their music differently; that earthworms swallow and excrete soil and that this makes the soil light; and that ladybirds clean crops of other insects. It is noticeable, however, that it is not by using their 'natural' talents that the useful earthworm and ladybird find acceptance in 'the new country' of the fiction, and that it is only by using their natural talents fictionally that the rest do.

The narrator, too, engages in some explicit reader education, which has the further purpose of making the fantastic happenings of the story appear more credible. Just after the successful outcome of James' plan to lift the peach out of the ocean by lassooing seagulls with rope spun by the spider and the silkworm, the narrator explains why the sharks from which the travellers have now escaped have not caused much damage to the peach:

> A shark, you see, has an extremely long, sharp nose, and its mouth is set very awkwardly underneath its face and a long way back. This makes it more or less impossible for it to get its teeth into a vast smooth curving surface such as the side of a peach. Even if the creature turns on its back it still can't do it, because the nose

always gets in its way. If you have ever seen a small dog trying to get its teeth into an enormous ball, then you will be able to imagine roughly how it was with the sharks and the peach.

(1961/1990: 80–1)

This careful explanation of the less surprising event – that the peach is almost undamaged – draws attention away from the more surprising event that the peach is being transported through the air by 502 seagulls.

The Ladybird, significantly, says of the fact that the peach is not damaged: 'It must have been some kind of magic. . . . The holes must have healed up by themselves' (1961/1990: 81). This remark, like James' projection of his former life into a fairytale distance in the first chapter, complicates the relationship between fiction and reality, magic and the natural. It is a real fact about real sharks that would have prevented the fictional peach from having holes in it, had the fictional events actually taken place. The fictional ladybird, however, thinks that the holes of her imagination have been healed by magic. Similarly, when the centipede has sawn through the stem that connects the peach to the tree, which causes the peach to roll down the hill metering out just desert to the aunts on its way, the aunts' status changes from fictional reality to that of a fiction transported into reality:

And behind it, Aunt Sponge and Aunt Spiker lay ironed out upon the grass as thin and lifeless as a couple of paper dolls cut out of a picture book.

(1961/1990: 50)

James' aunts are among the most physically and verbally abusive of Dahl's adult characters, though their unpalatable characteristics are shared in some measure by adults in other stories.

The interlinked themes of imprisonment and punishment, too, recur in several other stories, including *The BFG*:

You got punished if you were caught out of bed after lights-out. Even if you said you had to go to the lavatory, that was not accepted as an excuse and they punished you just the same.

(1982/1984: 10)

Sophie is imprisoned in her bed at night by the rules imposed by the referents for 'they'. 'They' are excluded from this fiction except in a subsequent piece of direct speech by Sophie which introduces one of 'them' by name, but which, otherwise, simply expands on the information in the paragraph just presented:

> That place you took me from was the village orphanage. . . . The woman who ran it was called Mrs Clonkers and if she caught you breaking any of the rules, like getting out of bed at night or not folding up your clothes, you got punished. . . . She locked us in the dark cellar for a day and a night without anything to eat or drink. . . . It was horrid. . . . We used to dread it. There were rats down there.
>
> (1982/1984: 38–9)

This segregates 'them' more absolutely from Sophie than Lionel's Prime Minister and Chancellor were segregated from him (see above). Lionel's Prime Minister and Chancellor, too, are first introduced as unknown referents: 'Master Lionel, dear, they've come to fetch you' (Nesbit, 1900/Lurie, 1993: 203). However, they get to play fairly active roles in the story; Sophie's controllers never enter it in person.

Clearly, the regime Sophie describes recalls that of James's aunts, though in *The BFG*, the beatings to which James was subjected by the aunts is replaced by the consumption of a multitude of humans by nine giants. The overall structure of the narratives is identical in so far as the semi-realism of their beginnings turn faerie through a character's perception, and in so far as the endings of both books reveal a main character to be the narrator: 'But where, you might ask, is this book that the BFG wrote? It's right here. You've just finished reading it' (1982/1984: 207).

The BFG begins with a realistic description of Sophie's sleeplessness, which, however, falls under the chapter heading 'The witching hour'. Sophie's midnight impressions of reality takes us into the fairy realm:

> In the silvery moonlight, the village street she knew so well seemed completely different. The houses looked bent and crooked, like houses in a fairytale. . . . Across the road, she could see Mrs Rance's shop. . . . It didn't look real.
>
> (1982/1984: 10–11)

In both books, as we see, magic, beauty and escape are clearly linked with moonlight and night, from which children are, of course, usually excluded by bedtimes imposed by adults. Sophie's impending escape is triggered by the intrusion into her prison of a moonbeam. At a moment when she is intent on shutting out its disturbing light, her

longing to see the world overlaid by magic triggers the event which is
to lead to her release from adult control:

> She longed to . . . lean out of the window to see what the world
> looked like now that the witching hour was at hand. . . . The
> longing became so strong she couldn't resist it. Quickly, she
> ducked under the curtains and leaned out of the window.
>
> (1982/1984: 10)

Having adopted the fairytale mode of perception, Sophie perceives
'something' which she gradually defines in more and more detail:
'something black'; 'something tall and black'; 'something very tall
and very black and very thin' (p. 11); 'some kind of PERSON'; 'A GIANT
PERSON'; and, finally, 'the Giant' (p. 13). Since this part of the text
concerns Sophie looking out of the window, it is not surprising to find
that it contains a number of verbs of seeing. However, except for the
sentence 'Sophie could see it' (p. 12), it is not until Sophie has defined
the Giant for herself that the two of them are related as Sensor and
Phenomenon in Sophie's Mental process of seeing, as in 'she/Sophie
saw him/the Giant'. Then, however, they are placed in that relationship four times in one paragraph consisting of ten main clauses:

> She saw the Giant. . . . He bent over. . . . He took something. . . .
> It looked like. . . . He unscrewed. . . . Sophie watched. . . . She
> saw the Giant . . . and she saw him. . . . She saw the Giant . . . and
> *whoof*, he blew.
>
> (1982/1984: 13)

Here, even where the Giant is the Actor in a Material process, it is
clear that he is perceived as such by Sophie, because the paragraph
begins with the sentence in which Sophie sees him, and because her
seeing him is repeated regularly. In contrast, while the giant is still a
mere 'something', Sophie's only action is a freezing into inactivity
and out of the syntax:

> Suddenly she froze. *There was something coming up the street*
> *on the opposite side.*
> *It was something black . . . [sic]*
> *Something tall and black . . . [sic]*
> *Something very tall and very black and very thin.*
>
> (1982/1984: 11)

So, it is by going through a process of defining something mysterious
that shows itself to her that Sophie is enabled to relate to it; and
although the fact that Sophie has seen the Giant seems, initially, to

endanger both of them, in the end the interaction between the two
liberates both Sophie and the Giant, and humanity in general, from
perpetual imprisonment of one kind or another.

The Giant takes Sophie to a cave in Giant Country. If she leaves the
cave, the other giants will eat her, and the Giant himself refuses to take
her home because she might tell people about him. This appears worse
than her imprisonment in the orphanage, because she would eventually
have grown out of that; however, the Giant liberates her mentally:

> This extraordinary giant was disturbing her ideas. He seemed to be
> leading her towards mysteries that were beyond her understanding.
> (1982/1984: 102)

Thus liberated, she is able to think of a way for both of them to work
together to liberate themselves and every one else (except the nasty
giants, who end up in 'perpetual imprisonment' (p. 199) in a hole in
the ground). Her plan involves a traditional fairytale character, a
queen, except that this one is clearly recognisable as the contemporary Queen of contemporary England. The Queen has the power
required to effect the capture of the nine other giants, and the
acceptance into society as free agents of the BFG and Sophie.

A good deal of narration is given over to description of these
unpleasant-looking, bullying, meat-eating giants. It is therefore particularly effective when Dahl begins to compare them favourably
with humans. First of all, the BFG explains to Sophie that one reason
why no human being has ever had any suspicion of foul play when the
giants have eaten great numbers of them is that

> human beans is disappearing everywhere all the time *without* the
> giants is guzzling them up. Human beans is killing each other
> much quicker than the giants is doing it. . . . Human beans is the
> only animal that is killing their own kind.
> (1982/1984: 78)

There follows a scene in which Sophie attempts to defend her
species, and the BFG demonstrates the invalidity of her argument:

> 'But human beans is squishing *each other* all the time,' the BFG
> said. 'They is shootling guns and going up in aerioplanes to drop
> their bombs on each other's heads every week. Human beans is
> always killing other human beans.'
>
> He was right . . . and Sophie knew it. . . . 'Even so,' she said,
> defending her own race, 'I think it's rotten that those foul giants
> should go off every night to eat humans. Humans have never done
> *them* any harm.'

'That is what the little piggy-wig is saying every day,' the BFG answered. 'He is saying, "I has never done any harm to the human bean so why should he be eating me?"'

(1982/1984: 79)

The last two paragraphs in this quotation clearly set up a relationship of equivalence between the giants' action of eating humans and the human action of eating pigs, and, within that, interestingly enough, of equivalence between *both* giants and humans *and* humans and pigs:

Sophie: giants eat humans; humans have never harmed giants.
BFG: humans eat pigs; pigs have never harmed humans.

The fact that the meat-eating giants are described as greedy and dirty reinforces this multiple identity relationship: the giants to whom humans are being related behave like the (stereotypical) pigs to whom humans are also being related.

The BFG is an exception among giants: he is a catcher of dreams, of the mysterious: '"Dreams is full of mystery and magic" the BFG said. "Do not try to understand them"' (1982/1984: 128). Sophie is an exception among children: there are ten girls in her orphanage, but Sophie is the only one (as far as we know) with a longing for mystery and magic – for seeing the world at the witching hour.

The contrast between the sensitivity of the BFG and the greed of the other nine giants is symbolised by his having 'Marvellous Ears' (1982/1984: 38, chapter heading) while they have huge mouths: 'the mouth was huge. It spread right across the face almost ear to ear' (p. 57). With his ears, the BFG can hear '*all the secret whisperings of the world*' (p. 43) – dreams, the footsteps of a ladybird, the beating of a heart, 'faraway music coming from the stars in the sky' (p. 44) and the tiniest effect of the smallest action of wanton destruction:

'I can hear plants and trees.'
'Do *they* talk?' Sophie asked.
'They is not exactly talking,' the BFG said. 'But they is making noises. For instance, if I come along and I is picking a lovely flower, if I is twisting the stem of the flower till it breaks, then the plant is screaming. . . . It is screaming just like you would be screaming if someone was twisting *your* arm right off.

(1982/1984: 44–5)

The BFG's simile here, 'just like you would be screaming if . . .' obviously encourages Sophie and the reader to put themselves in the

place of the suffering plants and trees, and further encouragement to
do so follows immediately:

> If I is chopping an axe into the trunk of a big tree, I is hearing a
> terrible sound coming from inside the heart of the tree. . . . A soft
> moaning sound . . . like the sound an old man is making when he is
> dying slowly. . . . Trees is living and growing just like you and me.
> . . . They is alive. So is plants.
>
> (1982/1984: 45–6)

Giant Country, together with the neighbouring Dream Country, is
the nearest Dahl gets to inventing the 'other place' of fantasy. It is
described as 'not quite of this earth' (p. 21), but the Giant reaches it
by running across country, and not by any kind of magical transfer to
another realm. It may be, in fact, that the sense in which it is not quite
of this earth is not spatial, but hypothetical: it is how the world nearly
ended up or could end up, resembling, as it does, a post-nuclear world
far more than it resembles the traditional Giant's castle in the sky:

> He went . . . up over a range of hills as bare as concrete, and soon
> he was galloping over a desolate wasteland that was not quite of
> this earth. The ground was flat and pale yellow. Great lumps of
> blue rock were scattered around, and dead trees stood everywhere
> like skeletons. The moon had long since disappeared and now the
> dawn was breaking.
>   Sophie . . . saw suddenly ahead of her a great craggy mountain.
> The mountain was dark blue and all around it the sky was gushing
> and glistening with light. Bits of pale gold were flying among
> delicate frosty-white flakes of cloud, and over on one side the
> rim of the morning sun was coming up red as blood.
>
> (1982/1984: 21–2)

Here, the vocabulary of desolation, death and destruction – 'bare as
concrete', 'desolate wasteland', 'dead trees', 'like skeletons', 'red as
blood' – infects the sense of other lexical items, so that the scattering
of the rocks, the disappearance of the moon, the bittiness of the flying
pale gold and the flakes of clouds all suggest a general shattering of
wholes such as might occur after an explosion.

The description of Dream Country is reminiscent of the metaphor
of the mists of time, although its ashy greyness and its ghostliness
might also suggest the aftermath of a great disaster:

> They were in a country of swirling mists and ghostly vapours.
> There was some sort of grass underfoot but it was not green. It was

ashy grey. There was no sign of a living creature and no sound at all. . . . Sophie shivered and stared around her at the swirling mists and ghostly vapours.

'Where are we?' she asked.

'We is in Dream Country,' the BFG said. 'This is where all dreams is beginning.'

(1982/1984: 80)

If one takes it that this country contains ghosts and ashes, then this is clearly a highly anarchic vision, suggesting that new dreams can only be born subsequently upon the destruction of an old order.

By combining fragments of captured dreams, the BFG makes for the Queen of England a nightmare about the nine human-eating giants consuming English children, which she is to dream at about the time that this is actually taking place. She is further to dream that when she wakes she will find on her bedroom window-sill Sophie, who will tell her where she can find a Big Friendly Giant, who knows where the nasty giants live. As Sophie predicts, when the Queen sees her dream mirrored in reality, she believes it and acts to prevent any repetition of its nightmarish aspects.

Perhaps, then, since the dream-blender turns out to be the asserted narrator of the story, Dahl is hoping that the nobler (Queen-like) among his readers will react in a similar manner to the nightmarish aspects of the book – that is, take steps to prevent desolation, abuse of power by adults over children, by powerful humans over less powerful humans, and by humans over other species.

If so, then this book holds out more hope than those discussed earlier in this section. Treglown has pointed to the similarities between it and *The Witches*, published one year later:

> *The Witches* is *The BFG* after a series of sex-changes. An old woman and a little boy collaborate in overthrowing the forces of evil, represented by (female) witches. In *The BFG*, the characters are an old man, a little girl, and (male) giants.

(Treglown, 1994: 226)

He suggests that the shift in attitude evidenced in these two books results from the combined influences of Dahl's editor Stephen Roxburgh 'and of marital happiness' (Treglown, 1994: 225). Nevertheless, the overriding effect remains a questioning of what is possibly the most fundamental assumptions of modern civilisation: that the family is the natural environment for growth and development and that the human is a species superior to all others.

6 Fantasy fiction

INTRODUCTION

In chapter 5 above, we suggested that literary fairytales tend, in general, to conform fairly closely to the constraints which guide realist fiction. The fairytale remains within one time, one space and one world, and tells its story largely in chronological order. The fictional world of the fairytale is infused with magic, but, once this is accepted, everything proceeds in a recognisably natural manner.

Fantasy fiction, too, may incorporate a magical element, but when it does, the magical element, far from being assumed, is fantastic relative to the realistic aspects of the work: 'A fantasy is a story based on and controlled by an overt violation of what is generally accepted as a possibility' (Irwin, 1976: ix), even within the confines of the story. In Lewis's Chronicles of Narnia there are many mentions of the special nature of the other world, for example that it allows for 'the sort of thing that would have been quite impossible in our world' (1956/1990: 163). In particular, there are several instances of overt explanation of how people can disappear into the other world without losing any time of their own. For example, the Professor explains that if Lucy has been in the other world, he would 'not be at all surprised to find that the other world has a time of its own; so that however long you stayed there it would never take up any of *our* time' (1950/1988: 48). Formally speaking,

> literary fantasies have appeared to be 'free' from many of the conventions and restraints of more realistic texts: they have refused to observe unities of time, space and character, doing away with chronology, three-dimensionality and with rigid distinctions between animate and inanimate objects, self and other, life and death.
>
> (Jackson, 1981: 1–2)

According to Townsend (1965 [1990]: 71), the publication in 1865 of Carroll's *Alice's Adventures in Wonderland* confirmed the 1860s as 'The decade in which fantasy took wing', and in this section we examine, first, this work and its sequel, *Through the Looking-Glass, and What Alice Found There* (1871). Second, we examine two of the Chronicles of Narnia (see below). Both sets of text amply illustrate the formal freedoms just referred to.

Carroll's Alice finds herself transported from one place and situation to another; she moves to other worlds inside the earth and through the mirror; she interacts both physically and linguistically with animals, playing cards and chess pieces; she worries that she has become another; and she defies death when she falls into inner earth. The action contravenes the laws of nature in a variety of ways. For example, Alice, falling down the rabbit hole, is able to replace a jar of marmalade on a shelf – as Gardner (1865/1970: 27, note 2) points out, a physical impossibility unless Alice really is falling 'very slowly' (1865/1970: 26); but this is another physical impossibility. In the second story, Alice's manner of moving between squares on the chess board remains as mysterious to her as the King and Queen's movements from grate to table seem to them at the start of the story, when Alice picks them up.

Lewis's Chronicles of Narnia transport the main characters between worlds whose times are mutually independent, and in which they take on somewhat different psychologies: in the world from which they set out, they are ordinary children, whereas in Narnia they become regal. When they die, they die into an eternal life of greater perfection, purity and vitality than the life they leave behind.

Of course, freedom of form does not liberate fantasy fiction from its social context. Even though the fantasy may struggle against the limits of its social context, it must nevertheless 'take off' from it: 'Its introduction of the "unreal" is set against the category of the "real"' (Jackson, 1981: 4). Therefore, the fantastic elements in fantasy fiction depend no less upon their creators' conception of reality than do the magical worlds of literary fairytales.

In chapter 5 above, we discussed, first, reactions to the materialism of Victorian society in the wake of the Industrial Revolution. Carroll's criticisms of this materialism are twofold. It takes a particularly interesting linguistic form as he allows his puns to reflect the essential instability and uncertainty of the language through which material 'facts' are reported. Given this uncertainty, it also becomes difficult to maintain a clear distinction between fiction and reality.

Second, in chapter 5, we discussed Dahl's reactions to the modern world and its problems, including the parent–child relationship. By situating reality in a fairytale setting relative to the setting for the main narrative, Dahl achieves, first, a blurring of the borderline between fiction and reality, and, second, the creation of a fictional here-and-now into which his characters can escape, through personal development over time, into a future which is that of their own lives, and where they are liberated from adult control.

In this chapter, we discuss C.S. Lewis's almost diametrically opposed strategy of saving his child characters from the contemporary world of their present by sending them, first, into a fantastic world in which motifs from the biblical and medieval past are re-enacted, and, finally, by allowing them to gain absolute freedom as they die into a platonic absolute, and absolutely pure, reality. Lewis has much in common with George MacDonald, including distaste for the habit of passing children off, not, in Lewis's case, to nannies, but to (secular) boarding schools. However, he does not share MacDonald's interest in family life; most of his child characters' parents play only the most fleeting role in the stories. Lewis's divine universe is not modelled on the family with the mother at the centre, but on the holy (male) trinity of Father (Emperor-from-Across-the-Sea), Son (Aslan) and the Holy Ghost (the very deepest magic).

LEWIS CARROLL

Lewis Carroll is the *nom de plume* of Charles Lutwidge Dodgson (1832–98), raised in a parsonage, educated at Rugby School and at Oxford where, in 1855, he was appointed sub-librarian of Christ Church, and later a lecturer in mathematics.

Carroll wrote the two fantasies we examine here, *Alice's Adventures in Wonderland* (1865) and *Through the Looking-Glass, and What Alice Found There* (1871) (page references for both are to the Penguin revised edition: Gardner 1970), for Alice Pleasance Liddell, second eldest of the five daughters of the Dean of Christ Church.

It is well known that Carroll sent the manuscript of *Wonderland* to the MacDonald family, who warmly approved of it, and it is interesting to note a number of similarities between the two authors' approaches to their subject. The overriding difference is, perhaps, that while MacDonald's two book-length fairytales are overtly theist, there are no very apparent religious overtones in Carroll's works.

Both *Wonderland* and *The Princess and the Goblin* begin with the child character seeking to escape from boredom: 'Alice was beginning to get very tired of sitting by her sister on the bank, and of having nothing to do' (1865/1970: 25). We have seen (chapter 5 above) that the ultimate outcome of Irene's escape is the re-instatement, however briefly, of proper order in the country over which she comes to rule with Curdie upon the death of the old King. In the case of the *Alice* books, order is restored only when Alice wakes from her dreams. In the dreams, Alice is faced with dis-order, and although this dis-order frames a number of criticisms of the Victorian world, for Alice it is, on the whole, profoundly distressing.

As Secunda in the prefatory poem to *Wonderland*, Alice asks for 'nonsense'. Yet within the nonsense she is truly bewildered and longs to be back home: '"It was much pleasanter at home," thought poor Alice, "when one wasn't always growing larger and smaller, and being ordered about by mice and rabbits"' (1865/1970: 58). The curious changes she undergoes early on make her cry and feel 'desparate' (p. 37), and her comments on her loss of control of language (see below) are couched in regretful terms:

'Oh dear, what nonsense I'm talking!' (p. 36).

'"I'm sure those are not the right words", said poor Alice, and her eyes filled with tears again' (p. 38).

'Alice said nothing: she had sat down with her face in her hands, wondering if anything would *ever* happen in a natural way again. (p. 139).

According to Zipes, the *Alice* books adopt a child's perspective in order to highlight the absurdity of many of the 'rules and regulations of the adult Victorian world' (Zipes, 1987: xxii), and Caroll, like Nesbit and Dahl (see chapter 5 above), distances his dream-Alice from adults by making her refer to them with the third-person plural pronouns *them*, *their* and *they*:

'there'll be no one here to scold me away from the fire. Oh, what fun it'll be, when they see me through the glass in here, and can't get at me!'

(1871/1970: 185)

However, alone in Wonderland, Alice longs for these impersonal adults to come and rescue her:

'It'll be no use their putting their heads down and saying "Come up again, dear!" . . . – but oh, dear!' cried Alice, with a sudden burst of tears, 'I do wish they *would* put their heads down! I am so *very* tired of being all alone here!'

(1865/1970: 39)

A short story-time later, Alice in fact finds herself in the company of not only a mouse, but also 'a Duck and a Dodo, a Lory and an Eaglet, and several other curious creatures' who stay with Alice until she frightens them away by her childishly thoughtless mention of her liking for a particular small dog who is skilled at catching birds. The effect of all this is to highlight the child's dependence on adults and on the orderliness of social life and manners which is promoted by adults.

Carroll, like MacDonald, also expresses overt preferences for many of the modes of child behaviour which would have been generally applauded in his contemporary society (as, indeed, in our own). Secunda (Alice) of the prefatory poem to *Wonderland* speaks 'in gentler tones' than her older sister, Prima; she has 'a gentle hand', and engages 'in friendly chat with bird or beast'.

Both authors also link good behaviour with royalty. Carroll (1887) outlines the personality of his dream-Alice: Loving, gentle, trustful, curious and 'courteous to *all*, high or low, even as though she were herself a King's daughter' (quoted in Gardner, 1970: 26, note 1). In Carroll's case, the association of good behaviour with royalty, however, does not spill over into the fictions, where royal characters (in so far as playing cards and chess pieces can be said to be truly royal) act absurdly – even savagely and 'like a wild beast', in the case of the Queen (1865/1970: 99, 125, 109 and Ch. VIII: *passim*). However, it is interesting that although it is incidental to his story, Carroll marks some characters off from the majority, and from Alice, by making them use non-standard accents and dialects.

The speech of the White Rabbit's gardener, Pat, suggests Irish English: '"Sure then I'm here! Digging for apples, yer honour!"'; '"Sure, it's an arm, yer honour!" (He pronounced it "arrum")'; '"Sure, it does, yer honour: but it's an arm for all that."' (p. 60); '"Sure, I don't like it, yer honour, at all, at all!"' (p. 61).

The lizard, Bill, the playing-card gardeners, the Gryphon and, occasionally, Humpty Dumpty speak in what appears to be Carroll's impression of a general rural English: '"No more, thank ye; I'm better now – but I'm a deal too flustered to tell you – all I know is, something comes at me like a Jack-in-the-box, and up I goes like a sky-rocket!"' (1865/1970: 62); '"this here ought to have been . . . if the Queen was to find out . . . afore she comes"' (p. 106); '"it's all her fancy, that; they never executes nobody, you know"' (p. 125); '"It's all his fancy, that: he hasn't got no sorrow, you know . . ."'; '"This here young lady," said the Gryphon, "she wants for to know your history, she do"' (p. 126); '"Ah, you should see 'em come round me of a Saturday night . . . for to get their wages, you know"' (1871/1970: 270).

In addition, the Victorian social class system is apparent in Alice's remark that 'If she [the governess] couldn't remember my name, she'd call me "Miss," as the servants do' (1971/1970: 224).

It is true that some aspects of adults' relationships with children are satirised in the stories. For example, Alice imagines a scene in which she puts off obeying her nurse, while obeying an order issued by Dinah, the cat:

> 'Miss Alice! Come here directly, and get ready for your walk!'
> 'Coming in a minute, nurse! But I've got to watch this mouse-hole till Dinah comes back, and see that the mouse doesn't get out.'
> 'Only I don't think,' Alice went on, 'that they'd let Dinah stop in the house if it began ordering people about like that!'
>
> > (1865/1970: 56)

Clearly, adults order people about; yet they would not accept this type of behaviour from cats, or, by implication, from children. The ways in which adults order children about are satirised in the Red Queen's remarks to Alice:

> 'Where do you come from?' said the Red Queen. 'And where are you going? Look up, speak nicely, and don't twiddle your fingers all the time.'
>
> . . .
>
> 'Curtsey while you're thinking what to say. It saves time.'
>
> . . .
>
> 'It's time for you to answer now,' the Queen said, looking at her watch: 'open your mouth a *little* wider when you speak, and always say "your Majesty".'
>
> > (1871/1970: 206)

> 'Speak in French when you can't think of the English for a thing – turn out your toes as you walk – and remember who you are!'
>
> > (1871/1970: 212).

> 'Speak when you're spoken to!' the Queen sharply interrupted her.
>
> > (1871/1970: 318)

In addition, the Queen's habit of belittling Alice's experiences by comparing them with her own clearly satirises another common adult strategy *vis-à-vis* children:

'When you say "garden" – *I've* seen gardens, compared with which this would be a wilderness.'

. . .

'When you say "hill," the Queen interrupted, *I* could show you hills, in comparison with which you'd call that a valley.'

. . .

'You may call it "nonsense" if you like,' she said, 'but *I've* heard nonsense, compared with which that would be as sensible as a dictionary!'

(1871/1970: 206–7)

Of course, given Carroll's awareness of the difficulties associated with the notion of meaning (see below), which is the domain of dictionaries, the satire here may be double-edged: not only does the Queen's behaviour parody the adult habit of self-aggrandisement by taking it to extremes in the example of the Queen; in addition, her faith in the dictionary may be mistaken.

Adults' faith in their own understanding of what is best for children does not go unremarked either. When Alice declares herself 'hot and thirsty', the Queen remarks, 'I know what *you'd* like! . . . Have a biscuit?' (1871/1970: 211). When Alice is in the railway carriage going between squares, the other passengers begin making senseless suggestions about what 'must' happen to Alice:

'She must be labelled "Lass, with care," you know – ' And after that other voices went on . . . , saying 'she must go by post, as she's got a head on her – ' She must be sent as a message by the telegraph – ' 'She must draw the train herself the rest of the way –,' and so on.

(1871/1970: 219).

The child's perspective is also clearly evidenced in a number of passages concerning education. There are repeated references to the learning of lessons as something unpleasant; for example, if Alice were the despised Mabel, she would have 'ever so many lessons to learn' (1865/1970: 28), a prospect which makes her contemplate never returning home. Again, the prospect of 'always to have lessons to learn! Oh, I shouldn't like *that*!' (p. 59) outweighs the advantages of never having to grow old.

Carroll's criticism of the Victorian education system and its methods range from gentle mockery to overt satirisation. Gentle mockery of the practice of 'translating' the Latin case system into 'corresponding' English expressions is at play when Alice addresses a mouse as 'O Mouse' because she has 'seen, in her brother's Latin Grammar, "A mouse – of a mouse – to a mouse – a mouse – O mouse!"' (1865/1970: 41). Similarly, Alice addresses the same mouse (Alice thinks the mouse might be French because it has not replied to a question previously put to it in English) with 'the first sentence in her French lesson-book': 'Où est ma chatte?'. The mouse's reaction to this sentence gives Alice what appears to be her first lesson in the importance of being appropriate to context. The mouse 'gave a sudden leap out of the water, and seemed to quiver all over with fright' (p. 42).

The emphasis on form of expression at the expense of understanding of content both in education and in society at large is perhaps more seriously satirised in a number of passages, including the following three:

'I must be getting somewhere near the centre of the earth. Let me see: that would be four thousand miles down, I think – ' (for, you see, Alice had learnt several things of this sort in her lessons in the schoolroom, and though this was not a *very* good opportunity for showing off her knowledge, as there was no one to listen to her, still it was good practice to say it over) '– yes, that's about the right distance – but then I wonder what Latitude or Longitude I've got to?' (Alice had not the slightest idea what Latitude was, or Longitude either, but she thought they were nice grand words to say.)

(1865/1970: 27)

'How funny it'll seem to come out among the people that walk with their heads downwards! The Antipathies, I think – ' (she was rather glad there *was* no one listening, this time, as it didn't sound at all the right word).

(1865/1970: 28)

'I move that the meeting adjourn, for the immediate adoption of more energetic remedies – '

'Speak English!' said the Eaglet. 'I don't know the meaning of half those long words, and, what's more, I don't believe you do either!'

(1865/1970: 47)

There is also a suggestion that schools neglect social education:

'Manners are not taught in lessons,' said Alice. 'Lessons teach you to do sums, and things of that sort.'

(1871/1970: 320)

Carroll shares MacDonald's predilection for puns, and though in Carroll's case the overriding theme which the puns reinforce is his preoccupation with the nature of language, some of his puns serve other purposes too. For example, he plays on the meanings of *dry* – both 'not wet' and 'uninterestingly expressed' – in order to reinforce his criticism of Victorian educational practices: the mouse attempts to dry off the soaking assembly by reciting a passage from a history book used by the Liddell children (see Gardner, 1970: 46, note 1). According to the mouse, the passage in question is 'the driest thing I know' (1865/1970: 46). However, the dry educational tale does not have the desired effects in the 'real' world in either of its senses. Alice complains, 'it doesn't seem to dry me at all' (p. 47); and the narrator remarks, 'with all her knowledge of history, Alice had no very clear notion how long ago anything had happened' (pp. 41–2).

According to Gardner (1970: 10), Carroll was a sincere, orthodox believer in the teachings of the Church of England (except for the doctrine of eternal damnation) and in Tory politics. Nevertheless, the Alice books are almost void of the overt moralising tendency characteristic of much Victorian fairytale and fantasy fiction. In fact, Carroll explicitly satirises the tendency of Victorian writers to attach 'morals' to everything, in Alice's conversation with the Duchess in chapter IX (1865/1970). The Duchess draws a moral from virtually every remark made during the conversation, and most of the morals bear only the loosest imaginable relationship to the remarks.

Gardner (1970: 336, note 11) notes that it is possible to argue that Alice's victory over the Red Queen introduces 'a faint moral' into the second story because the red chess pieces have 'fierce vindictive temperaments' whereas the white pieces 'are good and gentle characters'. On the whole, however, most of the adult-like characters in both books act absurdly, and Zipes considers that Caroll's books 'served to liberate the fairytale from moralism and encouraged young readers to think for themselves and question the accepted norms of the adult world' (Zipes, 1987: 73). In the passage below, Carroll appears to be both satirical and overtly critical of such moralism:

> It was all very well to say 'Drink me,' but the wise little Alice was not going to do *that* in a hurry . . . for she had read several nice little stories about children who had got burnt . . . and other unpleasant things, all because they would *not* remember the simple rules their friends had taught them: such as, that a red-hot poker will burn you if you hold it too long; . . . and she had never

forgotten that, if you drink from a bottle marked 'poison', it is almost certain to disagree with you, sooner or later.

However, this bottle was not marked 'poison', so Alice ventured to taste it.

(1865/1970: 31)

It is ironic to call stories of the kind described 'nice', and the passage shows that, in fact, Alice has not been made 'wise' by being instructed by her 'friends', the writers of instructional tales. For, from the fact that some bottles of poison are labelled as such, she wrongly reasons that if a bottle is not thus labelled, then its contents will not be poisonous.

In the fantasy worlds, Alice loses her ability to control what she says more and more. This loss of control over her own utterances begins in Chapter II when she utters the famous exclamation 'Curiouser and curiouser!' because 'she was so much surprised, that for the moment she quite forgot how to speak good English' (1865/1970: 35). In the same chapter, Alice also loses control of her knowledge of geography – 'London is the capital of Paris' etc. – and we encounter Carroll's first parody of a moralistic children's song, Watt's poem 'Against Idleness and Mischief' (from *Divine Songs for Children*, 1715; see Gardner, 1970: 38, note 4). Whereas Watt uses the example of the busy bee to encourage children to spend their time usefully employed, Carroll makes Alice voice a rhyme that describes a crocodile which grins cheerfully as little fishes swim into his mouth of their own volition. In Chapter V, Carroll uses Alice's loss of control of language to parody a didactic poem by Southey (see Gardner's note 2 to p. 69) about how to prepare in youth for a comfortable old age. Alice's rendering of 'You are Old, Father William' presents a distinctly unconventional old man. There are further examples of this loss of linguistic control throughout the first book, particularly in Alice's attempts at repeating songs and poems. In the second book, Alice loses the ability to name anything at all, including herself, in the wood where things have no name (1871/1970: 226).

As in the case of MacDonald's nameless creatures, however, this namelessness is only temporary. Jackson (1981: 40) suggests that in Carroll we meet creatureless names, and she considers that Carroll's nonsense and portmanteau words evidence 'a shift towards language as signifying nothing, and the fantastic itself as such a language'. However, within the fictions, all of Carroll's invented names refer to invented creatures – in fact all his 'nonsense terms' have meanings assigned to them (see, for example, the extensive notes on the poem 'Jabberwocky', 1871/1970: 191–7). Even though Alice does not fully grasp these meanings, the poem fills her head with ideas, and she knows that '*somebody* killed *something*: that's clear, at any rate' (p. 197). It is, rather, the familiar terms of everyday language, such as 'it' and 'muchness' which are shown to lack reference, both in the fiction and in reality (see below).

Jackson maintains that 'fantastic art draws explicit attention to the *process* of representation. It moves towards an "anarchic discourse" by combining units in new relations' (1981: 84), and it is true that Carroll employs this strategy. For instance, we see Alice reordering logical premises and conclusions in what might be considered a socio-critical way, when she declares 'That's the judge . . . because of his great wig' (1865/1970: 144). Of course, the judge is not a judge because he has a wig; rather, he has a wig because he is a judge. It could be, however, that Carroll wants to suggest that Alice is right – that in the case of many judges, their wig seems to be their most obvious qualification for being a judge. However, Carroll's linguistic anarchy resides as much in his use of everyday language as in his 'nonsense'. Both features of his discourse demonstrate his awareness of the complex nature of the link between language and reality, and between reality and fiction.

Alice was ten years old when she asked for the story. But Carroll tells a story of a seven-year-old 'dream-child' (1865/1970: 23). It is clear from the poems which accompany the stories that this child is part of the past. The language of the final stanza of the prefatory poem 'All in the golden afternoon', implies an older Alice as its addressee, describing the story as 'childish', and appealing to a person for whom 'Childhood's dreams' are already 'in Memory's mystic band', and comparable to 'pilgrim's withered wreath of flowers / Pluck'd in a far-off land.'

The connotations of death and decay contained in the image of the pilgrim's withered wreath of flowers find friends throughout both tales. In many cases, these take the form of the kind of black ironic humour we can perceive in the narratorial comment, '(which was very likely true)', on Alice's remark, 'Why, I wouldn't say anything about it, even if I fell off the top of the house!' (1865/1970: 27). In other cases, Alice speculates about her own possible annihilation, for example when she is shrinking and 'felt a little nervous about this; "for it might end, you know . . . in my going out altogether, like a candle"' (p. 32). In the second story, the Rose remarks to Alice, 'You're beginning to fade, you know', and 'Alice didn't like this idea at all' (1871/1970: 204). In the first book, Alice is presented as being seven years old. In the second, she is seven and a half. According to Humpty Dumpty, it would have been better for her to 'have left off at seven' which she might have managed 'with proper assistance' (p. 266), a remark which connotes both murder and the possibility of Carroll not having written the second book at all.

These sombre notes crescendo in the profound sadness of the 'terminal poem', as Gardner aptly describes it (1970: 354, note 1). Here, the dream-child is a phantom that haunts the poet, and the skies under which she moves were 'never seen by waking eyes'. The fifth stanza introduces an apparently hopeful tone of reference to future children:

> Children yet, the tale to hear,
> Eager eye and willing ear,
> Lovingly shall nestle near.

However, in the very next stanza, it becomes profoundly unclear whether the poet is referring to future children, or whether he is lingering on the three children of the past, captured forever in his fiction, endlessly drifting and dreaming during endlessly dying summers:

> In a wonderland they lie,
> Dreaming as the days go by,
> Dreaming as the summers die:

> Ever drifting down the stream –
> Lingering in the golden gleam –
> Life, what is it but a dream?

The question on which the poem ends blurs the line, Dahl-like, between fiction and reality, which the stories appear to set up so clearly, in the case of the first in the dream motif, and in the case of the second, through Alice's movement through the looking glass between worlds.

But the fact/fiction line is actually also blurred within the story itself. The fictional Alice of *Wonderland* realises that she is in a fairytale and considers: 'There ought to be a book written about me, that there ought!' (1865/1970: 59). The text immediately following suggests that (although Carroll, of course, has physically sat down and written the story), Alice, for whom, in the story, 'there's no room to grow up any more *here*' has guided his hand, just as she guides the hand of the White King in the second story (1871/1970: 190). In other words, Alice has used Caroll as a mouthpiece to write her story as much as he used her: '"And when I grow up, I'll write one – but I'm grown up now," she added in a sorrowful tone' (1865/1970: 59). Alice is Carroll's creature in the story, but as she is the source for his creature, the dream-Alice is as much, if not more, the creation of the real Alice as of Carroll.

In the second story, Alice enters a 'Looking-glass House' (1871/1970: 180) that is of her own invention within the 'realistic' part of the story. The dream helps her to get into this world to see more of it, but the dream, it turns out, is ambiguously attributable: 'Only I do hope it's *my* dream, and not the Red King's' (p. 293), and from time to time, as in the first story, there are references to the 'real' Alice talking about the dream later. Of these, the following may be particularly significant, if, as Gardner (1970: 307, note 8) suggests, the White Knight is a caricature of Carroll himself:

> Of all the strange things that Alice saw in her journey Through the Looking-Glass, this was the one that she always remembered most clearly. Years afterwards she could bring the whole scene back again, as if it had been only yesterday – the mild blue eyes and kindly smile of the Knight.
>
> (1871/1970: 307)

The story ends with the narrator addessing the reader directly with exactly this question of whose dream it was: 'Which do *you* think it was?' (p. 344).

There is also, within the story itself, a scene which is clearly related to the terminal poem through the images of the boat drifting down the stream and Alice's eager eyes, and which, unlike most of the text, casts the narrator so clearly in an observer role that it is difficult not to perceive the passage as an image of the real Alice, on a real occasion, held in Carroll's memory:

> So the boat was left to drift down the stream as it would, till it glided gently in among waving rushes. And then the little sleaves were carefully rolled up, and the little arms were plunged in elbow-deep, to get hold of the rushes a good long way down before breaking them off – and for a while Alice forgot all about the Sheep and the knitting, as she bent over the side of the boat, with just the ends of her tangled hair dipping into the water – while with bright eager eyes she caught at one bunch after another of the darling scented rushes.
>
> (1871/1970: 256)

It is this blurring of the line between fiction and reality, profoundly non-conformist to Victorian values, which Carroll promotes implicitly in the language of both books.

The language of a dream-child

We suggested in the previous section that Carrol's main purpose in punning and in presenting Alice's confusions is to highlight the tenuous nature of the link between language and reality. His position appears to be that language gives an impression of certainty and orderliness, but that this impression is misleading in a number of ways.

First, much of language is ambiguous: one term can stand for several different kinds of phenomenon. In the examples below, the ambiguity only exists in speech:

'Mine is a long and sad tale!' said the Mouse . . .
    'It *is* a long tail, certainly,' said Alice . . . 'but why do you call it sad?'

(1865/1970: 50)

'That's the reason they're called lessons,' the Gryphon remarked: 'because they lessen from day to day.'

(1865/1970: 130)

'The twinkling of *what*?' said the King.
    'It *began* with the tea,' the Hatter replied.
    'Of course twinkling *begins* with a T!' said the King sharply.

(1865/1970: 148)

'Am I addressing the White Queen?'
    'Well, yes, if you call that a-dressing,' the Queen said. 'It isn't *my* notion of the thing, at all.'

(1871/1970: 245–6)

However, in many cases, ambiguity is present in both the written and spoken form of words:

'there's a large mustard-mine near here. And the moral of that is – "The more there is of mine, the less there is of yours."'

(1865/1970: 121–2).

'Now, I give you fair warning,' shouted the Queen, stamping on the ground as she spoke; 'either you or your head must be off, and that in about half no time! Take your choice!'

The Duchess took her choice, and was gone in a moment.

(1865/1970: 123)

'I'm a poor man, your Majesty,' he began. 'You're a *very* poor *speaker*,' said the King.

(1865/1970: 149)

'In most gardens,' the Tiger-lily said, 'they make the beds too soft – so that the flowers are always asleep.'

This sounded a very good reason, and Alice was quite pleased to know it.

(1871/1970: 203)

Alice . . . explained . . . that she had lost her way.

'I don't know what you mean by *your* way,' said the Queen: 'all the ways about here belong to *me*.'

(1871/1970: 206)

'Well, if she said "Miss," and didn't say anything more,' the Gnat remarked, 'of course you'd miss your lessons.'

(1871/1970: 224)

'. . . only I don't sing it,' he added, as an explanation.

'I see you don't,' said Alice.

'If you can *see* whether I'm singing or not, you've sharper eyes than most,' Humpty Dumpty remarked severely.

(1871/1970: 273)

'. . . it took hours and hours to get me out. I was as fast as – as lightning, you know.'

'But that's a different kind of fastness,' Alice objected.

The Knight shook his head. 'It was all kinds of fastness with me.'

(1871/1970: 303)

As the examples above illustrate, ambiguities need not hinder comprehension, and speakers may exploit ambiguities to suit their purposes. However, there are cases in which such exploitation of the system causes difficulties in communication. Such problems may be only temporary:

'The master was an old Turtle – we used to call him Tortoise – '

'Why did you call him Tortoise if he wasn't one?' Alice asked.

'We called him Tortoise because he taught us,' said the Mock Turtle angrily. 'Really you are very dull!'

(1865/1970: 127).

'But what could it [a tree] do, if any danger came?' Alice asked.

'It could bark,' said the Rose.

'It says "Bough-wough!"' cried a Daisy. 'That's why its branches are called boughs!'

'Didn't you know *that*?' cried another Daisy.

(1871/1970: 202)

However, miscommunication may be more permanent. In the following passage, the breakdown in communication between Alice and the Sheep which arises from their different understandings of the meanings of 'feather' and 'crab' is not resolved; instead, the two drift, via their agreement about Alice's use of the term 'bird', into agreement about the extended meaning of 'goose' in the Sheep's final remark:

'Can you row?' the sheep asked. . . .

'Yes, a little . . .' Alice was beginning to say, when suddenly . . . she found they were in a little boat . . . so there was nothing for it but to do her best.

'Feather! cried the Sheep. . . .'

This didn't sound like a remark that needed any answer: so Alice said nothing, but pulled away. There was something very queer about the water, she thought, as every now and then the oars got fast in it, and would hardly come out again.

'Feather! Feather!' the Sheep cried again. . . . 'You'll be catching a crab directly.'

'A dear little crab!' thought Alice. 'I should like that.'

'Didn't you hear me say "Feather"?' the Sheep cried angrily. . . .

'Indeed I did,' said Alice: 'you've said it very often – and very loud. Please where *are* the crabs?'

'In the water, of course!' said the Sheep. . . . 'Feather, I say!'

'*Why* do you say "Feather" so often?' Alice asked at last, rather vexed. 'I'm not a bird!'

'You are,' said the Sheep: 'you're a little goose.'

(1871/1970: 254–5)

In fact, the unresolved question of the two senses of *crab* arises again three pages further on, when Alice's oar gets stuck in the mud; again, Alice's misunderstanding of the Sheep's use of the term is allowed to remain.

In other cases, ambiguity causes a dialogue to loose direction:

'How is bread made?'

'I know *that*!' Alice cried eagerly. 'You take some flour – '

'Where do you pick the flower?' the White Queen asked. . . .
'Well, it isn't *picked* at all . . . it's *ground* – '
'How many acres of ground?'

(1871/1970: 322)

In addition, an inherently vague term can take on a particular, specific meaning for a user against the background of a particular context. In the example below, 'gone', which is inherently vague in so far as there are many different manners of 'going', is being used by the soldiers to refer to a state of being no longer present, whereas the Queen takes it to refer to the state of a head which has been severed from its body.

'You shan't be beheaded!' said Alice, and she put them in a large flower-pot that stood near . . .
'Are their heads off?' shouted the Queen.
'Their heads are gone, if it please your Majesty!' the soldiers shouted in reply.

(1865/1970: 110)

Finally, there are metaphorical extensions of meanings, as in the Duchess's saying 'flamingoes and mustard both bite' (p. 121).

Second, some terms stand for nothing at all. Carroll highlights the emptiness of some natural language words:

'"Stigand, the patriotic archbishop of Canterbury, found it advisable – "'
'Found *what*?' said the Duck.
'Found *it*,' the Mouse replied rather crossly: 'of course you know what "it" means.'
'I know what "it" means well enough, when *I* find a thing,' said the Duck: 'it's generally a frog or a worm. The question is, what did the archbishop find?"

(1865/1970: 47)

'. . . – you know you say things are "much of a muchness" – did you ever see such a thing as a drawing of a muchness!'

(1865/1970: 103)

Third, people can, and do, give expressions idiosyncratic meanings: the Dodo gives his own special meaning to the term, 'Caucus-race' – he demonstrates it as a general aimless running around in circles on the part of the wet creatures until they are dry (1865/1970: 48). In similar vein, the pigeon reminds us that the way in which we order the world into classes of things depends on our interests; that is, our taxonomies are not absolute, or determined by nature, but depend on criteria determined by us. The pigeon points out that, as far as she is concerned, if little girls eat eggs like serpents do, 'then they're a kind of serpent' (p. 76).

The powerful effects, both positive and negative, of linguistic classification, are explicated particularly clearly when Alice and the Fawn emerge from the wood where things have no names: the Fawn is delighted to find itself classified, but frightened to discover which class Alice falls into:

> So they walked on together through the wood, Alice with her arms clasped lovingly round the soft neck of the Fawn, till they came out into another open field, and here the Fawn gave a sudden leap into the air, and shook itself free from Alice's arm. 'I'm a Fawn!' it cried out in a voice of delight. 'And, dear me! you're a human child!' A sudden look of alarm came into its beautiful brown eyes, and in a moment it had darted away at full speed.
>
> (1871/1970: 227)

Finally, in set phrases, which are, of course, in very common use, terms can lose aspects of their sense:

> 'I beg your pardon?' said Alice.
> 'It isn't polite to beg,' said the King.
>
> (1871/1970: 280)

The impression of linguistic orderliness, too, is misleading for a number of reasons. First, many terms do not conform to those linguistic patterns which are commonly considered regular. For example, the regular way of forming adjectives in the so-called 'second degree' or 'comparative form' in English is to add '-er' to the adjective stem: *big – bigger; small – smaller.* This rule, however, does not apply to the adjective *curious*, and Alice's application of it results in the famous, oft-quoted 'Curiouser and curiouser!' (1865/1970: 35). Carroll's narratorial comment 'she was so much surprised, that for the moment she quite forgot how to speak good English' (p. 35) is, of course, ironic in so far as Alice is applying a perfectly good, English rule, only she is applying it to an adjective which does not conform to the rule. It is the language that is disorderly, not Alice.

Second, even if a particular function is always performed by one structural pattern, there may be apparently unprincipled restrictions on the generality with which the rule can be applied. For example, to the adjective *beautiful* corresponds a verb *beautify* and a noun *beautification*; but the same pattern is not found for the adjective *ugly* (at least not in Alice's vocabulary):

> 'I never heard of "Uglification,"' Alice ventured to say. 'What is it?'
>
> The Gryphon lifted up both its paws in surprise, 'Never heard of uglifying!' it exclaimed. 'You know what to beautify is, I suppose?'
>
> 'Yes,' said Alice doubtfully: 'it means – to – make – anything – prettier.'
>
> 'Well, then,' the Gryphon went on, 'if you don't know what to uglify is, you are a simpleton.'
>
> (1865/1970: 129).

Finally, identical surface forms can hide different underlying structures. A relatively simple example of this is provided in the following passages:

> 'I see nobody on the road,' said Alice.
>
> 'I only wish *I* had such eyes,' the King remarked in a fretful tone. 'To be able to see Nobody! . . .'
>
> (1871/1970: 279)

> 'Who did you pass on the road?' the King went on. . . .
>
> 'Nobody,' said the messenger.
>
> 'Quite right,' said the King: 'this young lady saw him too.'
>
> (1871/1970: 281–2)

Here it is clear that whereas 'nobody' performs the function of grammatical subject, just as *him* might have done: *I see him on the road*, the underlying logical structures of the two sentences,

I see him on the road
I see nobody on the road

are different. The sentence, *I see him on the road* has the structure: there is someone who is referred to as 'him', and I see him on the road ($\exists \times$(him $\times$ & I see $\times$ on the road)). But in the case of the sentence *I see nobody on the road*, the structure is: It is not the case that there is anyone who is such that I see them on the road (~$\exists \times$(I see $\times$ on the road)).

A far more complex example is provided in the following passage:

> 'Do you mean that you think you can find the answer to it?' said the March Hare.

'Exactly so,' said Alice.

'Then you should say what you mean,' the March Hare went on.

'I do,' Alice hastily replied; 'at least – at least I mean what I say – that's the same thing, you know.'

'Not the same thing a bit!' said the Hatter. 'Why, you might as well say that "I see what I eat" is the same thing as "I eat what I see"!'

'You might as well say,' added the March Hare, 'that "I like what I get" is the same thing as "I get what I like"!'

'You might as well say,' added the Dormouse, which seemed to be talking in its sleep, 'that "I breathe when I sleep" is the same thing as "I sleep when I breathe"!'

'It *is* the same thing with you,' said the Hatter, and here the conversation dropped.

(1865/1970: 95)

This passage raises (at least) two questions: is Alice right or wrong to claim that 'I say what I mean' is the same thing as 'I mean what I say'? And are the other speakers right to claim that the relationships between the pairs of sentences in their own examples is invariant between these and Alice's examples?

The reason why 'I breathe when I sleep' and 'I sleep when I breathe' is the same in the case of the Dormouse is that the Dormouse sleeps almost all of the time; and 'I sleep when I breathe seems to suggest 'Whenever I breathe (i.e., all the time), I sleep.' 'I breathe when I sleep', on the other hand, seems to suggest 'Whenever I sleep (which is, of course, not all the time for most people), I breathe.' So rather than saying that it is the same thing in the case of the Dormouse, we might say that both sentences are true in the case of the Dormouse, because of its habit of sleeping all the time. However, as our reformulation shows, the two sentences express two different relationships of implication between the situation in which the speaker is sleeping and the situation in which the speaker is breathing.

When and *whenever* bind clauses together. So if we want to formalise the two sentences' structures, we would need to specify the relationships they set up between the two clauses, 'I sleep' and 'I breathe'. We could do this by calling the clause 'I sleep' P, and the clause 'I breathe' Q. Then the underlying logical structure of the two sentences can be seen to be

A	B
If P then Q	If Q then P
(Whenever I sleep, I breathe.)	(Whenever I breathe, I sleep.)
(I breathe when I sleep.)	(I sleep when I breathe.)

However, Alice's, the Hatter's and the March Hare's examples have to be analysed differently, because *what*, in these examples, is an expression that stands in for individual items (the items, whatever they are, which are meant, said, seen, eaten, liked or obtained). The examples are:

A		B
1 'I say what I mean'	and	'I mean what I say'
2 'I see what I eat'	and	'I eat what I see'
3 'I like what I get'	and	'I get what I like'

Alice contends that statement 1 A 'is the same thing' as statement 1 B. The Hatter and the March Hare contend that it is not the same thing at all, any more than the other A-statements are the same as the other B-statements.

The second pair of statements allow reformulation along the following lines:

'I see what I eat' seems to suggest
'I see whatever I eat' – in other words
'Whatever I eat, I see' – in other words
'For all x, if I eat x then I see x'.

'I eat what I see' seems to suggest
'I eat whatever I see' – in other words
'Whatever I see I eat' – in other words
'For all x, if I see x then I eat x'.

Obviously, then, they do not mean the same thing at all, because it certainly does not follow from the fact that I see everything that I eat, that I eat everything that I see. Similarly, for the third pair of statements:

'I like what I get' seems to suggest
'I like whatever I get' – in other words
'Whatever I get, I like' – in other words
'For all x, if I get x then I like x'.

'I get what I like' seems to suggest
'I get whatever I like' – in other words
'Whatever I like, I get' – in other words
'For all x, if I like x then I get x'.

Again, it is clear that the two sentences do not mean the same thing at all, since it does not follow from the fact that I like whatever I get, that I get whatever I like.

It is also clear that the Dormouse is wrong in suggesting identity of underlying structures between its example and the examples given by the Hatter and the March Hare. The Dormouse's example can be analysed in terms of relationships between the clauses 'I breathe' and 'I sleep', but the Hatter's and the March Hare's examples need to be analysed in terms of quantification (For all) over individual variables (x) and in terms of the relationship of implication (if – then) between predicates which are parts of clauses ('eat' and 'see'; 'like' and 'get'), rather than between whole clauses.

We have, however, still to consider the March Hare's and the Hatter's suggestion that Alice's two sentences allow of the same analyses as their own examples. In the case of pairs 2 and 3, the underlying structure differs between the A and B sentences. Is the same true of the first pair of sentences? According to the March Hare's and the Hatter's contention that Alice's example is like their own examples, 'I say what I mean' should allow of reformulation along the lines suggested for 2A and 3A:

> 'I say what I mean' should suggest
> 'I say whatever I mean' – in other words
> 'Whatever I mean, I say' – in other words
> 'For all x, if I mean x then I say x'.

And 'I mean what I say' should allow of reformulation along the lines suggested for 2B and 3B:

> 'I mean what I say' should suggest
> 'I mean whatever I say' – in other words
> 'Whatever I say, I mean' – in other words
> 'For all x, if I say x then I mean x'.

Furthermore, the two final reformulations should 'not be the same thing at all'.

On the assumption that the two are not the same thing at all, we see immediately that in Alice's case it is the A sentence that is implausible. If 'mean' means something other than 'say' – something like 'have in mind', for example, then it is implausible that a person should be saying everything that they have in mind. But in the case of the Hatter's and the March Hare's sentences pairs, it was the B sentences that were implausible (eating whatever one sees, and getting whatever one likes). So the March Hare and the Hatter are at least imprecise in the parallels they draw.

But is it plausible that Alice's two sentences are not the same thing at all? Is it, in fact, possible to mean something independently of saying it? Meaning is a complicated notion, and there are, and were in Carroll's day, a number of competing theories of what meaning is, which cannot be discussed in detail here. Suffice it to say that if we mean by 'meaning' something which requires understanding by a hearer, then, given Alice's insistence that she means what she says (that is, she is not trying to mislead, or to hint at something other than what she says) 'meaning' cannot be used to refer to what a speaker has in mind but does not say. On that view, Alice is right to insist that her two sentences amount to the same thing.

The implausibility of Humpty Dumpty's later insistence that he is able to give a word whatever meaning he wants (1871/1970: 269) gives a good deal of support to our suggestion that it is 'meaning' in the sense of 'understood by a hearer' which is at issue here. This is so even though, as Gardner points out in his note to the Humpty Dumpty passage in question, Carroll in fact accepted that writers might use words in whichever sense they wished, because the passage in which Carroll declares this to be acceptable makes it plain that it is only acceptable when the writer makes it clear to a reader that the word in question is to be understood to have a particular sense. Carroll (1895/ 1958: 165) writes, 'If I find an author saying, at the beginning of his book, "Let it be understood that by the word '*black*' I shall always mean '*white*', and that by the word '*white*' I shall always mean '*black*',"' I meekly accept his ruling, however injudicious I may think it.' Carroll engages in this practice of defining his own meaning for terms at one point in the first story:

> Here one of the guinea-pigs cheered, and was immediately sup- pressed by the officers of the court. (As that is rather a hard word, I will just explain to you how it was done. They had a large canvas bag, which tied up at the mouth with strings: into this they slipped the guinea-pig, head first, and then sat upon it.)
>
> (1865/1970: 149–50)

The discussion above amply demonstrates that to decide who is right and who is wrong about questions of meaning can be a matter of rather more working out than people tend to engage in when conver- sing. A more typical strategy is that adopted by Alice and the Hatter about one page further on. Alice remarks, 'I don't quite understand you', whereupon the Hatter changes the subject (1865/1970: 97).

However, as one might expect from someone concerned with the link between language and reality, Carroll keeps coming back to the question of meaning, and it is when the meaning becomes intolerably loose for Alice that she wakes from her dream.

The court has tried to make sense of the poem which begins, 'They told me you had been to her'. This poem is perfectly structured, but because it contains no nouns for its pronouns to stand in for, and because there is no apparent natural connection between the phenomena mentioned in those clauses which are linked together with connectives which imply such connections, the court is able to use the poem as evidence for the guilt of the accused. Finally, when the Queen insists on sentencing the accused before a verdict has been reached, Alice, who has now grown to her full size again, says 'Who cares for *you*? . . . You're nothing but a pack of cards!' (1865/1970: 161), and wakes from the fantasy.

Similarly, when Alice arrives in the Looking-Glass world, she is initially 'too much in awe of the Queen' to question whether her advice on behaviour is useful or not (1871/1970: 206). However, when the Queen begins to talk what Alice conceives to be nonsense, Alice is quick to object, her awe giving way to astonishment:

> 'When you say "hill"', the Queen interrupted, 'I could show you hills, in comparison with which you'd call that a valley.'
> 'No, I shouldn't,' said Alice, surprised into contradicting her at last: 'a hill *can't* be a valley, you know. That would be nonsense.'
> (1871/1970: 207)

It is, however, only in a fiction that we can wake from the deceptions of language, or walk into a more ordered world. And since a great deal of learning comes to us through language, human knowledge inherits a significant degree of instability from language. We think we have a grip on reality through language, but this apparent anchorage is often illusory, and it is likely that the illusion is greater than we think. Therefore, all of life may be as dreamlike as the stories themselves, as the final line of the poem appended to the end of the last story suggests: 'Life, what is it but a dream?' (1871/1970: 345). This view is, of course, highly subversive of the commonsense conception of language as a good tool for representing a concrete, material reality which is straightforwardly available to the senses. It also makes a mockery of adult desires to instruct children and to make them believe in the fixedness of human truths about life's realities.

C.S. Lewis, the subject of the remaining sections of this chapter, shares Caroll's mistrust of some human truths. But, instead of accepting this uncertainty, as Carroll does, albeit with some regret, as an aspect of human existence, Lewis seeks to absolve it in the certainty that at least some truths exist and filter down to human life from a higher reality than ours. This enables Lewis to be interestingly selective in his criticisms of relationships of power and of social life in general.

C.S. LEWIS

Clive Staples Lewis (1898–1963) was born in Belfast, Northern Ireland, into a conservative, Protestant, middle-class family (Wilson, 1990: 8). However, although, as Townsend (1965 [1990]: 221) points out, Lewis's Narnia stories are Christian allegories, they embody a strong element of

> what one could loosely term Neo-Platonism. It was the sense of another world which drew him; the sense he got from MacDonald . . . of Heaven being penetrable through dreams and the subconscious and the exercise of the imagination.
>
> (Wilson, 1990: 137)

Lewis read *Phantastes* (MacDonald, 1858) in 1916 (Wilson, 1990: 45), and MacDonald remains the major literary influence on Lewis, although, as a teacher at the University of Oxford, Lewis became a friend of J.R.R. Tolkien and an admirer of his work. Other important influences include E. Nesbit and Charles Williams, on whose Lion of Strength, from the novel *The Place of the Lion*, Lewis based his Aslan (Wilson, 1990: 150).

According to Wilson, Lewis began work on *The Lion, the Witch and the Wardrobe* towards the end of 1939, but it was an encounter in debate with the philosopher Elizabeth Anscombe in 1948 which gave Lewis the impetus to resume work on the book and to persevere with the genre (Wilson, 1990: 211–15). Anscombe, herself a devout Christian, had effectively demolished Lewis' argument for the existence of God, as set out in his theological work, *Miracles* (1947). This encounter affected Lewis so strongly that *Miracles* remains his last work of Christian apologetics. He turned, instead, to fantasy as 'another way of talking about the reality of things . . . the way of *Phantastes* – in which another world opens up to the Dreamer through a piece of bedroom furniture . . . another way "further up and further in"' (Wilson, 1990: 214–15).

It is difficult to say precisely when the Narnia books were written. According to Wilson.

> *The Lion, the Witch and the Wardrobe* was begun at the end of 1939 but not resumed and finished until 1948 or 1949. . . . *The Voyage of the Dawn Treader* was finished by February 1950; *The Horse and His Boy* seems to have been written by the middle of 1950. . . . By March 1953, Lewis had told his publisher that he had finished the seventh story in the series, *The Last Battle*.
>
> (Wilson, 1990: 220)

Here, we discuss the two books Lewis appears to have completed first and last, *The Lion, the Witch and the Wardrobe* and *The Last Battle*. (The former was first published by Godfrey Bles in 1950; our page references are to the Lions edition, 1988. The latter was first published by The Bodley Head in 1956; our page references are to the Lions edition, 1990.)

Wilson stresses the dependence of *The Lion, the Witch and the Wardrobe* on the gospel narrative of the Resurrection, and his remarks on *The Last Battle* highlights the similarity between its ending and the ending of MacDonald's *The Princess and Curdie*. Wilson describes *The Last Battle* as

> the Apocalypse in which there is a final conflict with the forces of evil. The old heaven and the old earth pass away, Narnia is destroyed, and then remade for eternity.
>
> (1990: 228)

The first book introduces 'four children whose names were Peter, Susan, Edmund and Lucy', and describes what 'happened to them when they were sent away from London during the war because of the air-raids'. The story is thus situated in a fairly specific time, and is, in addition, set in a fairly specific place: 'They were sent to the house of an old Professor who lived in the heart of the country' (1950/1988: 9). This Professor is, in the final story, revealed to be Digory of *The Magician's Nephew*, the book which relates how humans first came to enter the other world, and how Aslan created Narnia. In the last book, 'Everyone you had ever heard of (if you knew the history of these countries)' (1956/1990: 167) comes together in 'Chapter One of the Great Story which no one on earth has read: which goes on forever: in which every chapter is better than the one before' (p. 172). Only Susan is excluded because she has, in Wilson's words 'committed the unforgivable sin of growing up' (1990: 228) – more precisely, she has grown up in the wrong way:

'My sister Susan,' answered Peter shortly and gravely, 'is no longer a friend of Narnia.'

'Yes,' said Eustace, 'and whenever you've tried to get her to come and talk about Narnia . . . she says, ". . . Fancy your still thinking about all those funny games we used to play when we were children."'

'Oh Susan!' said Jill. 'She's interested in nothing nowadays except nylons and lipstick and invitations. She always was a jolly sight too keen on being grown-up.'

'Grown-up indeed,' said the Lady Polly. 'I wish she *would* grow up. She wasted all her school time waiting to be the age she is now, and she'll waste all the rest of her life trying to stay that age.'

(1956/1990: 127–8)

This passage demonstrates Lewis's strategy of selective criticism. It operates by differentiation between good and bad realisations of a category, though in this case several categories come under scrutiny: grown-ups, interests and children. Susan represents the wrong type of each, but there is no suggestion that every member of any category is wrong. This stance is strikingly similar to that of MacDonald. In essence, the status quo is right, but its categories may be misused by those who occupy them: 'places' in a category may be misappropriated. The central aim of the stories is to describe how, in Aslan's words, names can 'be restored to their owners' (1950/1988: 127). This desire to see the status quo functioning perfectly is strikingly different from Dahl's almost total rejection of, for instance, contemporary views of the adult–child relationship, and from Carroll's profound scepticism about our ability, as humans, to perceive and represent to ourselves whatever order it is that our language obscures so severely.

Another close resemblance between MacDonald and Lewis can be seen in their blurring of the lines between youth and age. In MacDonald's deity, youth and age come together in the timelessness of her eternity, as youth and age are related in the divine family-line to which both Princesses Irene belong. In Lewis's case, all questions of time fall away as all who are united in the inner world live 'happily ever after' (1956/1990: 172), and the notion of age is replaced by that of freshness. For example, the Professor is introduced in the first story as

a very old man with shaggy white hair which grew over most of his face as well as on his head, and they liked him almost at once; but on the first evening when he came out to meet them . . . he was so

odd-looking that Lucy . . . was a little afraid of him, and Edmund
. . . wanted to laugh.

(1950/1988: 9)

Again, in *The Last Battle*, Tirian sees him first as 'an old man with a
white beard' (1956/1990: 45). By the end of the story, the Professor is
not said to be young, but to be 'a man whose golden beard flowed
over his breast and whose face was full of wisdom . . . the Lord
Digory' (p. 127), and previously young characters, too, acquire an
aura of agelessness:

> Now she looked cool and fresh, as fresh as if she had just come
> from bathing. And at first he thought she looked older, but then he
> didn't, and he could never make up his mind on that point.

(1956/1990: 126)

Language 'Further up and further in'

'Further up and further in' is the title of the penultimate chapter of the
last of the Chronicles of Narnia, and variations on its form runs
through both stories like a leit-motif.

The house where the children's adventures begin lies 'in the heart
of the country' (1950/1988: 9); from there, the journey further in
begins with Lucy's entry into Narnia through the wardrobe: 'She
immediately stepped into the wardrobe. . . . Soon she went further
in. . . . She took a step further in – then two or three steps – . . . going
still further in . . . and went on a step or two further' (pp. 12–13).

Next, the expression is used by the Beaver who will lead the
children to Aslan: '"Further in, come further in. Right in here.
We're not safe in the open!"' (1950/1988: 63), and it is used
repeatedly throughout the final chapters of *The Last Battle*, when
the goodly company travels towards the real, inner place, away
from the Shadowlands (1956/1990: 146 ff.). We have used the
expression in the title of this section as a metaphor for Lewis's
preferred strategy for getting his meaning to stick.

Where Carroll uses the pun to demonstrate the basic instability of
language, Lewis creates a narrative which is unambiguous on the
surface, but which nevertheless explicitly invites several compatible
interpretations on 'higher and higher' planes, depending on the reader's sophistication and prior knowledge of the Christian tradition
upon which Lewis's work draws. For example, it is possible to read
'Professor' simply as the academic title of the children's host. How-

ever, as Peter and Susan's discussion of Lucy's peculiar behaviour with the Professor demonstrates, the old Professor is also one who professes his opinion and his faith and who teaches them to the children. In the process, he places himself and his own teaching in contrast with the teachers ('they') and teaching of the children's schools:

> 'Logic!' said the Professor half to himself. 'Why don't they teach logic at these schools?' (1950/1988: 47).
> 'I wonder what they *do* teach them at these schools.' (p. 49)
> 'Bless me, what *do* they teach them at these schools?' (p. 171)

In fact, it is Edmund's school that is blamed for his misdemeanours in the story: 'That horrid school which was where he had begun to go wrong' (p. 163). The manner of his going wrong is, so to speak, Cartesian. Edmund appears to have been taught to doubt, rather than to have faith, as indicated by his repeated suggestions that others should not be taken on trust, that one should not put one's faith in them unless one *knows*:

> 'We're following a guide we know nothing about. How do we know which side that bird is on?'
>
> (1950/1988: 59)

Peter replies that 'That's a nasty idea', that robins are 'good birds in all the stories' and says 'I'm sure a robin wouldn't be on the wrong side' (p. 59). But Edmund's desire for knowledge persists:

> 'How do we know that the Fauns are in the right and the Queen (yes I know we've been *told* she's a witch) is in the wrong? We don't really know anything about either.'
> 'The Faun saved Lucy.'
> 'He *said* he did. But how do we know?'
>
> (1950/1988: 60)

The high incidence in this passage of expressions in Edmund's speech in which he suggests that knowledge is superior to faith is particularly significant because it occurs in a context where the children are being led by a robin, a bird traditionally associated with Christ and Christmas, and the robin is the children's first guide on their journey towards Aslan.

Their second guide is the Beaver, and on encountering him, Edmund again remains doubtful, while the others are prepared to put their faith in the Beaver:

'I know what it is,' said Peter; 'it's a beaver. I saw the tail.'
'It wants us to go to it,' said Susan. . . .
'I know,' said Peter. 'The question is, are we to go to it or not?
What do you think, Lu?'
'I think it's a nice beaver,' said Lucy.
'Yes, but how do we *know*?' said Edmund.
'Shan't we have to risk it?' said Susan.

(1950/1988: 62)

At this point, Lucy has already been shown to be trustworthy, kind
and truthful, and Edmund to be spiteful and a liar, and the stress on
his demand to know indicates more than pronunciation.

The Professor's two first remarks quoted above occur in a context
in which he is professing/teaching faith in Lucy, in her story and in
the possibility 'that there could be other worlds – all over the place,
just round the corner – like that' (1950/1988: 49), as Peter puts it, a
possibility which the children find difficult to countenance, but of
which the professor convinces them. So it is the secular teaching in
contemporary schools that is found wanting, not teaching as such.
Secular teaching fails on two counts: it fails to instruct its pupils in
logical reasoning and it fails to emphasise faith. The Professor
demonstrates by logical reasoning that Lucy cannot be lying. But
the children have been schooled not to believe what they cannot
understand, and their incredulity has interfered with their ability to
reason out the truth. However, the value of instruction as such is not
in question, as the truth of the Professor's teaching demonstrates.
Similarly, though the four children, now installed on the thrones of
Narnia, liberate 'young dwarfs and young satyrs from being sent to
school', they do this as rulers who have 'made good laws' (p. 166). It
is not anarchy that is being advocated, but good order kept by good
rulers.

By the stage of the narrative where we find the Professor profes-
sing, the other world which is in question in the passage has already
been infused with a Christian symbolism which Lewis reinforces
through a variety of linguistic means, including the explicit and
frequently repeated use of biblical names which most children
would recognise. When the Faun first encounters Lucy, he
enquires: 'should I be right in thinking that you are a Daughter of
Eve?' As Lucy does not quite understand, the Faun checks that she is
a human and a girl before remarking that he has 'never seen a Son of
Adam or a Daughter of Eve before'. He then addresses her as 'O Lucy
Daughter of Eve' (1950/1988: 16), thus providing three instances of

this biblical naming on one page, against one mention of 'girl'. These instances included, the ten pages which constitute Chapter 2 – of which approximately two and two-thirds are given over to illustrations – contain eleven mentions of 'Daughter of Eve'and two of 'Son of Adam', against two of 'human(s)' and one of 'girl'. These expressions continue to be used about and to the children by the good characters in the story, including Father Christmas and Aslan himself. The Witch also uses them when she is trying to trap Edmund, though once she has him in her power, she refers to him, irreverently, as 'the human creature' (1950/1988: 102ff.).

There is a further reminder of the Christian aspects of the story in the Faun's description of how the White Witch has caused Narnia to be in a state of eternal winter. The description ends with the remark: 'Always winter and never Christmas; think of that!' (1950/1988: 23). Lucy repeats this to Edmund: '"And she has made a magic so that it is always winter in Narnia – always winter, but it never gets to Christmas"' (p. 42), and subsequently to the whole group: '"she's a horrible witch, the White Witch. Everyone – all the wood people – hate her. She has made an enchantment over the whole country so that it is always winter here and never Christmas."' (p. 57).

The significance will not be lost on children schooled to consider Christ the redeemer who appears 'in the deep midwinter'. However, in the second mention quoted above, the Witch is also portrayed as a usurper of aspects of a character to whom few of Lewis's prospected readers would fail to relate, namely Father Christmas: 'And she drives about on a sledge, drawn by reindeer' (1950/1988: 42). In this way, the passage has a double resonance; it relates at once to the two major foci of one of the great Christian festivals: the religious focus on the birth of Christ, and the more earthly focus on Father Christmas.

The same dual focus is found in the image of the robin 'with such a red breast' (1950/1988: 58), '(you couldn't have found a robin with a redder chest or a brighter eye)' (p. 59), which guides the children on the first stage of their journey towards Aslan: according to legend, the red of the robin's breast is made by a drop of Christ's blood, and for this reason the robin is often used on Christmas cards and placed on the top of Christmas trees.

In fact, the children meet Father Christmas before they encounter Aslan, and the description in the relevant passage shows what a poor substitute the White Witch was: 'It *was* a sledge, and it *was* reindeer with bells on their harness. But they were far bigger than the Witch's reindeer, and they were not white, but brown' (1950/1988: 98). Father

Christmas, who addresses the children as 'name + Adam's Son/Eve's Daughter', gives each child a gift which proves vital in their subsequent battle, on the side of Aslan, against the forces of the Witch, and he departs expressing sentiments which again link him closely with the divinity: 'Merry Christmas! Long live the true King!' (p. 101).

Christ, of course, does not figure in person in either story. The 'Deeper magic from before the dawn of time' of the heading of Chapter 15 (1950/1988: 142) is represented in the stories by the Lion, Aslan, 'the son of the great Emperor-beyond-the-Sea' (p. 75). Aslan is introduced into the story by a Narnian creature, the Beaver, so that he can be presented as known, without immediate explanation: 'They say Aslan is on the move – perhaps has already landed' (p. 65). However, the significance of Aslan is highlighted in a twenty lines long narratorial comment on the effect his name has on the children. This comment forms a paragraph on its own, addresses the reader directly as 'you' at least five and arguably seven times (some mentions are ambiguous between the *you* of second person address and the *you* of general reference) and begins with a sentence which explicitly marks its significance: 'And now a very curious thing happened.' Particularly significant expressions in this narratorial comment include the following: 'something which you don't understand'; and 'enormous meaning' (p. 65). In addition, Edmund is further condemned and set off from the other children through his reaction to the name of Aslan: 'Edmund felt a sensation of mysterious horror'; the others' reactions are linked with bravery and a desire for adventure (Peter), delicious scents and delightful music (Susan) and holidays and summer (Lucy). Given the wintry state of Narnia, and the significance of Christmas, Lucy's reaction is highly significant.

Aslan's name continues to have differentiating effects on the children in subsequent conversations about him: 'the mention of Aslan gave him [Edmund] a mysterious and horrible feeling just as it gave the others a mysterious and lovely feeling' (1950/1988: 82). The Beaver goes on to explain that Aslan is 'the King. He's the Lord of the whole wood' (1950/1988: 74). He is 'the King of the wood and the son of the great Emperor-beyond-the-Sea . . . the King of Beasts. . . . A lion – *the* Lion, the great Lion . . . the King' (p. 75), in other words, for those who know, Judah's Lion. Aslan, the Beaver assures the children, will 'settle the White Queen all right' (p. 74). This White Queen is the anti-Christ to Aslan's Christ, and is more commonly referred to as the White Witch. Lewis' characterisation of the White Witch is particularly interesting in so far as he manages to associate her whiteness, which is extreme – her arms are elsewhere described as 'terribly white' (p. 124) – and itself linked with the extreme cold of snow and ice (icing sugar) – with the opposite extreme heat of fire, thereby connoting the extremes of heat and cold suffered by the inhabitants of hell and embodied in its ruler, Lucifer.

The reindeer's 'hair was so white that even the snow hardly looked white compared with them', but 'their branching horns were gilded and shone like something on fire. . . . In the frosty air the breath coming out of their nostrils looked like smoke.' The Witch's 'face was white – not merely pale, but white like snow or paper or icing-sugar, except for her very red mouth'. The coldness suggested by snow and ice is immediately afterwards assigned to the Witch's personality, as this is reflected in her face: 'It was a beautiful face in other respects, but proud and cold and stern' (1950/1988: 32–3). The Witch's eyes, however, like the smoke issuing from the nostrils of the reindeer, suggests an inner fire: 'she rose from her seat and looked Edmund straight in the face, her eyes flaming' (p. 35). Even the dwarf who drives the Witch's sleigh is attired in a similar symbolism: 'He was dressed in polar bear's fur and on his head he wore a red hood' (p. 33). The White Witch reinforces the linking of Father Christmas with Aslan through the vehemence of her fury when she discovers that Father Christmas has returned: 'What?' roared the Witch . . . "He has not been here! He cannot have been here!"' (p. 106)

The children who enter this world are differentiated partly according to the relationships they form with it and its inhabitants, though there are also more explicitly linguistic signs of the differentiation between them. These include pure narratorial comment about the children's moral qualities, which differentiate Lucy from Edmund, and Lewis's descriptions of how the children deal with the wardrobe door, contained within his regularly expressed warnings to children about this matter:

Lucy 'wanted to be truthful and yet not be too hard on him' (1950/ 1988: 24); 'was a very truthful girl' (p. 29), and 'proved a good leader' (p. 55). Edmund, on the other hand, 'could be spiteful' (p. 29), 'was becoming a nastier person every minute' (p. 45), and has 'horrible ideas' coming 'into his head' (p. 67). Peter, who understands Edmund perfectly well, declares: 'I believe you did it simply out of spite'; 'it's just spite' (p. 45). When Edmund meets Lucy after spending a considerable time with the Witch eating Turkish Delight and telling her about his brother and sisters, he tells Lucy 'I've been looking for you everywhere' (p. 41); this sets Edmund up as a liar, in sharp contrast with the truthful Lucy.

Lucy invariably treats the wardrobe door with due care. She leaves 'the door open, of course, because she knew that it is very foolish to shut oneself into any wardrobe' (1950/1988: 12); 'She had, of course, left the door open, for she knew that it is a very silly thing to shut oneself into a wardrobe' (p. 14); and 'She did not shut it properly because she knew that it is very silly to shut oneself into a wardrobe' (p. 30). Edmund, in contrast, 'jumped in and shut the door, forgetting what a very foolish thing this is to do' (p. 30). Peter acts like Lucy with respect to the wardrobe door: 'Peter held the door closed but did not shut it; for, of course, he remembered, as every sensible person does, that you should never shut yourself up in a wardrobe' (p. 52).

By these means, then, Lucy is shown to be truthful, caring, a good leader, and neither foolish not silly. Edmund is proved to be spiteful, a liar, receptive of horrible ideas and foolish. And Peter is classed as a sensible person. The storyline reinforces these impressions. Lucy, the good girl, meets a basically good character, the Faun, when she enters Narnia. She subsequently brings out the good qualities in the Faun, who repents of his sin. Edmund, who is spiteful and wants to tease and hurt Lucy, meets the evil White Witch when he first enters Narnia, and the White Witch is able to use him as an instrument in her plan to capture all the children. The evil that befalls Edmund is thus seen to be his just desert. He endangers his fellows by being greedy (for both Turkish Delight and power: the Witch promises to make him a king) and selfish, and it is partly the courage of his betters which saves them all and restores summer to Narnia. The good children are prepared to act out a reflection of Aslan's self-sacrifice through which all the children are finally saved. This sacrifice is in turn a clear allegory of Christ's dying to save human-kind, and by means of these layers of interlocking themes Lewis relates the individual to the universal in a manner reminiscent of MacDonald's parallelisms between the divine family and individual, earthly families.

However, Lewis also introduces a more concrete symbolism. When Edmund has consumed the several pounds of Turkish Delight with which the Witch tempts him, he ends up 'feeling very sick' (1950/ 1988: 43), a predicament with which Lewis probably assumed that most children could identify. Later, Peter gives voice to the full symbolic value of this sickness, linking Edmund with the serpent through the metaphor of poison, while Lewis links his case with that of the fall from Eden through the metaphor of the dead silence:

'So you really were here', he said, 'that time Lu said she'd met you in here – and you made out she was telling lies.'

There was a dead silence. 'Well, of all the poisonous little beasts – ' said Peter.

(1950/1988: 55)

The significance of the food is further hammered home when the Beaver remarks that Edmund, now on his way to betray the others to the White Witch, 'had the look of one who has been with the Witch and eaten her food . . . something about their eyes' (p. 80).

On the purely narrative level, of course, the fact that Edmund gives himself away (by mentioning the lamp-post before the party has reached it) provides an instructive instance of a liar being caught by his own carelessness. Edmund, however, remains unrepentant at this point, as Lewis inserts yet another warning, this time against self-righteousness: the others' attitude simply reinforces Edmund's disease and the danger this presents to them all:

but Edmund was saying to himself, 'I'll pay you all out for this, you pack of stuck-up, self-satisfied prigs.'

(1950/1988: 55)

Edmund's road to redemption begins when 'Edmund for the first time in this story felt sorry for someone beside himself' (p. 107). We know that this is the beginning of his salvation, because it mirrors the Faun's feeling for Lucy when he weeps at having been bad enough to have wanted to kidnap 'a poor innocent child in the wood' (p. 23) to hand it over to the White Witch, a sin which Lucy forgives because the Faun repents.

The beginning cleansing of Edmund's soul coincides with the beginning thaw in Narnia. In describing this process, Lewis employs a number of onomatopoetic expressions, which render the description particularly vivid to reinforce the contrast between the thawing-out process and the previous stultification of Narnia by the frost:

It was the noise of running water. All round them though out of sight, there were streams, chattering, murmuring, bubbling, splashing. . . . And much nearer there was a drip-drip-drip from the branches of all the trees.

(1950/1988: 108)

Edmund is finally redeemed by conversing with Aslan, a conversation which the narrator declares that there is no need to report, but after it, Edmund apologises to the other three children (p. 126) and joins in the battle courageously.

As in MacDonald's works, being good is for Lewis commensurate with siding with nature. Edmund 'felt sure the others would all be on the side of the Fauns and the animals; but he was already more than half on the side of the Witch' (1950/1988: 42–3). It is, of course, significant that the narrator, reporting Edward's psychological state, refers to the white apparition as 'the Witch'. This indicates that Edmund, whose state it is that is being referred to, knows she is a witch, but that he sides with her in spite of this; Edmund has to be a willing, knowing disciple of evil, not just a small, gullible boy. This knowingness is reinforced again in a later scene where all four children witness the destruction the Witch has wrought on the Faun's home and Lucy declares the Witch to be a Witch hated by all the wood people (see p. 57). Finally, it is stated explicitly by the narrator that 'deep down inside him he really knew that the White Witch was bad and cruel' (p. 83).

According to Lewis's ethics, however, one of Edmund's worst crimes is betrayal. The severity of this crime is clearly signalled in the narratorial comment in the following passage:

> And now we come to one of the nastiest things in this story. Up to that moment Edmund had been feeling sick, and sulky, and annoyed with Lucy for being right, but he hadn't made up his mind what to do. When Peter suddenly asked him the question he decided all at once to do the meanest and most spiteful thing he could think of. He decided to let Lucy down.

> (1950/1988: 44)

This passage works on several planes: on the linguistic, explicit level it reinforces Edmund's spitefulness and the impression of him as a liar, because he goes on to deny that he has been with Lucy in Narnia, explaining that the two of them have merely been playing. Edmund, then, lets Lucy down. More implicitly, this shows that Edmund is a betrayer. This places him apart from the other children, who are later shown willing to try to save Edmund from the Witch, but on the more allegorical plane, it also places Edmund on the side of evil. Christianity links self-sacrifice with love, and love with divine goodness. By implication, therefore, betrayal is linked with Satanic evil. It is interesting to note that although Lewis describes Edmund's various feelings using a variety of negatively loaded adjectives, the adjective he selects to describe Edmund himself and his action, is 'spiteful'. 'Spite' connotes oppositeness, as suggested in the expression *in spite of*; in particular, however, it connotes oppositeness to another's will, as we see in such common expressions as *They did it to spite me*. Edmund is the chief opposer, the wilful opposer.

In contrast, Peter does his best to believe in Lucy's story, and, once she has been proved right, he apologises immediately for not believing her: 'Peter turned at once to Lucy. "I apologise for not believing you," he said' (1950/1988: 53–4).

By clearly differentiating between the children from the beginning of the story, Lewis ensures that his readers will find it easy to identify with the right side. The values he defends are bravery, resolution, good leadership and the willingness to fight for what one believes, all of which are associated with the children who are on the side of Aslan – on the side of the traditional Christian teaching. In this respect, Lewis resembles MacDonald. However, his and MacDonald's faiths are ultimately at variance. Whereas MacDonald explicitly associates himself with the female aspects of Christianity, Lewis upholds its male aspects. Whereas MacDonald's Apocalypse clears the way for absolute renewal, Lewis's eternity contains the status quo within it, albeit in a pure, cleansed and expanded form, 'More like the real thing' (1956/1900: 158):

> You are now looking at the England within England, the real England just as this is the real Narnia. And in that inner England no good thing is destroyed.
>
> (1956/1990: 170)

Give such comfort, conformity is eased. Lewis uses the strategy of eternalisation of what he considers good, together with differentiation, to suggest that although the world as we know it has its faults, it is, after all, good at heart. The heart in question is rural: it is in the heart of the country that the old Professor's house is situated, 'ten miles from the nearest railway station and two miles from the nearest post office' (1950/1988: 9).

Railway stations and post offices are parts of institutions which facilitate communion between people. However, such communion may draw attention away from the communion with nature to which the children look forward when they first arrive at the Professor's house (see 1950/1988: 10) and which they experience in even greater measure than expected among the talking animals in Narnia. It can lead to the destruction of the heart of the country, and Lewis shares Dahl's concern with preservation: the apocalypse of the last book in the series is preceded by the felling of the forest which the four children of the first story, as rulers of Narnia, had set out to protect: they 'saved good trees from being unnecessarily cut down' (p. 166). The felling of trees by the forces of evil in the last Chronicle is reported with great emotional emphasis and shown to be sinful because the trees are said to be holy:

> 'Woe, woe, woe!' called the voice. 'Woe for my brothers and sisters! Woe for the holy trees! The woods are laid waste. The axe is loosed against us. We are being felled. Great trees are falling, falling, falling.'
>
> (1956/1990: 20)

Communion among humans had also resulted in the two wars which Lewis experienced. The children are 'sent away from London during the war because of the air-raids' (1950/1988: 9) to the house of a Professor whose own Narnian experiences date from before either war: the action of his story, *The Magician's Nephew*, takes place 'long ago when your grandfather was a child. . . . In those days Mr Sherlock Holmes was still living in Baker Street and the Bastables were looking for treasure in the Lewisham Road' (1955/1990: 9). In other words, these are the times of Edith Nesbit, towards the end of the Victorian era, and it was then that 'all the comings and goings between our own world and the land of Narnia first began' (p. 9).

This suggests that although Lewis clearly shares Dahl's aversion to war, he looks back to the values of an earlier time for salvation. His children are 'sent away from London' and 'sent to the house' (1950/1988: 9). They enter Narnia by accident in the first book and are transported into Narnia by dying in a railway accident, as it happens, in the last. For all their activities and the high social status they achieve in Narnia, Lewis's children are basically followers: sent by adults, led by bird and beast and Aslan. They are quite different from the self-reliant children we meet in Dahl's fairytales, whose triumphs result largely from their own initiative and inventiveness, even though magic may lend them a helping hand. Lewis's children triumph because they follow a good leader, and they convey an essentially conformist message.

7 Last thoughts

As Hunt (1990: Introduction) points out, critical writing on literature written with children in mind is a young discipline. Hunt (1990: 3) cites Darton (1932) as 'the first example of extended first-class work in the field', though his own collection of critical essays begins with Fielding (1749). This, and other early critical work included in Hunt's collection, evidences a long tradition of concern among those engaged with the socialisation of children about the degree to which children may be influenced by the literary works to which they are exposed. It is also clear that a number of those who have produced such works have done so with a view to affecting child socialisation in various ways.

Since Darton, and particularly since 1980, a number of representative collections of criticism, including two edited by Hunt (1990; 1992), have appeared, and we also have Stephens' (1992) excellent, full-length book, *Language and Ideology in Children's Fiction*. None of this work, however, takes a specifically linguistic approach to the literature in question, and in this book we have attempted to fill a part of this gap in the discipline. In doing so, we have drawn on work in critical linguistics, in stylistics and in contemporary theory of ideology.

There is in contemporary theory of ideology a particular interest in language, which arises from the definition of 'ideology' as meaning in the service of power – as the mobilisation of language in attempts to establish and sustain relations of domination, of systematically asymmetrical relationships of power. In chapter 2, we suggested that the adult–child relationship is, in many respects, such a relationship; adults are, generally, more powerful than children. For this reason, it can be particularly instructive to study literature written by adults for children. Here, the relationship between writer and reader is, almost by definition, a relationship of domination, so such texts ought to illustrate particularly clearly just *how* language can be made to serve the ideological purpose in such a relationship. As Hunt (1988: 163) points out: 'the realisation of a text, and especially of a text for children, is closely involved with questions of control, and of the techniques through which power is exercised over, or shared with, the reader'.

It is a firmly fixed tenet of critical linguistics that the structure of texts and the language choices made in them can tell us something about the society in which the texts themselves are rooted, and that an awareness of patterns of textual structure and of language choices may provide information about how the writer wants his/her readers to view society. The study of such patterns is the province of stylistics. However, since any linguistic form may be used in the service of ideology, while none is necessarily thus used, it is important to bring to linguistic analysis some awareness of the social conditions in which texts are written and read.

In this book we have used the methods of both traditional and modern stylistic analysis in order to highlight two phenomena: we have attempted to show how writers of different persuasions, writing at different times, have used their texts to promote particular reactions to the social conditions prevalent at their time; and we have attempted to show how these conditions, in turn, have, at least partly, conditioned the means through which the writers have sought to achieve these goals. As Montgomery points out, writers do not operate in a vacuum when presenting their fictional worlds:

> Words [and, we would add, structures] . . . are selected from a determinate set for the situation at hand and have been previously shaped by the community or by those parts of it to which the speaker (or writer) belongs.
>
> (1986:176)

Of course, a fictional world may distort 'reality'. Nevertheless, the distortion is significant because it imposes this 'reality' upon its reader. In this 'reality', value systems may be taken for granted, and the writer may make assumptions about his or her reader, and about the latter's world knowledge. This 'implied reader', constructed by the writer can, then, be particularly significant, because he/she is 'situated in such a position that he can assemble the meaning toward which the perspectives of the text have guided him' (Iser, 1978: 38). Clearly a reader need not agree with these 'meanings'. However, unless a work is intended to be satirical, it is probably often the case that conscious disagreement by the reader with the values promoted by the author

> is a sign of the author's failure to carry the reader with him: like suspension of disbelief, suspension of dissent seems to be a sacrifice which the reader is ready to accept in embarking on the adventure of reading a novel.
>
> (Leech and Short, 1981: 277)

Aidan Chambers (1980: 252) comments:

> The idea of the implied reader derives from the understanding that it takes two to say a thing. In effect it suggests that in his book an author creates a relationship with a reader in order to discover the meaning of the text.

In creating this relationship, a writer of literature for children may attempt to control his/her child reader. Chambers (1980: 263–6) goes on to discuss 'tell tale gaps' in children's narratives. Some of these gaps reveal an author's assumptions about the implied readers' 'beliefs, politics, social customs, and the like'. *Tom Brown's Schooldays*, for example, is partly based on an understanding of the customs and hierarchy of the early nineteenth-century English public school. But to what extent can it be assumed that a young reader of *Tom Brown's Schooldays* in the 1840s was aware of these customs and this hierarchy?

If the gaps between, on the one hand, the writer's 'assumptions of commonality' with an implied reader, and, on the other hand, the real reader's actual background knowledge become too great, these gaps can, at worst, alienate the reader, and, at best, prevent the reader from forming the writer's intended responses to the text. As we saw in chapter 6, C.S. Lewis goes to great lengths in the construction of a narrative with several layers of meaning to try to ensure that the narrative can appeal to most child readers, whatever their understanding, or lack of it, of the Christian doctrine he wishes to promote in his Narnian Chronicles.

The texts we have discussed in this book were produced for communities of readers, defined by time and genre. In chapter 1 we saw how modern children's literature had its roots in the mid-nineteenth century when stories of a more entertaining nature began to take over from the overtly didactic narratives which predominated previously. We identified the genres of adventure and school stories, fantasy fiction and fairytales, and noted that genre boundaries in the late twentieth century are less clear cut.

We suggested that the notion of the social institution can be a useful starting point for linguistic analysis, and discussed the advantages which corpus based, computer-aided stylistic studies offer the analyst. These include the speed and precision with which structural and collocational patterns in texts can be established, and extensive reference was made to the results of computer aided analysis throughout chapters 3 and 4. These chapters dealt, respectively, with analyses of texts drawn from the genres of traditional juvenile fiction, and from a representative cross-section of modern children's literature.

Chapter 3 discussed the exploits of the Doers and the Sayers of the nineteenth century. Using lexical description and clause analysis, we considered the world views of Victorian writers as presented in early, nationalistic, God-fearing narratives, through to the height of empire. Excitement was much to the fore in these narratives, but they were by no means purged of didacticism.

In chapter 4, on children's literature from the twentieth century, we saw how the linguistic representation of mental processes could be used to sustain a narrative that is entertaining and home-based, and how powerlessness is the lot of children of all ages. We also saw how, occasionally, that powerlessness is not relieved, as evil triumphs over good.

Chapters 5 and 6, which dealt, respectively, with fairytale and fantasy, employed more traditional, primarily interpretively based stylistic analyses, coupled with fairly extensive reference to the writers' various persuasions. Texts of these genres tend to be more metaphorical than 'realist' fiction, so that it is more difficult to take their language literally. Nevertheless, it was made clear, particularly in chapter 5, on fairytales, that once a writer's intent and persuasion is clear, it can be instructive to observe how these can be reflected in the statistical predominance of particular linguistic choices and combinations. This was particularly evident in the comparison of the use made by MacDonald and Wilde of vocabulary related to precious stones and metals.

In chapter 6, on fantasy, we compared Carroll's essentially subversive emphasis on ambiguity and puns with Lewis's employment of multiple meanings to essentially conformist ends.

In these various ways, we have hoped to highlight the linguistic nature of ideology. We hope to have made it clear how extensively the nature of the societies in which writers live can influence both their purpose in writing and the linguistic choices they tend to make in the process. We have been concerned with a relatively short historical period, but it is a period in which profound social changes have taken place, and the differences we have found in, for example, the vocabulary in modern children's fiction and in traditional juvenile fiction, reflect cultural changes in terms of vanished or highly restricted words, and changes in patterns of collocation.

It is not unreasonable to assume that linguistic choices will, in turn, work effects in readers, particularly, perhaps, when readers are young. However, it must be said in conclusion that the detrimental or beneficial effects on children of reading particular kinds of literature (with some exceptions, of course) should not be overemphasised. Two of the most popular contemporary writers discussed in this book are Dahl and Lewis. Ideologically speaking, these have little in common; yet large numbers of children read both with equal delight, and without displaying the least evidence of psychological trauma as a result of trying to reconcile the conflicting values promoted by the two authors. Writing and reading are both constraining and constrained. As a writer must use what is given to construct something that may be new, a reader can only assimilate the new within what is already known. What a child takes on board from any one socialising agent will be greatly influenced by what it has already received from other quarters, and socialisation is a continuing, lifelong process. Literature, as mentioned in chapter 2, although it may be an important socialising agent, is still only one among a very vast array.

References

Abrahamson, J. (1983) 'Still Playing It Safe: Restricted Realism in Teen Novels', in R. Bator (ed.) *Signposts to Criticism of Children's Literature*, Chicago: American Library Association, pp. 319–23.

Abrams, M.H. (1957) *A Glossary of Literary Terms* (3rd edn 1971), New York: Holt, Rinehart & Winston.

Aiken, H.D. (1956) *The Age of Ideology: The Nineteenth-Century Philosophers*, New York and Scarborough, Ontario: New American Library; London: New English Bibliography Library.

Aikin, J. and Barbauld, A.L. (1792–6) *Evenings at Home*, (1875) London: George Routledge.

Alcott, L.M. (1868) *Little Women*, Boston, MA: Roberts.

Anstey, F. (1882) *Vice Versa, or a Lesson to Fathers*, London: Smith & Elder.

Arnold, G. (1980) *Held Fast for England: G.A. Henty, Imperialist Boys' Writer*, London: Hamish Hamilton.

Avery, G. (1965) *Nineteenth-Century Children*, London: Hodder & Stoughton.

—————— (1975) *Childhood's Pattern: A Study of the Heroes and Heroines of Children's Fiction 1770–1950*, London: Hodder & Stoughton.

Ayto, J. (1990) *Bloomsbury Dictionary of Word Origins*, London: Bloomsbury.

Ballantyne, R.M. (1858) *The Coral Island*, (1966) London: Bancroft Classics.

—————— (1861) *The Gorilla Hunters*, London: Nelson.

Bator, R. (ed.) (1983) *Signposts to Criticism in Children's Literature*, Chicago: American Library Association.

Bawden, N. (1957) *Devil by the Sea*, London: Collins.

—————— (1973) *Carrie's War*, (1974) London: Penguin.

—————— (1975) *The Peppermint Pig*, London: Gollancz.

Baynton, M. (1988) *Jane and the Dragon*, London: Sainsbury Walker.

—————— (1990) *The Dragon's Purpose*, London: Sainsbury Walker.

Biber, D. (1991) *Variation across Speech and Writing*, Cambridge: Cambridge University Press.

Blishen, E. (1975) *The Thorny Paradise: Writers on Writing for Children*, London: Kestrel.

Blume, J. (1975) *Forever*, (1986) London: Pan.

———— (1970) *Are You There God? It's Me, Margaret*, Englewood Cliffs, NJ: Bradbury Press.

Briggs, J. (1987) *A Woman of Passion: The Life of E. Nesbit 1858–1924*, London, Hutchinson; (1989) London, Penguin.

———— (1989) 'Reading Children's Books', *Essays in Criticism*, vol. XXXVIX, no. 1, pp. 1–17.

Briggs, K.M. (1970), *A Dictionary of British Folk-Tales in the English Language: Incorporating the F.J. Norton Collection*, London: Routledge & Kegan Paul.

Buchan, J. (1915) *The Thirty-Nine Steps*, London: Hodder & Stoughton.

Burnett, F. Hodgson (1911) *The Secret Garden*; (1992) London: Sainsbury Walker.

Cadogan, M. and Craig, P. (1976) *You're a Brick Angela: A New Look at Girls' Fiction from 1839–1975*, London: Gollancz.

Campbell, R. (1982) *Dear Zoo*, London: Abelard-Schuman; (1984) London: Picture Puffins; (1987) London: Campbells.

Carpenter, H. (1985) *Secret Gardens: A Study of the Golden Age of Children's Literature*, London: George Allen & Unwin.

Carpenter, H. and Prichard, M. (1984) *The Oxford Companion to Children's Literature*, Oxford and New York: Oxford University Press.

Carroll, L. (1865) *Alice's Adventures in Wonderland*; (1970) *The Annotated Alice*, ed. M. Gardner, London: Penguin.

———— (1871) *Through the Looking-Glass, and What Alice Found There*; (1970) *The Annotated Alice*, ed. M. Gardner, London: Penguin.

———— (1887) 'Alice on the Stage', *The Theatre*, April.

———— (1895) *Symbolic Logic*; (1958) *Symbolic Logic and the Game of Logic*, London: Dover.

Carter, R. (1987) *Vocabulary: Applied Linguistic Perspectives*, London: Allen & Unwin.

Chambers, A. (1980), 'The Reader in the Book', in N. Chambers (ed.), *The Signal Approach to Children's Books*, London, Kestrel, pp. 250–75.

Chatman, S. (1978) *Story and Discourse*, Ithaca: Cornell University Press.

Childe-Pemberton, H.L. (1882) 'All my Doing; or Red Riding-Hood Over Again', in *The Fairy Tales of Every Day*; reprinted in J. Zipes (ed.) (1987) *Victorian Fairy Tales: the Revolt of the Fairies and Elves*, New York and London: Methuen, pp. 211–48.

Chilton, P. (1982) 'Nukespeak: Nuclear Language, Culture and Propaganda', in C. Aubrey (ed.), *Nukespeak: The Media and the Bomb*, London: Comedia, pp. 94–112.

Chomsky, N. (1979), *Language and Responsibility*, Brighton: Harvester Press.

Cleaver, P. (1978) 'William Mayne', in D.L. Kirkpatrick (ed.), *Twentieth Century Children's Writers*, London: Macmillan, pp. 848–9.

COBUILD (1987) *COBUILD English Language Dictionary*, London and Glasgow: Collins.

Coolidge, S. (1872) *What Katy Did*, Boston, MA: Little Brown.

Cormier, R. (1975) *The Chocolate War*, (1992) London and Glasgow: Lions Tracks, HarperCollins.

Coupland, N. (ed.) (1988) *Styles of Discourse*, London: Croom Helm.

Craig, P. (1978) 'Judy Blume', in D.L. Kirkpatrick (ed.), *Twentieth-Century Children's Writers*, London: Macmillan, pp. 136–7.

Crouch, M. (1962) *Treasure Seekers and Borrowers: Children's Books in Fiction*, London: Library Association.

Culler, J. (1975) *Structuralist Poetics*, London: Routledge & Kegan Paul.

Dahl, R. (1961) *James and the Giant Peach*, (1990) London, Penguin.

———— (1967) *Charlie and the Chocolate Factory*, London: Allen & Unwin.

———— (1975) *Danny, the Champion of the World*, (1987) London: Penguin.

———— (1981) *George's Marvellous Medicine*, London: Cape.

———— (1982) *The BFG* (1984) London, Penguin.

———— (1983) *The Witches*, London: Cape.

———— (1988) *Matilda*, (1989), London: Penguin.

Darton, F.J. Harvey (1932) *Children's Books in England: Five Centuries of Social Life*, 3rd edn revised by Brian Alderson, Cambridge: Cambridge University Press, 1982.

Day, T. (1783–9), *The History of Sandford and Merton* (1875) London: George Routledge.

Defoe, D. (1719) *Robinson Crusoe*, London: Taylor.

De Morgan, M. (1877) 'A Toy Princess', in *On a Pincushion and Other Tales*; reprinted in J. Zipes (ed.) (1987) *Victorian Fairy Tales: The Revolt of the Fairies and Elves*, New York and London: Methuen, pp.165–76.

Dixon, B. (1977) *Catching Them Young*, vol. 1: *Sex, Race and Class in Children's Fiction*, London: Pluto Press.

Ellis, J.M. (1983) *One Fairy Story too Many: The Brothers Grimm and their Tales*, Chicago and London: University of Chicago Press.

Eyre, F. (1971) *British Children's Books in the Twentieth Century*, London: Longman.

Farrar, F. (1858) *Eric, or Little by Little*, (1971) London: Hamish Hamilton.

Fenn, G.M. (1907) *George Alfred Henty, the Story of an Active Life*, London: Blackie.

Fielding, S. (1749) 'Preface' to *The Governess or Little Female Academy*, (1968) Oxford: Oxford University Press; (1987) London: Routledge & Kegan Paul; (1990) extracts in P. Hunt (ed.) *Children's Literature: The Development of Criticism*, London and New York: Routledge, pp. 16–17.

Firth, J. (1957a) *Papers in Linguistics 1934–1951*, London: Oxford University Press.

———— (1957b) *A Synopsis of Linguistic Theory 1930–55*, (special volume of the Philological Society), Oxford: Basil Blackwell.

Forster, E.M. (1927) *Aspects of the Novel*, London: Edward Arnold; (1962) Harmondsworth: Penguin.

Fowler, R. (1977) *Linguistics and the Novel*, London: Methuen.

Gardner, M. (1970) *The Annotated Alice*, revised edn, first published Clarkson N. Potter, 1960.

Garner, A. (1960) *The Weirdstone of Brisingamen*, London: Collins.

———— (1963) *The Moon of Gomrath*, London: Collins.

———— (1967) *Elidor*, London: Collins.

———— (1967) *The Owl Service*, London: Collins.

———— (1973) *Red Shift*, London: Collins.

Garnett, E. (1937) *The Family from One End Street*, London: Muller.

Godden, R. (1947) *The Doll's House*, London: Joseph.

Goudge, E. (1946) *The Little White Horse*, London: University of London Press.

Grahame, K. (1908) *The Wind in the Willows*, London: Methuen

Haggard, H.R. (1885) *King Solomon's Mines*, London: Cassell.

Hallett, M. and Karasak, B. (eds) (1991) *Folk and Fairy Tales*, Peterborough, Ontario: Broadview Press.

Halliday, M. (1966) 'Lexis as a Linguistic Level', in C. Bazell, J. Catford, M. Halliday and H. Robins (eds), *In Memory of J.R. Firth*, London: Longman, pp.148–62.

————— (1971) 'Linguistic Function and Literary Style: An Inquiry into the Language of William Golding's *The Inheritors*', in S. Chatman (ed.), *Literary Style: a Symposium*, London and New York: Oxford University Press, pp. 330–65.

————— (1978) *Language as Social Semiotic: The Social Interpretation of Language and Meaning*, London: Edward Arnold.

————— (1985) *An Introduction to Functional Grammar*, London: Edward Arnold.

Hawkes, T. (1983) *Structuralism and Semiotics*, London: Methuen.

Henty, G.A. (1886) *For Name and Fame or Through the Afghan Passes*, London: Blackie.

Hodge, R. (1990) *Literature as Discourse: Textual Strategies in English and History*, Cambridge: Polity Press.

Hoey, M. (1983) *On the Surface of Discourse*, London, Boston, MA and Sydney: Allen & Unwin.

Hollindale, P. (1988), 'Ideology and the Children's Book', *Signal* 55, pp. 3–22; reprinted in P. Hunt (ed.) (1992), *Literature for Children: Contemporary Criticism*, London and New York: Routledge, pp.19–40.

Hughes, T. (1857) *Tom Brown's Schooldays*, (1880) London: Macmillan.

Hunt, P. (1988) 'Degrees of Control: Stylistics and the Discourse of Children's Literature', in N. Coupland (ed.) *Styles of Discourse*, London: Croom Helm, pp. 163–82.

————— (ed.) (1990) *Children's Literature: The Development of Criticism*, London and New York: Routledge.

————— (ed.) (1992) *Literature for Children: Contemporary Criticism*, London and New York: Routledge.

Inglis, F. (1981) *The Promise of Happiness: Value and Meaning in Children's Fiction*, Cambridge: Cambridge University Press.

Irwin, W.R. (1976) *The Game of the Impossible: A Rhetoric of Fantasy*, Urbana, Chicago and London: University of Illinois Press.

Iser, W. (1978) *The Act of Reading: A Theory of Aesthetic Response*, London: Routledge & Kegan Paul.

Jackson, R. (1981) *Fantasy: The Literature of Subversion*, London and New York: Routledge.

Jakobson (1960) 'Concluding Statement: Linguistics and Poetics', in T. Sebeok (ed.) *Style in Language*, Cambridge, MA: Massachusetts Institute of Technology, pp. 350–77.

Jeffries, R. (1882) *Bevis, the Story of a Boy*, (1952) London: Cape.

King, C. (1963) *Stig of the Dump*, London: Penguin.

Kingsley, C. (1855) *Westward Ho!*, Cambridge (no publisher listed).
———— (1863) *The Water Babies*, London: Macmillan.
Kingston, W.H.G. (1851) *Peter the Whaler*, (1909) London: Cassell.
———— (1860) *Ernest Bracebridge; or, Schooldays*, (n.d.) London: Gall and Inglis.
———— (1873) *The Three Midshipmen*, (1909) London: Cassell.
Kipling, R. (1899) *Stalky and Co.*, (1987) London: Puffin Classics.
———— (1906) *Puck of Pook's Hill*, London: Macmillan.
———— (1910) *Rewards and Fairies*, London: Macmillan.
Kirkpatrick, D.L. (1978) *Twentieth-Century Children's Writers*, London: Macmillan.
Kress, G. (1985) *Linguistic Processes in Sociocultural Practice*, Victoria, Australia: Deakin University Press.
Laski, M. (1950) *Mrs. Ewing, Mrs. Molesworth and Mrs. Hodgson Burnett*, London: Arthur Baker.
Leech, G.N. and Short, M. (1981) *Style in Fiction: A Linguistic Introduction to English Fictional Prose*, London and New York: Longman.
Leeson, R. (1980) *It's My Life*, (1981) London and Glasgow: Lions Tracks, HarperCollins.
———— (1985) *Reading and Righting*, London and Glasgow: Collins.
Lewis, C.S. (1947), *Miracles*, London: Geoffrey Bles, The Centenary Press; (1960) London, Fontana.
———— (1950) *The Lion, the Witch and the Wardrobe*, (1988) London: Lions.
———— (1955) *The Magician's Nephew*, (1990) London: Lions.
———— (1956) *The Last Battle*, (1990) London: Lions.
Lewis N. (1978) 'Introduction' to D.L. Kirkpatrick (ed.), *Twentieth-Century Children's Writers*, London; Macmillan.
Lively, P. (1973) *The Ghost of Thomas Kempe*, London: Heinemann.
Louw, B. (1993) 'Irony in the Text or Insincerity in the Writer? The Diagnostic Potential of Semantic Prosodies', in M. Baker, G. Francis and E. Tognini-Bonelli (eds), *Text and Technology: in Honour of John Sinclair*, Amsterdam and Philadelphia, PA: John Benjamins, pp. 157–76.
Lüthi, M. (1975) *Das Volksmärchen als Dichtung: Asthetik und Anthropologie*, Eugen Diederichs Verlag; English translation by Jon Erickson (1984) *The Fairytale as Art Form and Portrait of Man*, Bloomington: Indiana University Press.
Lyons, J. (1977) *Semantics*, 2 volumes, Cambridge: Cambridge University Press.
MacDonald, G. (1858), *Phantastes*, (1983) London: Dent.
———— (1864), 'The Light Princess', in *Adela Cathcart*; (1993) in A. Lurie (ed.), *The Oxford Book of Modern Fairy Tales*, Oxford and New York: Oxford University Press, pp. 61–98.
———— (1867a) 'Little Daylight', in *Dealings with Fairies*; (1993) in J. Mark (ed.), *The Oxford Book of Children's Stories*, Oxford and New York: Oxford University Press, pp. 102–17.
———— (1867b) *Unspoken Sermons: First Series*, London: Alexander Strahan.
———— (1871) *At the Back of the North Wind*, (1976) New York: Garland.
———— (1872) *The Princess and the Goblin*; (1990) in R. McGillis (ed.),

George MacDonald: The Princess and the Goblin and The Princess and Curdie, Oxford and New York: Oxford University Press, pp. 1–167.

—————— (1883) *The Princess and Curdie*; (1990) in R. McGillis (ed.), *George MacDonald: The Princess and the Goblin and The Princess and Curdie*, Oxford and New York: Oxford University Press, pp. 169–342.

McGillis, R. (ed.) (1990) *George MacDonald: The Princess and the Goblin and The Princess and Curdie*, Oxford and New York: Oxford University Press.

Maceherey, P. (1978) *A Theory of Literary Production*, London: Routledge & Kegan Paul.

Mark, J. (ed.) (1993) *The Oxford Book of Children's Stories*, Oxford and New York: Oxford University Press.

Marshall, M. (1988) *The World of Children's Books*, Aldershot: Gower.

Marryat, F. (1836) *Mr. Midshipman Easy*, (n.d.) London and Birmingham: Rylee Classics.

—————— (1841) *Masterman Ready*, (1889) London and New York: Frederick Warne.

Marx, K. and Engels, F. (1845–6), *The German Ideology* (not published in Marx's lifetime); (1939) The Marxists Library, vol. VI; (1947) ed. R. Pascal, New York: International.

Milne, A.A. (1926) *Winnie the Pooh*, London: Methuen.

—————— (1928) *The House at Pooh Corner*, London: Methuen.

Montgomery, M. (1986) *An Introduction to Language and Society*, London: Methuen.

Moore, Sir T. (1516) *Utopia*, (1910) London: Everyman.

Morris, W. (1890) 'News from Nowhere', (1993) in C. Wilmer (ed.), *William Morris: News from Nowhere and Other Writings*, London: Penguin.

Munsch, R.N. (1980) *The Paperbag Princess*, Toronto: Annick.

Murray, I. (ed.) (1979) *Oscar Wilde: Complete Shorter Fiction*, Oxford and New York: Oxford University Press.

—————— (1990), *Oscar Wilde: The Soul of Man and Prison Writings*, Oxford and New York: Oxford University Press.

Musgrave, P.W. (1985) *From Brown to Bunter: The Life and Death of the School Story*, London: Routledge & Kegan Paul.

Nash, W. (1990) *Language in Popular Fiction*, London: Routledge.

Nesbit, E. (1899) 'The Island of the Nine Whirlpools', *The Strand*; (1993) in J. Mark (ed.), *The Oxford Book of Children's Stories*, Oxford and New York: Oxford University Press, pp. 271–83.

—————— (1900) 'The Book of Beasts', in *The Book of Dragons*; (1993) in A. Lurie (ed.) *The Oxford Book of Modern Fairy Tales*, Oxford and New York: Oxford University Press, pp. 203–14.

—————— (c. 1900) 'The Last of the Dragons'; (1925) in *Five of Us – and Madeleine*; (1987) in J. Zipes (ed.), *Victorian Fairy Tales: The Revolt of the Fairies and Elves*, New York and London: Methuen, pp. 353–8.

—————— (1902) *Five Children and It*, London: Unwin.

—————— (1906) *The Railway Children*, (1992) London: Sainsbury Walker.

Norton, M. (1952) *The Borrowers*, London: J.M. Dent; (1993) London: Penguin.

Oxford English Dictionary (compact edn) (1971), Oxford: Oxford University Press.

Paton-Walsh, J. (1978a) 'Nina Bawden', in D.L. Kirkpatrick (ed.) *Twentieth-Century Children's Writers*, London: Macmillan, pp. 93–5.

————— (1978b) 'Robert Westall', in D.L. Kirkpatrick (ed.), *Twentieth Century Children's Writers*, London: Macmillan, pp. 1314–15.

Pearce, P. (1958) *Tom's Midnight Garden*, London: Oxford University Press.

Perera, K. (1984) *Children's Writing and Reading: Analysing Classroom Language*, Oxford: Basil Blackwell.

Peyton, K.M. (1970) *Seventeenth Summer*, (1994) London: Point, Scholastic Children's Books.

Prince, A. (1986) *Nick's October*, (1987) London: Teens, Methuen Children's Books.

Propp, V. (1968) *Morphology of the Folktale*, Austin, TX: University of Texas Press (orig. publ. in Russian, 1928).

————— (1976), 'Study of the Folktale: Structure and History', *Dispositio* vol. 1, pp. 277–92; revised version included as ch. 5 of A. Liberman (ed.), *Theory and History of Folklore*, tr. A.Y. Martin and R.P. Martin, Minneapolis: University of Minnesota Press.

Quigley, I. (1984) *The Heirs of Tom Brown: The English School Story*, Oxford: Oxford University Press.

Ransome, A. (1930) *Swallows and Amazons*, London: Cape.

Reed, T.B. (1887) *The Fifth Form at St. Dominic's*, (n.d.) London: 'The Boys' Own Paper' Office.

Rees, D. (1978) *The Exeter Blitz*, London: Hamilton.

————— (1984) 'Macho Man, British Style', in *Painted Desert, Green Shade* Boston, MA: Horn, pp. 115–25.

Rigby, E. (1844) 'Children's Books', *The Quarterly Review*, vol. 74, pp. 1–3, 16–26; extracts in P. Hunt (ed.) (1990) *Children's Literature: The Development of Criticism*, London and New York: Routledge, pp. 19–22.

Rimmon-Kenan, S. (1983) *Narrative Fiction: Contemporary Poetics*, London and New York: Routledge.

Röhrich, L. (1986) 'Introduction', in R. Bottigheimer (ed.), *Fairy Tales and Society: Illusion, Allusion, and Paradigm*, Philadelphia: University of Pennsylvania Press, pp. 1–9.

Ruck, B. (1935) *A Story-Teller Tells the Truth: Reminiscences and Notes*, London: Hutchinson.

Salinger, J.D. (1951) *The Catcher in the Rye*, (1969) London: Hamish Hamilton.

Salmon, E. (1888) *Juvenile Literature as it is*, London: Drane.

Salway, L. (ed.) (1976) *A Peculiar Gift: Nineteenth Century Writings on Books for Children*, Harmondsworth: Kestrel Books.

Scholes, R. and Kellogg, R. (1966) *The Nature of Narrative*, Oxford and New York: Oxford University Press.

Scott, M. and Johns, T. (1993) *Microconcord*, Oxford: Oxford University Press.

Scott, Sir W. (1819) *Ivanhoe*, 1st edn published anonymously: no details.

Shavit, Z. (1992) 'Introduction', *Poetics Today* vol. 13, no. 1, Children's Literature. Duke University Press, pp. 1–3.

Sinclair, C. (1839), 'Uncle David's Nonsensical Story about Giants and Fairies', from *Holiday House: A Book for the Young*, London: Ward, Lock; reprinted in J. Zipes (ed.) (1987) *Victorian Fairy Tales: The Revolt*

of the Fairies and Elves, New York and London: Methuen, pp. 3–12; also
in J. Mark (ed.) (1993) *The Oxford Book of Children's Stories*, Oxford and
New York, Oxford University Press, pp. 49–57.

Sinclair, J. (1966) 'Beginning the Study of Lexis', in C. Bazell, J. Catford,
M. Halliday and R. Robins (eds), *In Memory of J.R. Firth*, London:
Longman, pp. 410–30.

———— (1987a), 'The Nature of the Evidence', in J. Sinclair (ed.), *Looking
Up: An Account of the COBUILD Project in Lexical Computing*, London and
Glasgow: Collins, pp. 150–9.

———— (1987b), 'Collocation: A Progress Report', in R. Steele and T.
Threadgold (eds), *Language Topics: Essays in Honour of Michael Halliday*, vol. 3, Amsterdam: John Benjamins, pp. 319–31.

———— (1991), *Corpus, Concordance, Collocation*, Oxford: Oxford University Press.

Spenser, E. (1590) *The Faerie Queene*, (1978) Harmondsworth: Penguin.

Stables, G. (1901) *With Cutlass and Torch*, London: Nisbet.

Steedman, C. (1982) *The Tidy House: Little Girls Writing*, London: Virago
Press.

Stephens, J. (1992), *Language and Ideology in Children's Fiction*, London
and New York: Longman.

Stevenson, R.L. (1883) *Treasure Island*, London: Cassell

———— (1886) *Kidnapped*, London: Cassell.

Thompson, J.B. (1984) *Studies in the Theory of Ideology*, Cambridge: Polity
Press.

———— (1990) *Ideology and Modern Culture: Critical and Social Theory
in the Era of Mass Communication*, Cambridge: Polity Press.

Tolkien J.R.R. (1937) *The Hobbit*, London: Allen & Unwin.

———— (1955) *The Lord of the Rings* (The Fellowship of the Ring; The
Two Towers; The Return of the King), London: Allen & Unwin.

Toolan, M.J. (1988) *Narrative: A Critical Linguistic Introduction*, London:
Routledge.

Townsend, J.R. (1965) *Written for Children*, London: Garnet Miller; (1990)
5th edn, revised and reset, London: The Bodley Head Children's Books.

———— (1980), 'Standards of Criticism for Children's Literature', in N.
Chambers (ed.), *The Signal Approach to Children's Books*, London:
Kestrel Books.

Trease, G. (1949, 1964) *Tales Out of School*, London: Heinemann.

Treglown, J. (1994), *Roald Dahl: A Biography*, London and Boston, MA:
Faber & Faber.

Trimmer, S. (1786) *Fabulous Histories*, London: Longman.

———— (1802) 'Observations on the Changes Which Have Taken Place in
Books for Children and Young Persons', *The Guardian of Education*, 1;
extract in L. Salway (ed.) (1976), *A Peculiar Gift: Nineteenth-Century
Writings for Children*, Harmondsworth: Kestrel Books.

———— (1803) 'On the Care Which Is Requisite in the Choice of Books for
Children', *The Guardian of Education*, 2; extract in P. Hunt (ed.) (1990)
Children's Literature: The Development of Criticism, London and New
York: Routledge, p.18.

Tucker, C. (1858), 'The Green Velvet Dress'; (1993) in J. Mark (ed.), *The*

Oxford Book of Children's Stories, Oxford and New York: Oxford University Press, pp. 93–101.

Tucker, N. (1981) *The Child and the Book: A Psychological and Literary Survey*, Cambridge: Cambridge University Press.

——— (1989) 'Finding the Right Voice: The Search for the Ideal Companion in Adventure Stories', in C.F. Otten and G.D. Schmidt (eds), *The Voice of the Narrator in Children's Literature*, London and New York: Greenwood Press, pp. 141–7.

Turner, E.S. (1975) *Boys will be Boys*, Harmondsworth: Penguin.

Wall, B. (1991) *The Narrator's Voice: The Dilemma of Children's Fiction*, London: Macmillan.

Waller, G. (1986) *English Poetry of the Sixteenth Century*, London: Longman.

Watt, I. (1715) 'Against Idleness and Mischief', in *Divine Songs for Children*; reprinted in M. Gardner (ed.) (1970) *The Annotated Alice*, revised edn, London: Penguin, pp. 38–9.

Westall, R. (1975) *The Machine Gunners*, London: Macmillan.

Wilde, O. (1888a) 'The Happy Prince'; (1979) in I. Murray (ed.), *Oscar Wilde: Complete Shorter Fiction*, Oxford and New York: Oxford University Press, pp. 95–103.

——— (1888b), 'The Selfish Giant'; (1979) in I. Murray (ed.), *Oscar Wilde: Complete Shorter Fiction*, Oxford and New York: Oxford University Press, pp. 110–14.

——— (1891a) 'The Young King'; (1979) in I. Murray (ed.), *Oscar Wilde: Complete Shorter Fiction*, Oxford and New York: Oxford University Press, pp. 171–84.

——— (1891b) 'The Star Child'; (1979) in I. Murray (ed.), *Oscar Wilde: Complete Shorter Fiction*, Oxford and New York: Oxford University Press, pp. 237–52.

——— (1891c) 'The Soul of Man under Socialism'; (1990) in I. Murray (ed.) *Oscar Wilde: The Soul of Man and Prison Writings*, Oxford and New York: Oxford University Press, pp. 1–37.

Williams, C. (1931) *The Place of the Lion*, London: Mundanus (Gollancz).

Willis, L. (1985) '"Born Again": the Metamorphosis of Irene in George MacDonald's *The Princess and the Goblin*', *Scottish Literary Journal*, 12, 24.

Wilson, A.N. (1990) *C.S. Lewis: A Biography*, London: William Collins.

Wood, M. (1976) 'Tolkien's Fictions', in N. Tucker (ed.), *Suitable for Children: Controversies in Children's Literature*, London: Sussex University Press.

Yonge, C. (1853) *The Heir of Radclyffe*, London: Parker.

——— (1856) *The Daisy Chain*, London.

Zipes, J. (1979) *Breaking the Magic Spell: Radical Theories of Folk and Fairy Tales*, London: Heinemann.

——— (1983) *Fairy Tales and the Art of Subversion: The Classical Genre for Children and the Process of Civilization*, London: Heinemann.

——— (ed.) (1987) *Victorian Fairy Tales: The Revolt of the Fairies and Elves*, New York and London: Methuen.

——— (ed.) (1991) *The Penguin Book of Western Fairy Tales*, London: Penguin.

Index

Bold indicates key lexical items